The
Great Crown Jewels
Robbery of 1303

The
Great Crown Jewels
Robbery of 1303

The extraordinary story
of the first big bank raid in history

PAUL DOHERTY

CARROLL & GRAF PUBLISHERS
New York

Carroll & Graf Publishers
An imprint of Avalon Publishing Group, Inc.
245 W. 17th Street
NY 10011
www.carrollandgraf.com

First published in the UK by Constable,
an imprint of Constable & Robinson Ltd 2005

First Carroll & Graf edition 2005

ISBN-13: 978-0-78671-664-7
ISBN-10: 0-7867-1664-9

Printed and bound in the EU

This book is dedicated to Garry Francis Davey

Contents

Illustrations

Chronology

1276 First Welsh war

1306 Welsh rebellion crushed. Welsh leaders are killed or executed

1284 *April:* Edward II born at Caernarvon

1286 *March:* Alexander III of Scotland dies after falling from his horse

1290 Eleanor of Castile, Edward I's wife dies

1290 *Sept.:* Margaret the Maid of Norway dies

1294 War with France begins

1296 Scottish war begins

1297 *Sept.:* Battle of Stirling Bridge, Wallace defeats the English

1298 Battle of Falkirk, Edward I's troops defeat Wallace

1299 Edward I marries Margaret of France

1306 English Law courts organized into three parts: Kings bench, Court of Common Pleas and Court of the Exchequer

1301 *Feb.:* Edward of Caernarvon created Prince of Wales

1303 Fresh invasions of Scotland
       April–May: ROBBERY OF THE CROWN JEWELS

1304 *Aug.:* Wallace executed in London

1306   *Feb.:* Robert Bruce kills John Comyn in Dumfries, resumption of Scottish War

1307   *July:* Edward I dies. Edward II succeeds and promotes his favourite, Peter Gaveston, to be Earl of Cornwall and Regent whilst he travels to France to marry Isabella the daughter of Philip IV [*Jan. 1308*]

Prologue

'Mes cum fust endormie e tapist dreiture'

'Right and law be as if fast asleep'
Contemporary ballad

Today the Crypt of Westminster Abbey is, in both name and atmosphere, a gloomy and forbidding place. It lies buried beneath the Chapter House of the Abbey, octagonal in shape with walls seventeen to eighteen feet thick. The width of its floor is almost nine yards, the only light is provided by six windows with chamfered jambs and square heads. The jambs are set back almost two yards from the outer face of the wall, they have a segmental pointed arch in front of them. The windows are heavily barred, steel rods are embedded in the stone sill at the bottom and the square head of the window at the top. The floor inside is tiled, the ceiling, a stone vault, has chamfered ribs radiating from a thick-set rounded column in the centre of the crypt which has a moulded capital and base. This central column or pillar is about two feet in circumference and fashioned out of red brick, on close inspection it will be found that some of these

1

bricks can be removed to reveal hollow recesses behind them.[1]

The windows, as you look at them from left to right, peer out over what used to be the waste land and cemetery of the monks of Westminster. Through the window on the far left of the column can be glimpsed the pathway which still stretches from the south east door of the Abbey church leading to the main road across which stands the House of Lords. In 1303 this pathway led from the Abbey to the Royal Palace. The window to the far right of the column now overlooks one of the gardens of the Canons of the Abbey, in 1303 the window looked out over the most desolate of the Abbey grounds just below the Infirmary of the Black Monks of Westminster. This sixth window is, in 2005, quite different from the other five, it has no stone sill. The reason for this is that, between Tuesday 30th April 1303 and Friday the 3rd May 1303, the sill of this sixth window was hacked away by the mason John of St Albans and a carpenter called Philip under the direction of a former merchant, Richard de Puddlicott, in order to loosen the bars across the windows, this sill has never been replaced.

The entrance to the Crypt today is still as secure as it was in 1303 being entered by a doorway in the west wall down a corridor and turret-staircase east of St Faith's chapel, the ceiling above is barrel-vaulted. In 1303 the staircase was broken by a two yard gap which could only be spanned by a wooden bridge, in 2005 the gap has been closed by wooden steps. The doors to the staircase and Crypt are heavy with fortified locks. In 2005 these keys are held by the verger, in 1303 they were in the custody of high ranking officials of the Royal Treasury. In 2005 the area outside the crypt window is a narrow grassy verge and the private gardens of the Canons, in 1303 the entire area was wasteland, the rest God's Acre, the cemetery of the monks. In 2005 this gloomy Crypt has electric lighting but, in 1303, the six windows would be heavily shuttered by wooden boards behind the iron bars, the only light would be from cresset torches fixed in iron sconces on the walls or wax candles and oil lamps. In 2005 the Crypt holds nothing but some chests and an ironing board for altar cloths and other items. In 1303 however, the Crypt of Westminster was a treasure house containing most of the royal regalia of the Crown of England as well as jewels, silver and gold coins, goblets, jugs, chalices, cups, saucers, spoons, vases not to mention unique treasures such as the Cross of Neath; the Holy Cross of Holyrood [the Black Cross of St Margaret from Scotland]: the Sceptre or the Rod of Moses: the sword of King Athelstan from the ninth century, which had cut though the rock of Dunbar: the sword of Weyland the Smith last used to knight Henry II and the sword of the mythical prince Tristan which had been presented to King John by the Holy Roman Emperor. The Crypt also held important possessions of the reigning king, Edward I, [1272 to 1307], including the dagger used in an attempt to assassinate him whilst he had been on crusade in the Holy Land. According to one story, Edward had been resting in his tent near Acre when an assassin sent by the Old Man of the Mountain entered his tent with a poisoned dagger and tried to kill him. Edward had slain the assassin whilst his beloved wife Eleanor of Castile sucked the poison from the wound. Edward I had recovered and kept the dagger as a personal relic.[2] All these treasures, both family and personal, became the plunder of a band of robbers.

Introduction

'Et Tenebrae facta est'

'And darkness fell'

Scripture uses such a phrase to describe the betrayal of Christ by Judas. However, in the week beginning Monday 27 April 1303, some of the Benedictine Monks of Westminster Abbey had forgotten the truth of the Gospels and did not wish to recall the constant warnings of Christ and his prophets. How those things done in the dark would, one day, be judged in God's full light. Indeed, some of the Black Monks of the Great Abbey longed for the darkness to shroud the cemetery and wasteland which divided their Abbey from the King's great Palace of Westminster. Secretly, under the cover of dark, an unholy alliance had been forged between monks, supposedly dedicated to the love of God and their neighbour, and the turbulent underworld of medieval London. On Tuesday and Wednesday of that week a great conspiracy came to fruition in the Abbey: lights were doused, as were those in the Palace, men hooded and visored, armed with bows and arrows, patrolled the gates leading into that stretch of dividing land which included the King's delightful gardens, open wasteland and God's Acre. Here the deceased monks of Westminster lay shrouded in their graves, waiting to be wakened by the blast of the Angel's trumpet at that last moment of time when the elements would dissolve and Christ returned in judgement.

The frescoes and tympana at Westminster and elsewhere sharply depicted Christ Pantocrator, the supreme King in judgement, coming on the clouds of heaven to separate the sheep from the goats. Yet, that was for the future. '*Carpe diem* – seize the day' was more suited to some of the monks of Westminster and their equally sinister confederates. Naturally they had to be careful, yet the threat of retribution was much diminished. The King and all his company were fighting in Scotland, chasing Scottish rebels through the mist-strewn heather, the Abbot was rarely in residence and, even if he was, easily controlled, whilst the Royal Palace and its grounds were firmly under the thumb of one of the principal 'ordainers' of the projected robbery. Everything was ready. True, a wall separated the Abbey from the Palace but this assisted the robbers' plans, being easily patrolled and watched, whilst all gate-keys were in their hands. The escape route to King's steps on the river Thames had been clearly plotted out, carts and barges stood waiting under the protection of violent men who had prowled out of the sinister twilight of medieval society. Once the treasure was moved, it could be distributed to the greedy merchants of the city. Of course, despite such careful preparations, the robbery would be discovered but, like the warning from *Dies Irae*, of Celano's famous hymn, that was for the future:

> See what fear man's bosom rendeth,
> When from heaven the Judge descendeth,
> On whose sentence all dependeth.

On those warm April evenings such holy thoughts were totally ignored by the gang of thieves lurking amongst the thick hempen weeds deliberately grown across the monks' cemetery to conceal their blasphemous handiwork. Once they had forced a window into that great cellar, the Abbey Crypt, and lowered themselves into the King's Treasury, the weeds would screen their crime. The thieves had sprinkled the hempen seed the previous year; they were now eager to reap their own rich harvest. They had plotted and planned one of the most outrageous robberies in the history of the Crown of England, to storm the Royal Treasury and literally remove a king's ransom in wealth. They had acted with great cunning. People accustomed to use that stretch of land, be it farmers who had the right to pasture their cattle or those who wished to use the latrines built there, had been totally excluded. Gates and doors were locked and guarded. The person at Westminster Abbey responsible for lighting and security, in particular that area around the Crypt, was party to their plot as were others of his brethren. From their comfortable Abbey chambers, these monks could hear the gang whispering amongst themselves and the echoing rasp of hammer and chisel as the bars of the chosen window nearest in the Crypt were brutally forced.

The robbery did not take place within an hour but over three days. Once dawn arrived, the gang always withdrew whilst the thick tangled weeds concealed their handiwork. On the third day, with their guards watching doors and gates and working in the poor light of shuttered lanterns, the robbers achieved success. They broke through their chosen window and slid down into the Crypt to wrench open coffers and chests. Cups and goblets, dishes, plates, precious jewels, sacred relics, gold and silver coins, poured back up the narrow window shaft and into the hands of those waiting in the monks' cemetery. A few items were lost but the bulk was removed to the Palace or, across the wasteland and royal gardens, to barges waiting on the Thames. Some of the thieves had been drinking heavily after carousing in a local prison; others were sober, eager to move their ill-gotten wealth as quickly as possible. The leaders of the gang were very much aware of the danger. Edward I, King of England, was a hard man, his face set like flint. If they were caught, little mercy would be shown, no pardon offered. The horrors of Newgate Prison would be theirs, followed by an excruciating journey through the city on a hurdle to choke out their lives on one of London's many gallows. The rewards, on the other hand, were unimaginable – they would steal from a King to live like kings. By Friday, 1 May 1303, the crime had been committed. The Crown Jewels of England had been robbed.

Part One

1

The King's Tale

'Ry ne doit a feore de gere extra regnum ire'

'A King should not leave his realm to wage war'
Contemporary ballad

Edward I of England was in Scotland at Linlithgow when he heard news of the robbery.[1] The sixty-four-year-old king, now in the thirty-first year of his rule, had emerged as a redoubtable figure in his own kingdom as well as on the international scene. In his long reign Edward had crushed opposition and developed a vision of his own power and that of his kingdom. This was shared by the great lords and barons of his council, both spiritual and temporal and, above all, by the powerful clerks, who staffed the great offices of state, the Exchequer (or Treasury), the Royal Household (with its own treasury at Westminster and its wardrobe of stores in the Tower), as well as the Royal Writing Office or Chancery. Such clerks were Edward's allies, as well as his servants. Scholars of the Trivium and the Quadrivium when they had attended the schools and halls of Oxford and Cambridge, many had also studied law, so they could advise their king on a wide range of issues as well as act as his commissioners and judges. Edward I was very much aware of whose support he needed, so he had also tried to reach an accord with the powerful mercantile families, dominant in the great trading cities of London, Bristol, York, and the Cinque Ports along the south coast. London, however, was deeply suspicious of such an accord and jealous of its hard-won privileges.

The Crown of England was an autocratic institution where that famous precept of Roman legislation: 'The will of the Prince has force of law' played a major part. Nevertheless, Edward I's power had been limited, not only by his coronation oath but by the clauses of Magna Carta which had been reconfirmed countless times since its first great sealing in 1215 during the reign of his grandfather, King John. The troubles caused by Magna Carta, and the issues surrounding it, had dominated the reign of Edward's father King Henry III, when powerful opposition to the power of the Crown had been organized and led by Simon de Montfort, Earl of Leicester. By 1303 de Montfort had been dead for almost forty years but his legend still lingered, even though, Edward had crushed de Montfort, once and for all, at the Battle of Evesham in 1265, destroying his forces, executing or exiling his kin and allies. The great Earl's corpse was mutilated and, according to popular rumour, its severed flesh fed to dogs.[2]

When Henry III died in 1272 Edward I, accompanied by his wife Eleanor of Castile, returned from crusade in Outremer. Edward worked hard to avoid his father's mistakes. He recognized that England was changing, its arable fields being turned to pasture because the hunger for English wool abroad was becoming almost insatiable. Edward exploited this growing wealth by negotiating loans, raising money from his own merchants as well as merchant-bankers from Northern Italy, like the Frescobaldi. At the same time he recognized the growing political aspirations of his kingdom's land-owning classes and merchants. While business was usually conducted with his great lords, both spiritual and temporal, in meetings of the royal council, he extended political debate to the Commons, the representatives from the shires and towns who would meet for a 'Parlement' or talking session at Westminster or elsewhere. However, Edward certainly did not accept the legal axiom of a contemporary lawyer, Bracton: 'What affects all must be approved by all.' When the Commons did meet in the Chapter House of Westminster Abbey or in some annexe to Westminster Hall, they were obliged to listen to royal demands for taxes on 'moveable' and 'immoveable', property as well as witness Edward's new type of legal pronouncements, the statutes, covering a wide range of domestic and foreign issues.[3]

At such sessions, through both the Lords and the Commons, Edward I could promulgate his vision of a kingdom where the royal writ would run from Dover to the northern tip of Scotland and west through Wales to the wilds of Ireland, even beyond the Pale, the English fortified settlement around Dublin. Edward had ruthlessly pursued this vision. By 1303 English common law extended to Ireland, whilst Edward's Justiciar there vigorously enforced English policy. In fact, Edward I felt so confident about his control of that country that, in 1301, he had issued 184 personal writs for military service to Irish lords to join him in his Scottish war.[4] By 1303 Wales, too, was firmly under his writ but only after a bitter military struggle along its narrow valleys. The Welsh princes had subdued canton after canton, their land shared out among the great English families such as the Mortimers, Audleys, Despencers and de Clares. Massive fortified castles had been built in the principality such as those at Conway and Caernarvon. The Welsh princes had stoutly resisted, been crushed then risen in fresh revolt, only to be brutally suppressed. Their leader, Prince Llewellyn had been killed, his brother David savagely executed. Terror and military might, not to mention bribes, had subdued the Principality for which Edward had created a new title, the Prince of Wales, for his eldest son and heir-apparent.[5]

However, Edward I's vision encompassed even more than this. He had turned on the independent, sovereign kingdom of

Scotland, a potential threat to his own northern shires. He had exploited the sudden, unexpected demise of Alexander III when, in March 1286, the young Scottish king had died in a riding accident. Edward immediately intervened, acting the honest broker, trying to mediate between the different claimants to the Scottish throne. Alexander had left only a young girl as his heir, Margaret the Maid of Norway, but she, too, died unexpectedly during her return to Scotland. The two principal claimants to the vacant throne were the noble Scottish families, the Comyns and the Balliols. Edward played one off against the other until he tired of the game and showed his true hand: Scotland was to be conquered and brought firmly under the English Crown so Edward marched north with his cavalry, pikemen, hobelars, men-at-arms and archers.

York became his military base as well as the seat of government. Forsaking London and his palace at Westminster, the king moved to York the great courts, Kings Bench and the Court of Common Pleas, not the mention the Chancery and the Exchequer under its flinty-eyed Keeper, Walter Langton, Bishop of Coventry and Lichfield. Edward turned York into his new capital, the mustering point for his troops. Then he moved across his northern march to wage total war, in the words of the ancient Consuls of Rome, 'by land and sea, by fire and sword'. It was a fierce, bloodthirsty struggle. Scotland had produced its own resistance fighters led by William Wallace and Simon Fraser who, time and again, defeated the English in sudden ambush, sly sortie and even pitch battle.[6]

Wallace's resistance surfaced in 1296 when Edward was at his most vulnerable, facing the two power blocs he truly feared: Philip IV of France and the powerful Church of Rome. Philip was as ambitious as Edward with his own vision of France's pre-eminence in Europe. The French king exploited Edward's difficulties in Scotland to raise the vexed question of Gascony, that rich, wine-producing province in south-west France, the only real relic of the Angevin Empire so abruptly lost by Edward I's grandfather, John, in 1214. The power of the Catholic Church proved equally threatening. Edward experienced serious difficulties with his own bishops and senior clergy. Not only had the clergy and many of the monastic communities grown fat, lax and corrupt but, led by Robert de Winchelesea, Archbishop of Canterbury, they also stubbornly resisted Edward I's desire to tax the church. This eventually brought the English Crown into conflict with Pope Boniface VIII. If Edward feared a war over Gascony with France, he was equally wary of conflict with the papacy. His grandfather King John had been excommunicated by the powerful Pope Innocent III. This had turned John into an outcast both at home and abroad, his Crown becoming the plaything for his own barons as well as foreign princes. Edward I did not want to go down that path.

The Church was a powerful international corporation. Edward depended on its bishops for moral and financial support, not to mention the smooth running of the machinery of state. Moreover, the Church comprised more than its bishops. Every village had its own chapel whilst the monasteries and friaries of the different orders – Carthusians, Benedictines, Cistercians, Franciscans, Augustinians and Dominicans – were many and rich, their members a powerful force for accepting royal authority or rejecting it.

Desperate to continue his war with Scotland and keeping an eagle eye on France, Edward I eventually reached an accommodation of sorts with the Archbishop. However, Church and State continued to watch each other warily especially as the cost of the King's wars in Scotland and elsewhere soared.[7] Edward had to send troops, not only to Scotland but also to Gascony, and order his ships to patrol the Narrow Seas of the Channel where Norman pirates, displaying 'Beaussons, streamers of red sandal' sent a message, well known amongst mariners, that it would mean 'death without quarter and war to the knife' for English sailors.

Edward I was equal to these crises, he was in every way a king and politician, a warrior of commanding appearance. He stood well over six foot, a striking, lean and muscular figure. He dressed simply, resentful of any ostentation. By 1303, Edward's blond curly hair had turned grey. He was handsome, though one eyelid drooped slightly and he had a faint lisp. Above all, Edward was a fighter. As a youth he had hotly pursued the notorious outlaw Adam of Gurdon into the Forest of Alton where, it is said, he trapped him, engaged him in hand-to-hand combat, and took the outlaw's head.[8] In 1264 in the civil war between his father Henry III and Earl Simon de Montfort, Prince Edward had been captured at the Battle of Lewes. The following year, still a prisoner, he left the town of Hereford for a ride, accompanied by his prison escort. According to the chroniclers, Edward had planned to escape. He asked his companions if he could try all their horses in turn. His gaolers were only too willing to indulge their royal prisoner and allowed him. Having found the swiftest, Edward dug in his spurs and rode off shouting: 'Lords, I bid you good day! Greet my father well and tell him that I hope to see him soon and free him from imprisonment.'[9]

The story has been elaborated over the years but it does capture Edward's cunning, audacity and bravery. Unlike his father, whose sole great building achievement was Westminster Abbey, Edward I's most notable buildings were the magnificent castles of Wales which kept that Principality under English rule. Edward did patronize the more peaceful arts, and continued to develop Westminster where a Chapel of St Stephen, begun in 1292, was still being completed. The new Royal Chamber at Westminster Palace was painted green by Walter of Durham and decorated with beautiful paintings of 'Christ in Majesty' accompanied by figures of the Four Evangelists. Walter was probably also involved in renovating the Painted Chamber at the Royal Palace with frescoed scenes from the Old Testament.[10] Edward also liked board games, such as chess, and dice.[11] He pursued the stag though his great love appeared to be falconry. He had a special mews built at Charing Cross with a garden and a lead bath supplied with running water pouring through a leopard-headed fountain for the birds. Edward truly loved his hunting hawks. On one occasion he had a wax image made of an ailing falcon which was then despatched to the Shrine of St Thomas à Becket at Canterbury in the hope of obtaining a cure. He adopted other customs of caring for his birds, such as bending a penny over the head of the sick hawk. This coin would then be sent to various holy shrines to ask for the intercession of heaven in healing the sick bird.[12]

Edward's greatest personal passion was his wife Eleanor of Castile. When she died at Holby in Lincolnshire in 1290, her corpse was brought by slow procession back to Westminster Abbey. At every place her coffin rested Edward built a magnificent Eleanor Cross in her memory. Perhaps her death distanced him from the softer things of life. Two years before her death, 125 minstrels had performed for Edward at one of his feasts. After her death, the music seems to have faded. The only proven time Edward asked for music was for a blood letting operation in 1297 when a harpist was employed to take his mind off the pain.[13]

Meanwhile, Scotland was slowly turning from an open sore to a running ulcer. That same year an English army under the Earl of Surrey and Cressingham, Edward's Treasurer in Scotland, advanced from Berwick to Stirling. Surrey proved to be an incompetent commander who slept late on the morning that Cressingham led a clumsy English advance across a pontoon bridge over the Forth to attack Wallace. The Scots refused to fight by the book and caught the English as they were half-way across: those who reached the north side of the river were brutally massacred. Cressingham was killed, his corpse skinned by the victorious Scots, some of it being preserved to make a sword belt for Wallace.[14] The Battle of Stirling was the greatest military defeat Edward I faced in his thirty-five-year reign and committed him to total war. A year later, the King himself led an English army across the border to encounter Wallace at Falkirk. During the battle Edward received a fierce blow from a horse's hoof which broke his ribs but he still kept in the saddle and pursued the Scots that day, not resting until he returned to Linlithgow, the same place he was occupying in June 1303 when news of the robbery arrived.[15]

War, of course, meant money. Edward used up all his available resources, then sent his commissioners, such as John de Drokensford, Keeper of the King's Wardrobe, to search for more. The royal liberality and princely generosity of earlier days was now a thing of the past. After his Coronation in 1274, for example, Edward had held a magnificent feast at Westminster where the great Earls of Lancaster, Cornwall, Gloucester, Pembroke and Surrey came before him, each followed by a retinue of 100 knights. All dismounted and the horses were then set free for anyone to keep if he managed to catch one.[16] Such generosity was now rare as the war in the north escalated. In his campaign of 1303 Edward needed to build moveable bridges at Kings Lynn to bridge the Forth. He even bought sulphur for cannons and had to find the means to maintain over 3,500 men in the field as well as 173 ships at sea.[17] He used the wealth from the wool taxes and any other sources of income he could lay his hands on. In the final resort, he could pledge his crown jewels, that marvellous treasure hoard stored in the Crypt of Westminster Abbey.

At the beginning of June 1303, however, a courier from London arrived at the English camp with the startling news that the Royal Treasury at Westminster Abbey had been looted of tens and tens of thousands of pounds of precious coin, jewels and plate. Such items were now being discovered in the London money market and scattered in the fields and meadows around Westminster and elsewhere in the city. Edward's councillors were stunned. The Crypt was hallowed ground. More importantly, it was supposed to be secure behind huge thick walls. The chamber was underground, with a great stone roof and floor not to mention and three heavily locked doors. The stairs, without their wooden bridge, were unmanageable whilst the keys to the treasury were held secure in sealed pouches by senior officials of the King's Wardrobe. How could any thief have penetrated such thick walls or burrowed beneath them? Such a venture would need siege engines of extraordinary strength. No robber could surely have done this without the connivance of the Black Monks, the Benedictines housed at Westminster? But, surely, priest-monks, dedicated to their vows, would have had nothing to do with such a blasphemous felony?

The King's first reaction was probably to dismiss such reports as nonsense. But then his council would have reminded him how, only seven years before, a similar attempt had been launched by one John the Cook of Lechesman.[18] Also, in 1300, some of those very monks had allegedly made a further, – though again unsuccessful – attempt to force the treasury, – an event hastily hushed up after the Abbot of Westminster, Walter de Wenlok, had bribed the King. The avarice of some of the good brothers of the Benedictine community at Westminster was truly amazing. A group of them had even been involved in stealing a £100's worth of silver from the money the King had sent so chantry Masses could be sung for the repose of the soul of Queen Eleanor.[19] The King must have felt particularly betrayed at this: the Westminster monks managed the family mausoleum which housed his father's corpse and his brother's and, above all, his beloved Eleanor whose tomb was surmounted by an exquisite silver-gilt bronze effigy.

While the King's anger at earlier depredations had been molli-fied by bribes and the sweet words of Abbot Wenlok, when he heard the news of this fresh outrage, his notoriously hot temper boiled over. Matthew Paris the Chronicler reports how, when Edward was still in his teens, he and his retinue had attacked a young man, cut off his ear and gouged out an eye. The Chronicler bitterly asked what this young prince would grow into?[20] Edward's violent temper was a problem which he had tried to curb, yet it would flicker through the investigation into the robbery at Westminster, and would be responsible for the final indignities inflicted on its chief perpetrator. It was a streak of character which could turn Edward from a legalist to a vicious street fighter, a bully quite prepared to use the great robbery to achieve other ends.

Edward strove to control his temper, though he displayed a very aggressive attitude towards subordinates who did not obey. He once chased a falconer, who had lost control of one of his beloved hunting birds, and almost killed him with his sword. He had thrown one of his own daughter's coronets into the fire, but later paid for its repair. At the marriage of another daughter he beat a squire for no apparent reason, but later apologized and paid almost ten marks in compensation.[21] Edward's favourite oath was to swear by a part of God's anatomy. When his second queen, Margaret of France, fell ill, probably of the measles or chicken-pox, Edward I instructed her physician that she was not to travel until she was fully better. If he did not follow this instruction, 'By God's thigh,' Edward wrote, 'he would suffer for it.' When Blanche, Margaret's sister, died in Austria, Edward told her confessor to break the news as gently as possible and give her every consolation. However, if the queen grieved too much, the priest should point out to her that Blanche was as good as dead as soon as she had left France to marry the Duke of Austria![22] Edward's attitude to the plundering of the Royal Treasury would swing between these two extremes of mood: a desire to observe all the protocols and a ruthless desire to avenge such felonious insults. In Edward I's mind, theft from him was synonymous with treason and someone would have to pay.

Of course in the thirteenth and fourteenth centuries, theft was as common as it is now, though its detection and the pursuit of those responsible could be a matter of personal idiosyncrasy. Professional searchers, equivalent to modern bounty hunters, could be hired such as Giles of Spain.[23] Even magic was used. The *Grands Chroniques de France* describe a theft from the Cistercian Abbey of Serquigny, which took place at around the same time as the robbery at Westminster. The monks, desperate to recover their wealth, turned to Jean Prevost, who in turn hired a sorcerer – Jean Persant. He buried a live cat in a coffer at a crossroads, a location special to necromancers and, with the cat, placed bread soaked in holy water and sacred oil for the cat to eat, pipes leading from the coffer to the surface ensured the poor animal could breathe. The monks intended to remove the cat after three days, make three thongs from its flayed skin, which would then be used to form a circle. The magician, who had nourished himself on the same diet as the cat, would stand in the circle and invoke a demon, Berich. Once summoned, this demon would have to name those responsible, as well as reveal all other details about the robbery. Unfortunately, for all concerned, including the cat, some shepherds heard the creature's cries, and dug up the chest. The local magistrate was summoned. He, in turn summoned all the local carpenters to a meeting to identify the workmanship of the offending chest. The carpenter was none other than Jean Prevost, who, under torture, revealed his fellow conspirators, including a monk of Citeaux, the Abbot of Serquigny and certain canons. Jean Persant died before judgement could be carried out. Jean Prevost was burned at the stake, with the cat tied round his neck, while the others were imprisoned for life.[24]

Edward of England, however, was not a prince to put his trust in such macabre methods, be it black magic or torture which was forbidden under English law. When the Templars, for example, were suddenly arrested in England in 1308, the Pope had specifically to order Edward II to use torture and, even then, the king imposed limits.[25] Edward I believed that the law and its processes would uncover evil, bring it to judgement and punish it. Edward had a passion for the law – even his opponents (including the Black Monks of Westminster) recognized this.

An incident which took place well after the burglary reveals Edward's passion for the law and the trust imposed by oaths. In April 1304, Edward laid siege to the great Scottish fortress of Stirling, he demanded that it surrender, and its commander, William Oliphant, cede to him as his liege lord. Oliphant argued that he had never sworn fealty or done homage to Edward, who, of course, replied with equally explicit legal objections. An impasse was reached so both sides decided to settle the issue by force of arms. In the ensuing siege, Edward used 'Greek Fire', tossed into the castle in earthenware pots, and a massive battering ram called the 'War Wolf'. The garrison surrendered, barefoot with ashes on their heads, but, according to the rules of war, all were spared – except for the traitor who'd first betrayed the castle to the Scots in 1299.[26] When the Scottish leader, the Earl of Atholl, was captured, many English nobles, as well as Edward's wife, Princess Margaret, pleaded that Atholl be spared because of his birth. Edward I retorted that the Earl of Atholl, by breaking his oath, still deserved death and ordered his gallows to be built higher than the rest. Another Scottish chieftain, Simon Fraser, a former knight from Edward I's own household, suffered even more when captured; Fraser was dragged through the streets of London to a horrific death by disembowelling, his corpse later quartered. Edward was so incensed about the treachery of Fraser, who had taken a special oath to him, that he even ordered the gallows on which Fraser was hanged to be burnt.[27]

Edward's absorption with the law and its procedures is reflected in his legal enactments: the statutes. The First Statute of Westminster (1275) had devoted over half of its Chapters to judicial issues whilst these in turn were supplemented by the Statute on the Office of Coroners (1275), the Statute of Rageman (1276), the Statute of Gloucester (1278), and the Second Statute of Westminster (1285). If the law did err, Edward would try to fix it. In 1289, after he returned from a three-year stay in Gascony, Edward decided to investigate, 'A clamour of accusations' against leading officials and judges. He instituted a far-reaching inquiry proclaiming that all who had grievances against his ministers should come to Westminster on the morrow of St Martin (12 November 1289) to have their grievances redressed before a specially appointed panel of Justices.[28]

The robbery of the royal treasury would be investigated in the same thorough, judicial way. Edward's anger is more than obvious in the letter he dictated on 6 June 1303 from Linlithgow which instigated one of the greatest criminal investigations of the era.

John de Drokensford, Keeper of the King's Wardrobe would be despatched into London to investigate, while his justices, Roger de Southcote, John Bakewell, Walter of Gloucester and Ralph de Sandwich, would hold court in that city Edward had such difficulty with.

A translation of the royal letter reads as follows:

Edward by the grace of God, King of England, Lord of Ireland and Duke of Aquitaine, to his well beloved and faithful Ralph de Sandwich, Walter of Gloucester, John Bakewell and Roger de Southcote greetings.

We have accepted, and learnt from the testimony of faithful and loyal people, that certain malefactors and disturbers of our peace have, by force of arms, broken into our treasury within the Abbey at Westminster and have taken out and carried elsewhere a great part of our treasure deposited in the aforesaid place and have committed terrible crimes in clear contempt of us and inestimable damage against our peace. We, wishing a hasty remedy to this, have assigned you to enquire, on oath, from the Knights and other upright and law-abiding men of our city of London and of the neighbouring Shires of Middlesex and Surrey, who are known to us by their good life, to discover:

- Who are the malefactors?
- Who knew about the robbery?
- Who offered and gave the robbers help, counsel and assistance?
- Who knowingly received the said treasure?
- How was the said treasure taken and how much?
- In whose hands is the treasure now, as well as all other circumstances surrounding the said robbery and do whatever is necessary to elucidate the full truth of this

matter. Therefore, we command you, on certain days and at certain places, that you make a full inquiry and that all who are guilty of this deed, or have helped and advised in it, or received the said treasure, be arrested without delay and be kept safe and secure in our prison until we have reached a decision on the matter. Whatever treasure is found in the hands of these malefactors, you must deposit in a safe and secure place in accordance with our instructions. Know that we have instructed our sheriffs in London, Middlesex and Surrey to arrange to bring, on certain days and at certain places assigned to them by you, as many knights and upright men as is needed so you can establish more clearly the truth of this matter. In testimony of which we have issued these our letters patent witnessed by me, at Linlithgow 6th June, the 31st year of our reign (1303).[29]

The word *Malefactores* – malefactors – implies that more than one individual was named. The phrase *'vi et armis'* indicates the robbers broke into the treasury by force of arms, which points to an organized, well-equipped gang. That 'they took a great part of our treasure and carried it away' illustrates that royal officials had already entered the treasury and were able to calculate the magnitude of the losses. Given the conditions of the roads in the early 1300s, a messager from London would take about a week to reach the royal camp in Linlithgow, perhaps less if he came by ship from the Port of London. So, the robbery must have been discovered sometime in the week beginning Monday 27 May. The royal letter mentioned the source of this information 'the testimony of faithful and worthy [men]', a reference, possibly, to two men who would play a major role in the investigation into the robbery: Sir Ralph de Sandwich, Constable of the Tower of London and John de Drokensford, the royal official in charge of the treasure in that gloomy crypt beneath the Chapter House of Westminster Abbey.

Both Drokensford and Ralph de Sandwich were in London that summer. Drokensford, as Keeper of the King's Wardrobe was busy collecting money for his master, whilst de Sandwich's important post required his constant presence there. They, in turn, however, must have been alerted by other 'faithful and worthy men', a reference to the possibility that not all the monks of Westminster looked the other way when the robbery took place.

2

The Monk's Tale

'Lors Perit seinte Eglise, quant orgoil la mestrie – '

'The peace of the Church perishes when pride is the Master'
Contemporary ballad

The monk, Robert of Reading, who would become Chronicler of the Benedictine Abbey of St Peter at Westminster in 1307, would certainly remember the tumultuous events of 20 June 1303. In later years he would recite the 'Passion of the Monks of Westminster' by his predecessor John of London, in his *Flores Historiarum* (*The Flowers of History*). This Benedictine chronicle of St Peter's Westminster would, a few years after the event, provide its own unique interpretation of what happened in summer 1303 and deliberately set out to protect the monks' good name by claiming that the robbery was the work of only one man.[1] Chaucer's favourite phrase, '*Cacullus non facit monachum* – The cowl does not make the monk', may well have been in common usage long before the great poet's time even though Robert of Reading tried to prove the opposite. Almost a hundred years after the robbery of 1303, Chaucer savagely lampooned the Benedictine Order with his depiction of one of the Black Robes as a hunter, astride a plump horse, booted and spurred with an eye for the ladies and a love of the chase. Despite his public utterances even Robert of Reading in his more honest moments, must have acknowledged his Order's venal tendencies.

Certainly, 20 June 1303 marked the beginning of the 'Passion of the Monks of Westminster' – the ordeal the good brothers would endure at the hands of their King. Until then, the Abbey of which Robert of Reading was a member had been one of the most prestigious in the Benedictine Order. The Black Monk Community had been in existence at Westminster even before the invasion of William the Norman. The last Anglo-Saxon king, Edward the Confessor, had patronized the Abbey, whilst the Confessor's Norman successors not only developed the church but built their own hall and palace nearby, which came to house the great offices of state, as well as the developing Courts of Law, Kings Bench, the Courts of Common Pleas and of Chancery, these all sat in the different recesses and alcoves of the Great Hall of Westminster, first built by William Rufus at the end of the eleventh century. Around both palace and abbey, Westminster had expanded like the mustard seed of the Gospels. Once the Island of Thorns, a plot of land formed by Tyburn stream as it forked and flowed into the Thames, Westminster came to dominate that stretch of land by the great river as it curved in its flow through London.

The Abbey itself was huge. Not only was there the Collegiate Church of St Peter, but many domestic granges, courtyards, gardens, orchards, fish-ponds, vineyards, mills and other possessions. The entire ecclesiastical complex was bounded by a curtain wall cut by different gateways (see Figure II page 31). A traveller coming by land from the City would pass the Temple holdings, those of the Carmelites, or the White Friars, the Royal Mews at Charing Cross, then proceed down Kings Street on to the Royal Way which ran to its junction with the aptly named Thieving Lane. If he wished to bypass St Peter's, he would continue along

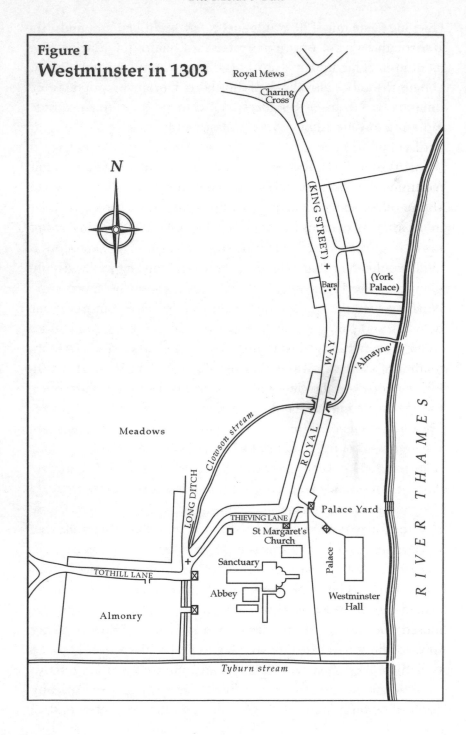

Figure I
Westminster in 1303

Royal Mews

Charing Cross

N

(KING STREET)

Bars

(York Palace)

WAY

'Almayne'

ROYAL

Meadows

Clowson stream

LONG DITCH

RIVER THAMES

Palace Yard

THIEVING LANE

St Margaret's Church

Palace

TOTHILL LANE

Sanctuary

Abbey

Westminster Hall

Almonry

Tyburn stream

Thieving Lane but, if he wanted to enter the Abbey, he would do so through its great northern entrance, a soaring double-arched gatehouse. The upper storey of the gatehouse served as the Abbey prison because the Abbot of Westminster was a Seigneur, a manor-lord in his own right, with the power to punish, correct and hang, on the Abbey stocks, pillories and gallows standing in nearby Tothill Lane.

On 20 June 1303, Robert of Reading, a monk of some years at Westminster, would ruefully reflect that the physical layout of the Abbey buildings must have played its part in the great scandal now gathering over his house. Travellers from the City, like those powerful lords who arrived to inspect the Royal Treasury in June 1303, would enter that gateway and find themselves in the Abbey precincts. Northwards from the gatehouse stretched the Sanctuary. In theory, such an area covered the entire Abbey but this was simply not practical; the monks occupied the south side, whilst the Sanctuary consisted of marshland north of the Abbey buildings. Sanctuary was an ancient right at Westminster, dating back even before the time of William the Norman, but codified during the reign of twelfth-century abbots such as Gilbert Crispin. To the south of the gate lay the church of St Margaret of Antioch, Parish Chapel of the Westminster community, built to cater for their needs so the laity would not interfere with the good brothers, at least that was the theory. St Margaret's stood independently, very close to the wall which divided the Abbey from the Palace of Westminster. However, stately though it was, St Margaret's architecture was nothing compared to the soaring mass of the Abbey which had been rebuilt and renovated by the King's father, Henry III of blessed fame. Henry III had trans-formed the Benedictine House into a Royal Mausoleum, which housed the shrine of his great patron saint, the Holy King Edward the Confessor. Henry had spared no expense. He had studied the best designs of France and hired master masons to carve out of Reigate stone and Purbeck marble, a breathtaking vision of stone, many-sided with an apse, or end, composed of chapels radiating out like jewelled stems, soaring walls, turrets and towers all supported by a double tier of lofty buttresses. Inside the Abbey church stretched a nave lit by windows with aisles and side chapels and, at its centre, the glorious sarcophagus of the Confessor. The stewards of all this splendour in stone were the Abbot and his Benedictine community, lords in their own right, to whom the royal heralds later ascribed a coat-of-arms, a blue shield bearing a gold cross, with fleur-de-lys and five golden doves. This insignia was everywhere, even emblazoned on the refectory silver which so mysteriously disappeared during those turbulent days of 1302–3.

The monks, the shrine keepers, were supposed to pray for Henry III and others of his family, Edmund Crouchback, the king's younger brother, Eleanor of Castile, the King's first wife, as well as their pathetic children, many of whom never survived the perils of childbirth. The monks also managed the Chapel of the Blessed Virgin Mary which held that sacred relic, the girdle-cord once worn by the Mother of the Saviour, as well as the Shrine of the Confessor – though this had never become as popular amongst pilgrims as Henry III would have wished, being outshone by the shrine to that most ardent opponent of royal authority, Thomas à Becket, at Canterbury.

Between the Abbey and the curtain wall to the south stretched the main monastic buildings, the houses and apartments of the abbot and prior, the cloister garth, refectory, kitchen and guest house. Further east stood the infirmary which stretched down almost to the Palace wall and overlooked the Pyx Chamber and Chapter House. The latter was an octagonal building, the windows of the Crypt beneath it, stretching out like the splayed fingers of a man's hand. The Abbey Crypt would be one place relatively unknown to the likes of Robert of Reading: it was reached by the eastern entrance in the south transept and was cut off from the rest of the Abbey by a number of stout doors. These were connected by a steep winding staircase where certain steps had been hacked out to deter unwanted visitors, the gap only

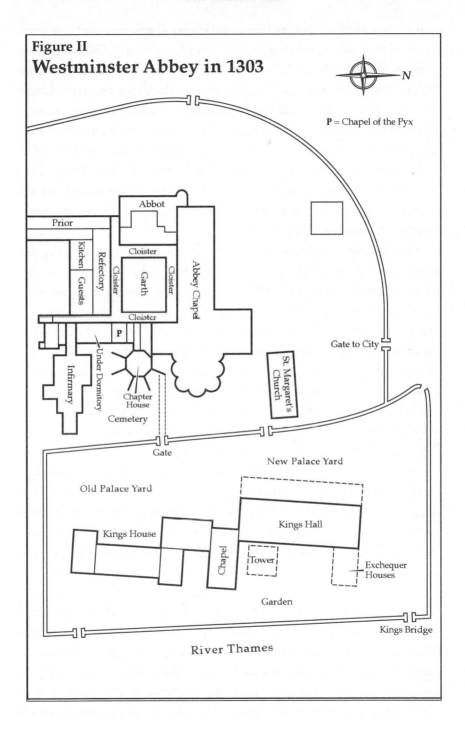

Figure II

Westminster Abbey in 1303

N

P = Chapel of the Pyx

being spanned by a portable set of wooden steps. The windows of the Crypt overlooked grassy wasteland as well as the monks' cemetery. Local farmers had leased the right to pasture their cattle here, whilst visitors to the Abbey could use the latrines built in the grounds. This wasteland stretched down to the Palace wall which, in turn, was cut by two gateways: one directly opposite the Crypt the other near St Margaret's church. Naturally the paths through these gateways were in continuous use by servants and pilgrims, as well as people milling between the Abbey and Palace where so much royal business was executed by hundreds of officials, lawyers, judges, stewards and bailiffs.

In 1303, however, such frenetic activity had ceased. The important offices of the state had, in 1298, been moved to York, to be near the king. Edward I had returned to Westminster in 1302 to hold two parliaments in July and October but, early in spring 1303, he had moved north again to prosecute bloody war against Wallace of Scotland. Monks such as Robert of Reading should have welcomed the peace which descended upon the Abbey precincts but the King's withdrawal had been the signal for mayhem and outrage which came to threaten the Abbey's very existence.

Robert of Reading later dismissed the great robbery of 1303 as the work of one man but, in his heart, he must have recognized the truth and secretly tabulated the causes. First was the problem of their Abbot, Walter de Wenlok, against whom four years later, Robert of Reading would be in fierce conflict. Wenlok, a Shropshire man, had been unanimously elected Abbot by the Benedictine community twenty years previously.[2] Now, in his Rule, the founder of the Order, St Benedict, had entrusted a sacred duty of care for his community to the abbot. This duty was to be shared with the cellarer but, as the Order expanded, other officials of the monastic community (or obedientiaries) were brought in to assist. In turn these obedientiaries were assisted by '*socii*' or helpers. By 1303 there were thirty-five such officers or obedientiaries at Westminster out of a community of about fifty.

These officers enjoyed considerable privileges. They could leave the Abbey for the town of Westminster, whilst the almoner, sacristan and cellarer could virtually travel where they wished.[3]

Such freedom of movement posed problems. Nevertheless, these paled into insignificance when compared to those of finance. The Abbey at Westminster had a wide range of income, from estates like the Honour of Eye and the Manor of La Neyte in Middlesex, as well as other holdings in Buckinghamshire, Oxford, Surrey, Berkshire and Gloucestershire, not to mention the royal manors formerly belonging to Queen Eleanor. Edward I had granted these to the monks so that they would light tapers round the tomb of his first wife, pray for her soul and sing the Requiem Mass on the anniversary of her death.[4] Other sources of income for the Abbey were equally far-ranging: the offerings of pilgrims at the tomb of the Confessor, the generosity of clerks such as Gerard de Aspale who diverted the profits of Haggheleford Manor to the Abbey so that two monk-chaplains would sing daily Mass for his soul.[5] The obedentiaries and the rest of the monastic community had the right to share in all this Abbey revenue. Such a sharing-out, termed the 'compositions', led to complex financial negotiations between the Abbot and his community as well as between the monks themselves. Robert of Reading, for example, would have known about the agreement sealed on 25 February 1303, some four months before the great scandal broke, between two officials of the Abbey: the precentor, or leader of the monastic choir, and the cellarer. According to this, the profits of the meadow land near the Abbey's vineyard which had gone to the precentor would now go to the cellarer, who also enjoyed the profits of the vineyard. He, in turn, would pay the precentor six shillings every year on the first Sunday of Lent. Accordingly, the monks of Westminster in 1303 had a great deal of freedom of movement as well as regular sources of income which they could augment through a series of business deals.[6]

Matters, however, might not have got out of hand, had Abbot Wenlok followed his own rule and cared for his community but, in truth, he was immersed in his own cares, keener to look after his family and retinue than his community of monks. The popular proverb: 'When the cat's away, the mice will play!' certainly applied to the monks in Westminster in 1303. Indeed, Wenlok appears to have shown little paternal care over the Westminster community or even any liking for the Abbey. He was often absent, preferring to stay in his manors, especially La Neyte in Middlesex or journeying to the Abbey estates such as Islip in Oxfordshire. Of course, he would return to Westminster for the great feasts of Christmas, Easter and the Commemoration of Edward the Confessor on 13 October, yet these appeared to be more state visits than a father caring for his community.[7]

Worse still, Wenlok, a passionate Shropshire man, was more devoted to his kith and kin than his fellow monks. Despite his promotion to abbot and his patrician ways, Walter remained devoted to his local parish of St Milburg at Wenlock. He was equally devoted to his family. He used a high-ranking monk of the Order, Alexander de Pershore, to buy his mother property around Ellesmere. Moreover, the surname Wenlok became a common one in the Abbey after Walter's election as abbot: at least three monks bearing that name joined the monastic community which proves another proverb – 'Blood is thicker than water'. These, too, profited, for example in 1296 Alexander de Pershore was ordered to pay the considerable sum of twenty shillings from the Abbey treasury, to a relative 'Father John de Wenlok'.

The Abbot's care for his family, especially his mother, is praiseworthy but it certainly interfered with his abbatial duties. He travelled to be near his mother in 1286/1287 and Wenlock in Shropshire was a considerable distance from Westminster at a time when travelling was both slow and dangerous. Sums of money were also sent to Walter's mother, whilst between 1289/1290 the abbot's mother, Lady Agnes, travelled in great state, along with the abbot's sister, to Westminster, stopping at Abbey holdings like the Manor of Pyrford in Surrey where she was given more money and gifts. The old lady stayed at Westminster for months, being royally entertained, along with other relatives, with feastings and minstrels. Such a state of affairs continued for the next eight years until the old lady's death in 1298. However, once mother was gone, Abbot Walter turned both his resources and those of the Abbey towards his sister. Other members of the family were also recipients of Walter's generosity including a so-called 'cousin', Christine de Evesham, who was brought up to Westminster and given lodgings nearby. Such generosity and largesse made Abbot Walter de Wenlok vulnerable and, as shall be shown, open to possible blackmail. Indeed the Abbot's zeal to help his family may have covered his own dark, secret sin.[8]

Here then was an abbot, often absent from his monastic community, expending both his energies and wealth on his family. The drain on Abbey resources must have been considerable. Wenlok worsened the situation by living in high style and insisting that this be strictly observed. He was Abbot of Westminster for twenty-five years, yet the longest document issued by Wenlok was a list of strict instructions about his own household. The Norman French of this high-toned *diktat* provides ample proof that the good Abbot had wandered far from the spirit of St Benedict. It begins as regal as any letter from the Crown: 'Walter, by the grace of God, Abbot of Westminster to all his loyal retainers, greetings!' It is worth translating and transcribing, for it reflects both the character of the man and the community Wenlok was supposed to guide, as well as providing an insight into how that community should have been administered, had the same high principles been followed. It continues:[9]

Everyone who maintains a household should follow a certain system for protecting that household and his own reputation: therefore, let this system, set forth here, be observed in all its items:

We have certain receivers to whom the bailiffs and brothers deliver the income from our lands. Tallies must be kept by them for all such receipts. No livery, or release, must be made by them, or from our estates, unless our receivers keep an accurate record of it and unless there is a letter from us to authorize it. These receivers must deliver to the Wardens of our household the necessary money to make provision for it, keeping scrupulous account of each sum delivered. Every night calculations must be made of all the expenses of the household in front of the Officials and the Steward who must control all expenditure, whether for my private chamber or the household in general. If the Steward is absent, only with our permission or command, then such an account must be sealed until his return. The expenditure in the meantime must be recorded by each individual officer, to be entered on the main account which must be sealed every night with the Steward's own seal. Beside the Steward of the household, there is a Steward of our estates, so both together will make provision for our journey through income as they think is best for both our honour and profit. The Steward of our estates is our Deputy and the bailiffs must carry out his instructions. He may arrive at our household with three horses, his clerk and three pages and he must receive honour next after ourselves. The Steward of the household must produce the accounts for him. He must describe the state of provisions, the stock and the treasure available. He must consult with our Steward of the estates on any important matter and, if necessary, await his coming before anything can be put right.

In the household itself the Steward represents us and all must show him obedience. Everything done in the various offices of our household is to be registered in duplicate under his supervision. The Officers of our house must bring in their accounts each evening and, in the presence of them all, the steward must make a strict enquiry of any possible misdoing. For the first and second petty offence, officials may be removed and punished. On the third they face dismissal. For any great offence the steward must dismiss them immedi-

ately and any loss to us be made up. Those who are
dismissed may never return in the hope of being forgiven!

The Marshal of our household must be of good appearance, courteous and prudent. He must observe and report
each night how many places have been laid at the table and
how many meals are served. He must see that important
guests have the right precedence at the table, that the
musicians and messengers are placed by themselves and
served according to their condition. The pages must
assemble at the door of our Hall where we ourselves are
seated. Pages who do not belong to our household must be
seated first and honourably served according to their state.
After the meal, guests must rise. They must not linger
between the hall and the entrance, nor gather in other
rooms but go immediately to the stables without arousing
the neighbours.

The Marshal must rise early in the morning and see that
there is no mischief amongst the pages, our own or any
others. He must visit the stables and make sure that the
palfreys and other mounts are comfortably littered whilst the
stores and mangers arranged so there is no waste of hay
through carelessness. The Marshal must be the first to rise
and the last to go to bed, for he is, as it were, the master of
our household. The Marshal must not indulge in sport,
whether it be with dogs or birds. It is his duty to be always
ready and, unless he has the Steward's special leave, he must
never be absent. Meals must not be served in separate
offices: those who want food must either take them at the
table in our hall or not at all. The Marshal also must prevent
any gathering of single women, pages and others about the
place, so that quarrels and other kinds of trouble can be
avoided. Fires must be lit in the hall on 31 October and
cease to be lit on the eve of Easter. The delivery of candles
is a matter to be settled by both Steward and Marshal. The
Marshal must be careful to have our hall orderly arranged,

cushions, wash bowl, basins and other furnishings in their proper place.

The Butler is to have charge of the pantry and the wine cellar. He must see that the wheat for the Abbot's bread is clean and pure. He must make special bread out of the finest wheat.

The master chef is the chief keeper of the larder. He must be careful there is no wastefulness in our larder or kitchen. He must be very clean, no one is to approach the Abbot's own special dish or come into the kitchen unless he is on proper business. Those who serve my Lord Abbot with dishes must be sober and clean in every aspect. The master chef, in particular, is a body servant of the Abbot. He must never be absent without permission and must know about his Lord's future movements. The porter must be a man of sound morals and of good address towards everyone and must never leave the court where his Lord is residing. He must supervise the delivery of all goods. If there is anything suspicious, he must immediately inform the Marshal or Steward so that it can be stopped. No one must be allowed in until the porter examines their loads and he should keep them, if he has any suspicions, at the door until he has spoken to the Marshal. He must take particular great care of boys, bad characters and women, lest scandal occurs. If a stranger of doubtful appearance comes, or is not known by sight, he must be stopped at the gates until his identity is discovered through the Steward or the Marshal's courteous questioning.

The laundry woman must also stay at the Porter's Lodge and there receive the linen and napery and deliver them back to the servants of the household. At bedtime the porter must go round the entire court and see that no one remains within except trusted retainers. No one in the household must keep dogs or birds. If anyone brings a dog, a bird and stays longer than three days that animal becomes the

Abbot's property to dispose of as he wishes. No retainer is to have a horse or sumpter pony or harness, except those to whom the Lord Abbot has given permission. The Marshal should make sure that the Abbot's squires are ready each morning, robed in the same livery as far as possible, especially when his Lordship goes to Parliament or other important assemblies to meet other noble Lords.

This interesting document describes the very strict supervision of the Abbot's household. It is quoted in length because it is most relevant (as shall be shown) to the causes of the great robbery. It is certainly a tragedy that such supervision was not exercised in the Abbey itself, where another document, the *Customary*, also provides a detailed plan on all aspects of Abbey life. *The Customary of St Peter's of Westminster* describes the Abbot's status as, '*Abbas, qui Christi gerens vicem preest ceteris in Monasterio* – the Abbot, who acts as Christ's vicar, is pre-eminent to all others in the Monastery.' The *Customary* is based on the Rule of St Benedict and lays down in great detail the life of the community, the duties of the obedentiaries, the conduct of the monks and the organization of daily life in the Abbey. It had been drawn up by Richard of Ware, Wenlok's predecessor, and is a bureaucrat's delight. Robert of Reading and all the monks were expected to know and act on this *Customary* in both its spirit and letter. Walter of Wenlok was supposed to enforce it in all its clauses. It has, in all, forty-eight chapters, dealing with the most minor matters, such as that of Chapter XXXV: 'The ritual of obsequies to be followed if a brother dies either within the quinzaine [15 days] of Maundy Thursday or on Holy Saturday or during the night or day of Easter.' Or Chapter XIV which stipulates minute regulations about the refectory: the tables must be properly prepared; if there is space, the brothers must sit wide apart, there must never be a majority of monks on one side of the table; anyone guilty of spilling wine, or making an unseemly noise, must immediately prostrate himself until his superiors allow him to retake his seat.

Nuts are not to be cracked noisily whilst cups are to be held in both hands, and so on.[10]

One of the great paradoxes of Westminster Abbey in 1303, and this must have puzzled monks like Robert of Reading not implicated in the robbery, as well as investigators such as John de Drokensford, is this: How could the Abbot Lord Walter of Wenlok, pre-eminent in the Abbey and author of that detailed *diktat* on his own household, promulgator of the *Customary*, defender of the Rule of St Benedict, allow members of his community to eat, drink and fornicate with whores; to ignore the instructions of the Prior; to harbour felons and outlaws; to fraternize with shady characters, rob silver intended for the Requiem Masses of a queen, and become involved in such treasonable activities as plundering the Royal Treasury? More importantly, why didn't this abbot, who issued such strict instructions about the positioning of cushions in his own hall, not notice, between November 1302 and June 1303, that the silver from the refectory of his own Abbey had gone missing?

Matters might have been helped if Robert of Reading could look to a powerful lieutenant of the Abbot for leadership and guidance. However, the Prior, William de Huntingdon, was a shadowy figure, weak and feckless, unable even to prevent, or so rumour had it, some of his brothers consorting with ladies of the night in the gardens of the nearby palace at Westminster.[11] True power seemed to lie with Abbot Walter's friend and colleague from the Midlands, Alexander de Pershore who, in 1303 held the office of sub-prior. He had come to pre-eminence in 1284 when he had accompanied Wenlok to Rome to secure confirmation of his abbacy. Once Wenlok became abbot, Alexander de Pershore emerged as a power in the land, securing loans for the Abbot, buying land for the Abbot's mother, holding the offices of Sacristan, Keeper of the Abbot's household, almoner, receiver and envoy to Rome. He appears to have been the link between Wenlok and his community, and between the community and the outside world, including, as we shall see later, a whole coven of nefarious characters.[12]

In an isolated location the dangers of the outside world to the peace of a monastic community were limited, but the Abbey of Westminster, to use a phrase from the confessional, was surrounded by many occasions of sin. First, Westminster town itself had expanded with properties built along King Street, the Royal Way, Thieving Lane and beyond (See Figure I p. 28). The Palace of Westminster was the seat of government and the officials who worked there needed houses, tenements, rooms and chambers. Walter Langton, the Treasurer, held property in Westminster, as did his deputy, John de Drokensford, who owned more than one tenement in Westminster and, to protect his holdings in York Place, had, in 1298/1299, ordered a wall to be built sealing off his property from these new developments.[13] Of course, such a hive of activity required inns, taverns, cook shops and bakeries which attracted swarms of tradesmen who, in turn, needed servants and workers, so the stream of retainers in and around the Palace expanded rapidly. Such power and wealth would attract other sorts: thieves, pimps, prostitutes, all the conjurors and cunning men of London's seedy underworld. Westminster offered rich pickings to such low life, especially as this boom town enjoyed its rights free of London's interference. Henry III had little love for his capital city but lavished affection, as well as a torrent of silver, on his own foundation at Westminster. In 1252, for example, Henry III had ordered the sheriffs of Buckinghamshire, Kent, Sussex, Essex, Norfolk, Cambridgeshire, Northampton, Berkshire, Wiltshire and London to send to Westminster by the Wednesday before the feast of St Edward of Confessor [13 October]: 76 boars, 60 swans, 71 peacocks, 1,700 partridges, 500 hares, 600 rabbits, 4,200 fowls, 200 pheasants, 1,600 larks, 700 geese, 60 bitterns and 16,000 eggs. Henry III undoubtedly enjoyed his feast but the communities around Westminster would remember, and resent, the cost to themselves. Henry III also made it very clear that London should not interfere with the liberties of the Abbey or Westminster town whilst London and other cities were ordered unreservedly to support the fairs of Westminster which took place every Monday, as well as the Great Fair of St Edward the Confessor which opened each October.[14]

Accordingly Westminster Abbey and town lay beyond the bar of London, the City's sheriffs and aldermen could not interfere with those who flocked to Westminster for whatever reason. Such a small yet teeming little town with its varied population was hardly a shrine of peace and calm. Violence was commonplace in its crowded streets. In 1235 a famous murder at Westminster had been perpetrated, the slaying of Henry Clement, an envoy despatched to the English king by the Justiciar of Ireland. The subsequent inquisition, the recod of the crime is worth translating as it not only conveys the violence and the crowded nature of Westminster, but the style of criminal investigation which the inquiry into the robbery of the King's treasury of Westminster would follow. The accounts, given by different witnesses, read as follows:[15]

Henry Clement, messenger of the Justiciar of Ireland, killed at Westminster in the house of Master David the surgeon.

William Perdriz, messenger of the Lord King, then in the house [where Clement was staying] says he was in that house just after midnight, on the Monday next before the Ascension of Lord, when five or six or armed men came with many others. He did not know the exact number but they entered the house of the said surgeon, broke the door of the hall and afterwards entered the hall and climbed towards the solar [a large upper room]. They broke the door of the said solar and they killed the said Henry and wounded the aforesaid Master David. Questioned if he knew who they were, Master William said he did not. Questioned again about the murder, he replied that he did not dare say anything at the time out of fear. The above-mentioned armed men said to him that if he kept his peace, they would not hurt him. Master David believes there were several more assailants outside the house because the said Henry Clement wished to flee but, when he went to go through a window, he withdrew on account of the multitude of people he saw in the vicinity.

Brianus, also messenger of the Justiciar of Ireland, was sheltering in a certain stable. He says that he saw no one or knew anything before the deed was perpetrated but he later raised the hue and cry. He said that he did not know who the attackers were and William, page of the said Henry Clements, said he was lying in a stable in the courtyard and that he knew nothing before the deed was done. And William, the manservant of the above Perdriz, came and he said that he was lying in the Hall. Several men came into the house, about 12 or more, so it seemed that the house was full but he dare not cry out but hid his head beneath a cloth. He said that when they left he followed them to the cemetery of Westminster, one of them turned round and threatened to come back, so he returned to the house and dare not follow them any more. He claimed he saw three of the attackers enter the cemetery with drawn swords. Sander the Scott, page of Thomas the messenger, explained that he was lying asleep in Surgeon David's house and that he saw six armed men enter. One of them held a great torch. When they reached the solar and saw that Henry was in the solar, they extinguished the torch and entered to perpetrate what they had come to do. Alice, Landlady of the said Master David, said that she was asleep in a certain chamber of the house, her family likewise, her boys with her when she heard the door of the hall being broken. She wished to leave but dare not because of her family. She raised the hue and cry and opened a certain window towards the court but was unable to arouse any of her boys who were asleep in the stable.

And Hawisa, servant of the said Alice said similar, that she was in a chamber but did not see anyone or know anything. Roger of Norfolk, who was asleep in a tent before the door of the Lord King's court, said that he heard men crossing over the threshold and saw several more, about sixteen, many of whom were armed and had drawn swords but he recognised no one. He said that their horses were at the cemetery, several stood there holding them and one went towards the town.

Geoffrey Suter was also lying in his tent. He heard horses and a horse braying, and, after a small interval, the door of Surgeon David's house was broken down. Armed men entered it but he did not know what they did there, but he heard the blow of swords. Master David swore that he did not recognize anyone, but armed men, about fifteen or sixteen in number, came into the solar and they wounded him and that the said Henry Clement opened a window and tried to escape but he came back on account of the multitude of men who were in the vicinity.

This account conveys so accurately the violence of medieval England, the horror of dark nights in cramped lodgings, of torch lights being abruptly doused, of felons carrying through their villainy unchecked and how the law depended solely on witnessed evidence. The atmosphere conveyed by this document, almost 800 years old, is truly gothic in its depiction of medieval Westminster. The same atmosphere would permeate the Crown's investigation of 1303 into the great robbery of the King's Treasure at Westminster, beyond the bar of London, swarming with landless men and women, a shifting population of good and bad. The same macabre atmosphere pervades the great robbery: gates and doors being summarily closed, felons gathering in the darkness of the Abbey grounds or the courtyard of Fleet prison, men on guard against the law: villainy being perpetrated so brazenly that innocent folk could only hide and watch.

Westminster Abbey itself did little to help the situation and, perhaps, made it even worse with the protection offered by its Sanctuary. Robert of Reading would have known about that marshy area to the north of the Abbey precincts. Here, according to the law and ancient usage, felons fleeing from the law could shelter and, provided they stayed there, be protected. They would eventually have to abjure the realm but, as one of the principal robbers later proved, sanctuary could be used as a respite whilst the thief plotted his escape elsewhere. The Sanctuary of Westminster dated back at least to the abbacy of Gilbert Crispin in the twelfth century. His decree makes it obvious how the right of sanctuary was linked to the shrine of the Confessor.

Do you know that Jordan [a fugitive] sought the altar of St Peter at Westminster and the body of King Edward the Confessor. Consequently, we pray that he has, therefore, the liberty of his body and the peace of the King.[16]

Such close proximity of the sanctuary to both the Abbey and a town already packed with landless people looking for employment was an unholy mixture. Little wonder that when the authorities did swoop on Westminster in June 1303, they would find hiding there a former priest and professional church-breaker, the Lincolnshire man, John de Rippinghale, fresh from his most recent exploits at Woolnoth where he had helped himself to church goods, and John le Riche, supposedly a servant for the Abbey who, in his other life was an outlaw in Bedfordshire and liked to call himself John Ramage. Robert of Reading must have wondered why his Benedictine brothers moved so easily amongst such people, did business with them and even recruited them for their own households? Was it because what their Father Abbot could do, they would certainly imitate? Such household retainers needed feeding and supporting. Brother Adam de Warfeld, the Sacristan, had at least six pages in his retinue, about whom all kinds of rumours were swirling.

Robert of Reading could openly bewail the monks' ill-treatment in the 'Passion of the Monks of Westminster" but he and others had to close their eyes to sacrilegious theft, like that already mentioned, of £100's worth of silver intended for Masses for the repose of Queen Eleanor. The Abbey of St Peter was supposedly an enclosed community. However, even the most biased of chroniclers would have had to concede that the Abbey grounds were busier than the great October Fair, with comings and goings of a wide variety of people, including carpenters and masons working on the Chapel of St Stephen or repairing the damage caused by the Palace fire of 1298. Accordingly, it is understandable that such craftsmen would also fall under suspicion during the summer of 1303.

Through the windows of the Abbey buildings Robert of Reading could glimpse the towers and turrets of Westminster Palace, only a short walk across the monastic enclosure. If the Abbey was leaderless, the Palace was in a more parlous position. The Lords of the Soil, the Great Ones, who worked in the royal Palace and Hall as well as the nearby Exchequer and Chancery Buildings, had all moved to York. True, the King did return for a while, but his eyes were on Scotland, his heart set on conquest. In ordinary circumstances some control could have been exercised by John Shenche who had inherited the keepership of the Palace through his wife Joan. However, Shenche, too, was an absentee official, leaving the palace to his lieutenant William Palmer.

Robert of Reading must have known all about William, a veritable imp of Satan who had endeared himself to some of the leading monks, organizing special parties for Alexander de Pershore and others 'who, . . . within the gardens of that palace, played, ate and drank with women of bad reputation about which they were often reproved by their prior'. Intimate illicit relationships developed between these supposedly celibate monks and ladies of the town, no wonder the Sacristan of Westminster, Adam de Warfeld, was rumoured to have offered the daughter of William Russell a bracelet and gold ring so that 'she could become his friend'. Stories of such licentiousness and lechery could not be ignored nor could those of the likes of John

Rippinghale, John le Riche and other undesirables roaming the Palace and Abbey whenever and wherever they wished.

William Palmer, or William of the Palace, as he was also known, was deputy Keeper of the Fleet Prison in the City as well, so he too enjoyed close links with the villains of London's underworld – as if the Abbey did not have enough problems with the its own Sanctuary men. William Palmer was hardly fit company for Benedictine monks. He had left his own wife and openly consorted with his whore Edelina, daughter of Nicholas the Cook, a member of whose family had been imprisoned in Newgate some seven years earlier for an attempt on the Royal Treasury.

Now the great scandal over the robbery of the royal treasure was about to break, other rumours surfaced: how, three years earlier, there had been a fresh attempt to breach the Crypt in the year of the Great Jubilee [1300]. Then the Abbot had gone to the King and hushed the matter up but not this time. During May and June 1303 items from the royal treasure had been found in the cemetery and wasteland around the Abbey. The Coroner of Westminster, Henry de Cherring, had even come to investigate such finds whilst, in the early spring, Alexander de Pershore and Adam de Warfeld had shut the Abbey off, closing its gates and doors, refusing admission to people who had every right to enter.

Finally, there was the ominous presence of a clerk and former merchant, Richard de Puddlicott from Oxfordshire.[17]

3

The Clerk's Tale

'Dieu pur soun seintime noun, confideat errores
E ceux que pensent fere tresoun, et pacis pertubatares'

'May God, for his own sacred name, confound errors, traitors
and other disturbers of the peace'
Contemporary ballad

'*Descendam et Videbo!* – I will go down and see' was God's reply when he heard about the sins of the ancient cities of Sodom and Gomorrah. The text must have been foremost in the mind of John de Drokensford, when he entered London in early summer 1303. Drokensford, like other royal officials, recognized that King Edward's anger at the news of his Treasury at Westminster being violated would be boundless. What actually happened when the King's letter of 6 June 1303 arrived in London is a matter of some speculation. However, Drokensford must have slipped into the city like a thief in the night to take counsel with the justices appointed by the King: Ralph de Sandwich, Constable of the Tower, John de Bakewell, Walter of Gloucester and Richard de Southcote.

It is apparent from later evidence that Drokensford, the king's wrath incarnate, wished to make his preparations well. He was aware of London's hostile attitude to the King and more than conscious of the Abbey of Westminster's rights. After all, Drokensford's main offices adjoined the Abbey whilst he was directly responsible for the Treasury. Moreover, Drokensford owned property in Westminster and was on cordial terms with Abbot Walter and the monks of the community. Drokensford's family held 90 acres of land in Hendon from the Abbey of Westminster. Abbot Walter had even hired Drokensford as a *peritus*, a counsellor skilled in law, paying him a retainer of twenty-five pounds sterling seven years earlier while, only four years before, Drokensford had been the Abbot's favoured guest at a splendid meal where he had been royally entertained by specially hired minstrels.[1] Nevertheless, such favour had to be forgotten, the King's business was paramount. Edward I had chosen well, Drokensford, for all his City connections, was not a Londoner. He was not tainted with the seedy politics of the capital. He was the King's man, body and soul, to be with him in peace and war. Drokensford had been promoted by the Crown so that his loyalty was to the King, his own career and his family. He owed everything to royal favour, as well as to his own undoubted skill and expertize.

John de Drokensford was born in about 1260 in the hamlet of Drokensford near Bishops Waltham in the Meon valley of South Hampshire. Despite his glorious days as Keeper of the King's Wardrobe, he would always retain a deep affection for that little hamlet and, above all, the memory of his revered mother, a filial virtue he and Wenlok shared. The Drokensfords were manor lords, owning ninety acres in Hendon and a further 120 in Finchley, both still in the heart of the English countryside. The Drokensfords were of noble birth and had their own coat-of-arms: ('Quarterly Or and Azure, four birds heads adorsed and counter charged') as well as the wealth to put their able son on the path of preferment. The effigy on Drokensford's tomb in

Wells Cathedral depicts an intelligent, calm-faced man of medium height whose register of documents, still extant, attest to a dedicated individual, though one given to hot temper, an innate characteristic of a man with boundless energy. Unlike Abbot Wenlok, Drokensford was not arrogant, he recognized his faults. He was also generous. He often forgave debts and placed himself at the disposal of those he served. He was diligent, energetic and diplomatic; above all, he was loyal.

Drokensford's parents were dead before their son reached the pinnacle of greatness but he never forgot his roots. He later built a beautiful altar tomb for his mother in Drokensford church, with an exquisite marble effigy of her. She appears to be a lady of some status, the bodice gown arranged in folds: around her neck she wears a heart which is clasped in one hand, a symbol of widowhood, as well as deep affection for her dead husband whose heart was probably buried with her. Sometimes stones do speak and Drokensford's village church depicts wealthy, doting parents who loved each other and their clever son, for which he was eternally grateful. He lavished his wealth on his family, though not unfairly or to the detriment of his duties. Nepotism flourished in the fourteenth century: this was not just offering free meals and favours to kith and kin, Drokensford needed men he could depend on and who better than relatives? Unlike Walter of Wenlok's relatives, Drokensford's family members had to work for their bread.[2]

Drokensford emerges from the pages of history as a loyal, highly efficient and effective official, an ideal choice to hunt down the criminals who had ransacked the Royal Treasury, seize them, as well as recover the king's possessions. Drokensford had a keen mind. He was probably educated in the Halls of Oxford for he patronized that university liberally to the total exclusion of Cambridge. He must have studied law, becoming so skilled that several leading families hired him as their attorney. Nevertheless, Drokensford's real genius was finance. It was 1286, while he was with the English army in Gascony, that Drokensford had entered the byzantine financial world of Edward I. He had at first served as a simple Clerk of the Exchequer, but his skill was soon noticed and Drokensford was quickly introduced into the subtle intricacies of Edward I's developing financial systems. By 1290 the Exchequer still controlled the kingdom's finances under its Treasurer Walter Langton. The Exchequer supervised expenditure and receipt, received dues for the Crown and audited the Sheriff's accounts four times a year at Easter, Midsummer, Michaelmas and Hilary. However, the king was the centre of government, and where he went the administration followed, so that his needs and those of his vast household led to the emergence of another prominent office of state, the Wardrobe, which financed the king in war and peace. The Wardrobe covered all the varying accounts of the different households of the king, the queen and Prince of Wales: gifts, messengers, day-to-day expenses, as well as foreign and military activity. Drokensford soon proved that he had a flair for such administration, being appointed Cofferer, then Controller and finally, in November 1295, Keeper, a post he would occupy for the next twelve years.[3]

Drokensford was well paid for such high office, receiving £200 a year for his own household (a massive sum in those days), not to mention the revenues of certain ecclesiastical benefices which he did not have to occupy. Nevertheless, as a royal minister Drokensford had to work for his money, be it in London or on the Scottish march. He was to support the King in peace and war and knew from bitter experience that this could be both costly and dangerous.

The clerk who accompanied Drokensford into London in May 1303, and was present at the opening of the violated treasury, Walter de Bedwyn, was Cofferer of the King's Wardrobe, Drokensford's lieutenant. However, Walter only held this office because Drokensford's first appointment, his close friend and colleague, Ralph de Manton, had been killed in Scotland only a few months previously. On 26 February 1303, de Manton had been with an English force ambushed by the Scottish war-leader,

Sir Simon Fraser. The English launched a furious counter-attack but de Manton was already captured. He begged for his life, offering huge sums of money but the Scots taunted this clerk, 'Garbed in Steel Hauberk', before slicing off his hands and head.[4] De Manton's fate proved that being a royal clerk, a senior official of the Royal Wardrobe, was no protection against the rigours of war or violence. Drokensford himself had been part of Edward's battle group at Falkirk in 1298 whilst, a year earlier, Drokensford had fielded a force of three knights and twenty-nine mounted squires for the King's Flemish campaign and, in 1301, two knights and sixteen mounted squires for Scotland.[5] Drokensford was both clerk and a fighting soldier. He would need the qualities of both in resolving the crisis of Westminster at the height of summer 1303. He would also need that escort of military might to seal off the Abbey and Palace so as to conduct his own thorough searches.

Finally, if Drokensford was acquainted with the horrors of war, he was also acquainted with its cost. Edward I was desperate for money, searching for it through loans, taxes and extra customs dues and a variety of other schemes which even included ransacking the deposits of Parish chests. In the year of 1302/1303 the receipts of the King's Wardrobe totalled about £120,520 whilst expenses amounted to almost £140,000, and this did not include hidden debts etc. The gap between receipt and expenditure was a staggering £20,000 which, carried forward year after year, threatened to bankrupt the King. Accordingly, the royal treasure hoard, containing hundreds of thousands of pounds' worth of precious goods, was vital to the King. Edward could raise loans on its security – so the robbery not only inflicted a terrible blow to the royal pride but also to the royal pocket. Drokensford fully understood how urgent it was to rectify the situation, not only because of Edward's financial demands but also because the Treasury was directly under his control.[6]

In the reorganization of Edward's finances and possessions during the 1290s, the King's Wardrobe became responsible not only for the King's household but also its stores and treasures, a distinction being drawn between the great store-house in the Tower of London, placed appropriately close to the workshops of the royal armourers, smiths and fletchers, and that of the Treasury proper. In the early 1290s Westminster Abbey was chosen as a place to store this treasure. Thirty years earlier Henry III had finished building the splendid Chapter House with its massive central pillar soaring up to its concave roof, well lit by windows with its sedilia inbuilt against the wall. Now, the Benedictines already had their own treasury, the Pyx Chamber along the east cloister. The Pyx was part of the original undercroft of the old eleventh century church and lay just beneath the monk's dormitory. Part of this undercroft had been walled up and used as a security room, with only one entrance protected by a massive door with six locks; it was prevented from being fully opened by a high stone sill built into the floor. There is no doubt that both Crown and Abbey used the Chapel of the Pyx, or Pyx Chamber, to store both valuables and documents, especially the latter. The Pyx chamber was secure though its outside windows overlooked a blind spot, a secluded place near the infirmary. Consequently, it is understandable that later historians should claim that the Pyx Chamber was where the royal treasure was stored and the robbery took place. However, the evidence from the accounts, as well as a contemporary drawing of the robbery, (see Figure III p. 54) clearly indicates that the Treasury was in the Crypt which, in fact, was an ideal strong room.[7]

The Crypt lies beneath the Chapter House. And as we saw in the Prologue, its floor is about thirty feet in diameter, its walls seventeen to eighteen feet thick in places. Entrance through the roof was impossible and clearly open to detection. The windows of the Crypt are narrow and were probably covered by bars reinforced by metal plates, and stout wooden shutters or even slabs of concrete. Still, as with the Chapel of the Pyx, these windows constituted the 'Achilles Heel' in the Crown's security measures. As we have seen, access to the Crypt was only along a

Figure III

In the Cottonian ms. in the British Library, written in the year 1304, the chroniclor has made his own drawing of the robbery, which shows a sole thief at work breaking through one of the windows of the crypt, this done largely to exonerate the monks of the Abbey.

narrow passageway from the Abbey Church near the Sacristy, through stout doors then down steep steps, some of which were missing. The actual door to the Crypt was thick and reinforced, its keys held by important Wardrobe officials. The Crypt had been specially paved by the mason John le Convers. Drokensford himself had seen the account for the work, '*Subtus* – Under' the Chapter House of Westminster, for which £5s.10d. had been paid. Inside the Crypt was a further security measure: the squat, central pillar was used as a safe or strong box. Parts of this very thick stone column were ingeniously carved out to form secret recesses in which there were other recesses. Valuables could be stored within and then concealed by inserting the missing slabs of stone.[8]

The treasure held there was certainly great. Edward I's letter of November 1303 claims £100,000's worth of it was stolen,[9] which, at the beginning of the fourteenth century, was literally a king's fortune. Drokensford also had in his possession the ledgers of the unfortunate Ralph de Manton from November 1300 listing the precious items stored in the Crypt. Such accounts, curious enough, had been drawn up in the very year of an earlier abortive raid on the Treasury, involving some of the monks, though, as we have seen, this had been hushed up by Abbot Walter de Wenlok's pleading with the King. These previous failed attempts to rob the Royal Treasury simply proved that the Crypt was impregnable. Moreover, the thick walls and narrow fortified access were also enhanced by the sacred nature of the place. Westminster Abbey was the Crown's own chapel, the kingdom's most prestigious church, the shrine of the Confessor, the mausoleum of royalty, the place of Coronation. It was sacred. Any riffler or felon would incur excommunication for violating such a place, and would be cursed by bell, book and candle in all his [or her] doings and actions, denied Christian burial and damned to the fires of hell for all eternity. The King's lawyers would also argue that theft from such a place constituted treason. The guilty party would be put to the horn, to be hunted down and killed like a wolf or, if seized by the law, suffer the full rigours for the crime of treason. Edward I had, by statute, decreed the most horrid punishment for such a crime. The death of the Welsh Prince David, brother of the great Llewellyn, had been published to all. The Welsh prince had been hanged, his stomach cut open, his entrails and bowels ripped out and burnt, his head struck off, his corpse quartered then boiled and tarred and sent to decorate the bridges and gatehouses of certain cities.[10]

Edward I would have a personal vendetta against the felons who robbed the Crypt. The treasure house not only contained royal regalia dating back centuries, but personal gifts such as a ring and a lid of a cup, enamelled with jasper, which had been given to Edward by his sister-in-law, the Countess of Cornwall in 1294. The treasure also included the Cross of Neath much prized by the King as one of the great spoils from his victory over the Welsh princes, Llewellyn and David. In 1294, while he was at Conway recuperating after his victory in the principality, a group of Welshmen approached Edward 'with a part of the Holy Wood of the true Cross the Welsh call Crosseneyte which Llewellyn and the Princes of Wales, owned'. Edward had been so delighted by this symbolic token of conquest that he gave the man responsible, Hugo Ap Ythel, a robe worth twenty shillings and enough funds to study at Oxford. Edward often took the Cross of Neath on his travels and spent £105 on adorning its pedestal with gems set in gold. Edward was furious when this precious relic was reported missing.[11]

Such precious items were family heirlooms, personal gifts, royal regalia, sacred relics as well as solid bullion against which loans could be raised. The Wardrobe book of 1299–1300, which analyses Edward I's income and expenditure for that year, has an entire chapter of over twenty pages dedicated to the royal treasure and minutely describes the wide range of items and what they were used for. The treasure included the crown which the king wore at church and dinner, ornaments with sapphires, emeralds and eastern pearls: two stones from Mount Calvary in the Holy Land given to the king by John Ailward. A gold ring, with sapphires, said to belong to St Dunstan. These jewels and other goods were also used by the King as gifts or, in lieu of payment, such as the silver cup given by Queen Margaret to envoys going beyond the seas to her mother the Queen of Navarre. The robbers had struck at the very heart of Edward's power and he would retaliate.[12]

The King's instructions to his justices, proclaimed in his letter of 6 June 1303 regarding the robbery, are quite specific. He had posed certain questions in his letter. 'Who are the malefactors? Who knew about the robbery?' Who offered and gave the robbers help, counsel and assistance? Who knowingly received the said treasure? How was the said treasure taken and how much? In whose hands is it now? What were all the other circumstances surrounding the said robbery? The king did not send these questions to the law officers of London, but to his justices and the likes of Drokensford.

Naturally, news of the robbery had spread through the city. Goldsmiths were involved whilst precious items were being hauled from the Thames as well as found in ditches and fields around Westminster and elsewhere. Indeed, according to one jury, the Coroner of Westminster had already been alerted about these finds and gone out to the Abbey to enquire about certain treasure found in or near the cemetery of St Margaret's by an old woman called Isabella (or Margaret) Lovit (or Lovett). The indictment actually stipulates that the Coroner had visited the Abbey six weeks earlier. Now such evidence (to be discussed later) was presented on 5 July which means that by the 25 May 1303, people in the know in London and Westminster were already alarmed by rumours and were trying to establish the truth. The Coroner, of course, was given short shrift by the two leaders of the errant monastic community at Westminster, Alexander de Pershore and Adam de Warfeld. The officer was bluntly told that it was none of his business so he could do no other, the Charter of King Henry III had specifically forbidden unwarranted interference by the City of London or anyone else in the Abbey's affairs.[13]

Drokensford and the King's justices were a different matter. They had received specific instructions from the King. Nonetheless, how they were to carry these out without alerting the thieves who thought they could hide behind the privileges of the Abbey or the connivance of some of the great men of London was another matter. Silence and speed would be the order of the day. Nevertheless, like investigative officers in any period of history, they first had to appeal for information and hope for the best. They must have arrived in London, taken counsel with Mayor John le Blund and decided on issuing a proclamation. In the later insertions of the *Liber de Antiquis Legibus* (literally *The Book concerning the Ancient Laws*) and translated as *The Chronicles of the*

Mayors and Sheriffs of London there is the following undated proclamation about the robbery:[14]

[Notice given on the occasion of the robbery of the King's Treasury at Westminster: 31 Edward I]. We do command you, on behalf of our Lord the King, upon forfeiture of life and of limb and of lands of chattels and whatsoever else you may forfeit, that all those who found any of the treasure of our Lord the King, be it gold or silver or precious stone or anything whatsoever, whether within the city or without, in whatsoever place it may be, coming from his treasury at Westminster, which has been broken into, such a person shall come into the Guildhall before the Mayor and Sheriffs and restore what they have found between this and Sunday next by the hour of Vespers. We do also command, on behalf of our Lord the King, under the pain of forfeiture aforesaid, that all those who have sold or bought any of the said treasure, or know any persons who have sold or bought any of the said treasure, or know any persons have found any part of the said treasure, or have the same in their keeping, in any manner whatsoever, shall come into the Guildhall before the Mayor and Sheriffs and shall show and acknowledge what they know about it, between this and Sunday next at the hour of Vespers, in the manner as is before stated. Whoever shall not do this, on or before such a day, the King will hold them as felons against him.

The proclamation is stark and uncompromising. If anyone knows anything about the robbery at Westminster, that person must present themselves at the Guildhall by 'Sunday next before the hour of Vespers'. The proclamation was the work of Drokensford and the other royal commissioners, though they were keeping in the background. Edward I and his ministers were not popular in London.

Now, bearing in mind what was to happen on Monday, 17 June 1303, the Feast of St Botulph, as well as the phrase 'between this and Sunday next' the proclamation must have been issued on Sunday, 16 June 1303. Like any hunters, Drokensford and his colleagues hoped to flush someone, or something, out into the open and they were not to be disappointed. As we shall see, some of the culprits did panic and hastily moved treasure which brought them to the attention of other people. However, Drokensford was rewarded with an even greater prize, for on the day following the proclamation, William Palmer, Deputy Keeper of the Palace, appeared in the Guildhall. He wanted to confess, though, of course, it was a self-serving confession fashioned to protect both himself and others. The account of it, written in Norman French, reads as follows:[15]

On Monday, the Feast of St Botulph, 17th June, William Palmer, valet of John Shenche, Keeper of the Palace, came into the presence of Ralph de Sandwich, John le Blund, Mayor of London, John Clicot, Coroner of London and Simon de Paris, Sheriff of London. He claimed that Adam de Warfeld, Alexander de Pershore, Thomas de Dene and John Butterley [restorer of the fabric of St Mary's at Westminster] and a certain novice (who had lately arrived and had been ordained for that Chapel, of whose name he is ignorant) as well as John of St Albans the mason and a certain John his valet, and William, valet of Dominus Arnold de Campania, as well as a certain valet from Essex (who had returned into the City of London and whose name he did not know), together with John, son of Geoffrey [also referred to as Philip] the carpenter and Roger de Wenlok, valet of the Sacristan and Roger de Prestok who works in the cellar at the Abbey, together with Robert de Cherring, John de Noteley, John de Prescot and Thomas de Lichfield, all knew and were consenting to the burglary. William said that the Sacristan, Adam de Warfeld had given him ten shillings, through John of St Albans, that he might keep their plan secret.

This betrayal is startling. William Palmer was indicting leading monks of the Abbey of Westminster. Besides Alexander de Pershore, whose career has already been noted, John de Butterley was also a friend of Abbot Wenlok, and made payments on his behalf as far back as October 1297. Butterley was Steward of the Abbot's household and Keeper of the Chapel of Our Lady in the Abbey, a rich source of funds for the monastic foundation. Adam de Warfeld had also been in the Abbey for some years acting on behalf of Abbot Wenlok in October 1297. He, too, had served as the Abbot's Steward and acted as his attorney in dealing with property belonging to the Abbey. On 24 February 1303 he had been appointed Sacristan, a powerful position in the monastic community because he had access to the Abbey treasure as well as other precious goods owned by the Benedictines. More importantly, Adam de Warfeld, as Sacristan, was responsible for security. Thomas de Dene had been Abbot Wenlok's Keeper of the Larder as far back as 1295, becoming monastic treasurer in 1299, certainly a man trusted by the Abbot. John de Noteley had witnessed a charter at Westminster on 24 March 1297. Robert de Cherring was probably a young monk, as was Thomas de Lichfield.[16] The others were valets or servants to the Abbey, but it is interesting to note that, as early as this, craftsmen working within the Abbey or Palace precincts were also named: John Albon [or of St Albans], a mason working in the Abbey, is reported as playing a prominent part in the burglary.

At first glance it would seem that William Palmer had panicked and wished to protect himself by giving evidence against his former colleagues. A closer study of his confession demonstrates William's cunning, not so much in what he said but what he doesn't say. He doesn't actually blame the monks for breaking in but says that they were 'consenting to it'. There is no reference to who actually carried out the crime, except that besides the monks, certain valets and two craftsmen – a mason and a carpenter – were involved. William of the Palace was gambling, for Westminster Abbey was strictly off-limits to law officers of the City. The monks could refuse entrance to them by citing royal authority: they themselves could claim benefit of clergy so they could not be tried by the secular arm, whilst the likes of the mason, John of St Albans, together with Geoffrey (or Philip) the carpenter, could seek sanctuary in the Abbey grounds and later make their escape. William was, perhaps, hoping that the prospect of invading the Abbey would cause significant delay or, indeed, block any progress at all. After all, the Coroner of Westminster, Henry de Cherring, had already been out to the Abbey, because of treasure being found, and he had been sent packing. Why should it be any different again? Criminals often display arrogance; William of the Palace certainly did, although he had been tricked by that proclamation. There is no reference to Royal Commissioners or what was planned, just a general warning. The proclamation talks only of London officers waiting at the Guildhall for evidence to be presented. When William of the Palace appeared before them on 17 June he had totally underestimated the opposition facing him, particularly Drokensford, who immediately seized on the information supplied and took decisive action. Palmer's confession marked a defining moment in the investigation. The forces of law and disorder clashed, The '*Dies Irae* – The Day of Anger' had arrived.

William's confession also establishes a chronology, a context for the robbery. The Treasury was broken into and robbed between Tuesday 30 April and Friday 3 May 1303. From evidence submitted later, it appears that rumours of the crime were rife by Pentecost, on or around Sunday, 25 May. Those involved had begun to panic and were beginning to move treasure from Westminster along the river to fields in Kentish Town. The Coroner of Westminster had been alerted. He must have warned Ralph de Sandwich and John de Drokensford. There is considerable evidence that information was also supplied by monks inside the Abbey, such as Reginald de Hadham, a future Prior of Westminster and an obedientiary implacably hostile to Wenlok and Pershore. The above-mentioned royal officers, now fully alerted, visited the scene of the crime, entered the Treasury in the same way the robbers had and established that a considerable portion of the precious hoard had been taken. They then sealed the forced entrance. Around 28 May they despatched, by sea or road, couriers bearing the dreadful news to the King in Scotland. The robbers, of course, realized that their crime had been detected but were confident that their privileged status would keep them safe. On 6 June Edward I responded, his letter would have reached London by Friday 14 June at the latest. Once Drokensford and his colleagues received the royal writ, they issued the proclamation on Sunday, 16 June. William Palmer's confession was obtained on 17 June but what then? Drokensford certainly visited the Crypt on Thursday 20 June to carry out a formal audit which he supplemented with additional treasure seized from other people between the 20 and 23 June. More importantly, leaders of the break-in were quickly arrested between 16 and 20 June.

The following month, July 1303, the juries from the wards of London and the surrounding shires appeared before the Royal Justices to provide any information they could about the robbery. Their presentments, written down in dog-Latin or equally atrocious Norman French by the local ward clerk, provide a clear insight into what happened at Westminster Abbey in June, 1303. Drokensford and the Royal Justices arrived like avenging angels. Their military escort ringed the Abbey with a circle of steel, and the fiery royal clerk, the King's man, went to work. Drokensford and his colleagues carried out a thorough search of the Abbey and its grounds. A later indictment proves this referring to '*Le jour du cherch fet* – the day the search was made'.[17] They went out into the wasteland and cemetery around the Crypt. They inspected the hemp, long and thickly clustered, sprouting around the windows of the Crypt where the robbery had taken place. They soon established it had been sown deliberately to conceal the robbers' handiwork. Therefore, the crime had been planned for some time. Afterwards, they scoured the entire ground. One of the justices, Walter of Gloucester, actually discovered precious items in the cemetery grass, which were handed over to Drokensford.[18] The Sanctuary was also violated and a thorough search made – which accounts for the line from one of one of the indictments: that a certain John 'the Priest' or 'the Chaplain' had been captured and detained at Westminster. This was the defrocked priest John de Rippinghale who was immediately lodged in the Abbey prison above the gatehouse at Westminster.[19]

Drokensford carried out a similar search in the Abbey itself despite the protests of the monks, and later evidence suggests that the royal clerk did not balk at violence. When, later, in 1307 Abbot Wenlok became involved in an acrimonious dispute with Prior Hadham, Wenlok accused him of being instrumental in getting him [the abbot] summoned to the King's Exchequer '*Super roberia et factura camerae Prioris*, over the robbery and the breaking into of the Prior's Chamber'.[20] Though at first glance this might seem as if the Prior's Chamber was robbed, in fact it refers to Drokensford's behaviour during his investigations. The Prior at the time of the robbery was William de Huntingdon, the nonentity who had virtually lost control of the Abbey to Alexander de Pershore. The Prior was present when Drokensford arrived, as he witnessed the famous indenture of 20 June. Drokensford apparently broke into his chamber to carry out his search for evidence and stolen treasure. Before that he questioned the monks for information. Some, of course, remained silent: others like Roger de Hadham, totally innocent, were shocked at what had happened and, deeply resentful at their Abbot for allowing such a state of affairs to develop, undoubtedly cooperated with the royal visitors. Hadham provided any information he could which Drokensford seized on before he began his search. Some of the monks certainly resisted, which led to doors being forced and chambers searched.

This violence also accounts for Robert of Reading's description of the robbery. In his chronicle, *The Flowers of History*, he does not specifically describe the attack on the Treasury but compares it with a contemporaneous attack in 1303 on Pope Boniface VIII by the agents of Philip of France, due to a long-standing conflict between the French King and the papacy. Philip's agents brutally seized the Vicar of Christ at the town of Anagni and later ransacked his Palace.[21] At first glance there seems little comparison between the robbery of the Royal Treasury, aided and abetted by Benedictine monks, and the violence perpetrated against the Pope by the envoys of the King of France. Robert of Reading is, of course, being most economical with the truth. He is not specifically referring to the robbery but to the violence carried out by Drokensford and others in their search for the truth. Robert de Reading looked for any similarity between the two events and seized on one incident: Anagni had been ransacked and so had Westminster. Other evidence indicates resistance to the royal searchers. A later indictment would accuse Adam de Warfeld the Sacristan of hiding goods, not just from the City officials but also from the King's ministers, as well as a reference to jewels and precious goods found in the Sacristan's chamber. 'They say that Adam de Warfeld, Sacristan, knew of the burglary, in that he concealed part of the treasure from the *ministers* of the King.'[22]

It is highly unlikely that Adam de Warfeld gave these up voluntarily but was forced to do so. Two days later, on 22 June, Drokensford drew up a detailed indenture of the jewels found in Westminster Abbey treasury. (An indenture is a document drawn up in duplicate or triplicate then divided in a jagged fashion, validation is proved if the pieces fit exactly together.) In the appendix of that indenture is another heading: 'Jewels found in the custody of the Sacristan of Westminster'. The goods are then listed:

- A silver gilt-edged flagon with fleur de lys.

- A silver gilt-edged cup, the same used for the reservation of Christ's Body.[23]

So it would appear that the Abbey was ringed off and raided, chambers broken into, the grounds searched and sacristan Warfeld and others closely questioned. Any chatter about the Church's rights would be brutally swept aside. According to the lists of prisoners drawn up in July/August 1303, ten monks at Westminster were ensconced with others in the Tower:[24] Adam de Warfeld, Alexander de Pershore, Thomas de Dene, Robert de Cherring, John de Noteley, John de Prescot, Thomas de Lichfield and John de Butterley. Two more joined them, Ralph de Morton the cellarer and Roger de Bures. Ralph de Morton had been Chaplain of the Abbot in 1288, as well as Keeper of the Abbot's household. Roger de Bures acted as an important official for the Abbot and the entire community in their appeal against Peckham, Archbishop of Canterbury in 1290. Bures had also been archdeacon in 1293 and was often despatched on the Abbot's business. In 1302 Roger de Bures is described as cellarer which also meant that he exercised an important position in the monastic community.[25] Such humiliation of the Black Monks was unheard of. Undoubtedly these ten detentions were due to searches Drokensford carried out as well as his questioning of the Benedictines at Westminster. In doing so Drokensford had truly breached the robbers' real defence. They had put their trust in the rights of the Abbey, its independence and the clerical status of its community, yet these had been totally ignored as they would be for the next ten months. Drokensford and his colleagues interrogated the monks and obtained the names and whereabouts of their principal associates which led to the lightning arrests of Richard de Puddlicott together with the principal 'fence' John of Newmarket sometime during Tuesday 18 June and Wednesday 19 June 1303. They were seized in their homes in possession of stolen items. John of St Albans the mason being also arrested in or near Chartson Abbey.

Once this business was settled, Drokensford, on 20 June 1303, together with his witnesses, the Justice Roger de Southcote, John le Blund, Mayor, Ralph de Sandwich, Thomas Queorle, Cofferer of the Queen, Walter de Bedwyn and the Prior of Westminster were ready to view the damage and formally inspect the Treasury.[26] These men accompanied Drokensford as his witnesses. Drokensford had to be sure a proper accounting took place. He did not want to face later allegations that some of the precious items disappeared after he entered the treasury, Edward I did not take too kindly to corruption or theft by his ministers. Drokensford knew only too well what had happened during the purge of 1289 when Edward had returned from France to find that officials like Adam of Stratton had been helping themselves. Adam's punishment, and that of others, was ruthless and swift: seizure of property, total disgrace, imprisonment, heavy fines and banishment.[27]

The indenture, drawn up on 22 June 1303, formally records the event concerning the jewels stolen from treasury in the thirty-first year of the reign of King Edward.

When John de Drokensford, Keeper of the Wardrobe of Lord King of England, was sent by him to parts of London for certain business and to carry out certain orders of the King, the said John came, on 20th June in the 31st year of the King's reign, to Westminster where he had been given to understand that the Treasury of the Wardrobe of the aforesaid King had been broken into by thieves and the King's treasure feloniously taken away. On account of which Lord John, when he acknowledged this, in the presence of Lords Ralph de Sandwich, Constable of the Tower, John de Bakewell and Roger de Southcote, Justices of the Lord King, John le Blund, Mayor of the City of London, the Prior of the said monks of Westminster [William de Huntingdon] and Thomas Queorle Cofferer of the Queen's Wardrobe did, in a nearby place, examine the keys of the said treasury which had been brought in a pouch of leather, its seal unbroken, by Lord Walter de Bedwyn, Cofferer of the King's Wardrobe which he had with him by reason of the King's injunction. There, in their midst, he showed [John de Drokensford] the keys from the pouch with the seal unbroken and, in their presence, took out the keys and opened the doors of the treasury. Lord John de Drokensford entered the said treasury [with the above witnesses] and, when they did, found the treasury had been broken into, its coffers and chests shattered and many goods furtively taken away. Now, first, because many of the jewels which were taken by the thieves were later replaced and, secondly, many of the jewels stolen were afterwards found in different places, this indenture was made by witness of the above.

This document totally disabuses the idea of later historians that, somehow, the keys to the royal treasure were kept in the Abbey. This is simply not true. The keys were in the custody of a senior official of the King's Wardrobe and kept in a sealed leather bag which, until 20 June, had never been opened since it had last been sealed. The scrutiny of the keys took place 'in a nearby place', perhaps the sacristy, after which the '*Ostia*' or gates of the Treasury were opened. Once inside, in the glow of candles, lamps and sconce torches, the witnesses could view the devastation: coffers and chests forced open and goods scattered. Undoubtedly the secret places in the central column had also been ransacked, because it was later proved that the thieves spent at least a day and a night there gathering loot and breaking it up before taking it away.

Drokensford's first task was to impose order, the treasure had to be itemized, stored in chests and moved to a more secure place – the Tower. The first part of the indenture then goes on to list treasures not stolen. These were immediately taken up, placed in one great chest which, along with the suspected monks, was also transported to the Tower. The second part of the indenture describes those jewels and the list is lengthy. This, in turn, is followed by those jewels found in 'the care of the Sacristan'. Nothing betrays Drokensford's legal training more than this enigmatic phrase. The truth was that Adam de Warfeld had most reluctantly handed these jewels over. The Sacristan would have maintained such precious items, found in the Abbey grounds [as a later indictment declared], had been handed over to him and that he was 'Keeping them safe' – this was his defence. Drokensford, tongue-in-cheek, employed the same phrase when listing such goods, the King's judges would decide on whether Adam de Warfeld's explanation was acceptable.

The list is incomplete. It does not include all that was recovered later but simply those jewels found there on 20 June, as well as those later seized during the last week of June. In a letter of November 1303, Edward reveals that £100,000's worth of treasure was stolen. The indenture did not include the Cross of the Neath, nor did it refer to the precious coins which were filched and, some four months later, mysteriously appeared in the money markets as far away as Kings Lynn in Norfolk. What is important is that by 20 June 1303, Drokensford knew the full extent of the damage, he had contained it and re-imposed order, now he had to search for the rest of the treasure and bring those responsible for stealing it to justice.

4

The Sheriff's Tale

'De Vicecomitibis, Quam duri sunt pauperibus?'

'Concerning the Sheriffs – how hard they are to the poor!'
Contemporary ballad

Amongst the noble and famous cities of the world, London, the capital of England, is one of the most outstanding. It possesses above all others, abundant wealth, wide commerce, great grandeur and magnificence. It enjoys a healthy climate, professes the Christian religion and possesses strength in its fortresses, its location, the honour of its citizens and the chastity of its matrons. In sports, too, it is most pleasant and, in the rise of illustrious and famous men, most fortunate. Its citizens are not addicted to licentiousness or lewdry nor are they savage or brutal but kind and generous

As regards to Divine Worship they have St Paul's Church, an episcopal see. There are also in London and its suburbs, thirteen larger conventual churches besides one hundred and thirty-six parish churches. On the east rises the great

Tower, a fortress of huge size and strength. Its courtyard and walls were established upon very deep foundations, the mortar used on the buildings was tempered with the blood of beasts. On the west are two Castles strongly fortified [Montefichet and Castle Baynard]. The city walls are high and thick with seven double gates having, on the north side, towers placed at proper intervals. London used to have such walls and towers along its south side but, because of the excellent river Thames (rich in fish, whose waters ebb and flow with the tide), the southern walls have long disappeared. Further west high up on the bank of the river Thames, stands the royal palace of Westminster. An incredible structure furnished with bastions, the palace is situated in a popular suburb about two miles distant from the city. Adjoining the houses of the citizens are spacious and beautiful gardens, well endowed with fruitful trees. On the north side lies fresh pasture, delightful meadow land, cut by flowing streams on which stand mills whose clatter is most pleasing to the ear. Near the city lies a stretch of immense forest, with densely wooded thickets where game of every kind, stag, deer, boars and wild bulls are to be found . . .

The workers of the different crafts, the sellers of various commodities, and the labourers of every kind, each have their separate station which they take up every morning. There are also in London, on the north bank of the river, wine-shops and public eating houses. Every day, according to the season there can be found there meats of all kinds: roast, fried and boiled, fish large and small, coarser meat for the poor and more delicate for the rich, such as venison, fowl and other small birds . . .

According to the evidence of the chroniclers, London is more ancient than Rome: indeed, both derive their origin from the same Trojan ancestors. So it is, that even to this day, both cities use the same ancient law and ordinances. London, like Rome, is divided into wards; it has annual sheriffs instead of consuls; it has an order of senators and inferior magistrates . . . Every type of business, be it administrative, executive or judicial, has its own appropriate place and proper court. On stated days it has its own assemblies. There is no city in which more approved customs are observed; attending churches, honouring God's ordinances, keeping festivals, giving alms, receiving strangers, confirming betrothals, contracting marriages, celebrating weddings, preparing entertainments, welcoming guests, as well as the ordered arrangement of its funeral ceremonies and the burial of the dead. The only inconveniences of London are the immoderate drinking of foolish persons and its frequent fires. Moreover, almost all the bishops, abbots, and great men of England are, in a manner, citizens and freemen of London. They own magnificent houses in the city to which they resort, spending large sums of money whenever they are summoned to London for councils and assemblies by the king, or their archbishop, or are compelled to go there for their own business.

Fitzstephen's description of London, translated and transcribed here (and given in full in the Appendix), is compelling. And though written in the last quarter of the twelfth century, his description, albeit biased, does capture the great vibrancy and springtime freshness of a bustling city, eager to expand and manage its own affairs.[1] Another Chronicler, however, of the same period, Richard of Devizes provides a powerful insight into the seamier side of Edward I's capital city. Richard of Devizes describes the advice given to a young boy leaving for England. The boy is warned to avoid, at all costs, visiting London where every race brings its own vices and every quarter abounds in grave obscenities teeming with prostitutes, magicians, beggars and extortionists.[2]

In the early summer of 1303, Hugh Pourte was one of the two annually elected sheriffs of this exciting, sprawling, teeming, luxurious yet squalid city with its population of about 100,000. In shape the London of 1303 was a rough rectangle with six main gates dating from Roman times. On the south-east corner rose the Tower, William the Conqueror's great fortress to overawe Londoners with its soaring central donjon, the entire complex had been extended by Henry III and Edward I with girdling walls, towers and fortified gatehouses. This line of defence ran north to Aldgate, west to Bishopsgate and Cripplegate and down through Newgate to the Thames. By 1303 the city enclosed about 330 acres: beyond its walls, gates or 'bars' lay the 'Portsoken', or Liberties such as Southwark across London Bridge which need not acknowledge the authority of the City Fathers and was rapidly becoming a place of ill-repute with its ale-houses, taverns, stews and brothels. The city was a busy mix of nobles, tradesmen and merchants, as well as a growing, shifting population drawn to London by the prospect of wealth.

This variety of population was reflected in the contrast of buildings; hovels and huts giving way to high walls with imposing gateways which protected the wood and plaster or grey rag-stone mansions of the wealthy. The houses of the well-to-do in fourteenth century London were grandiose affairs. Thomas Mocking, a fishmonger, owned a palatial residence which he called 'The Castle on the Hoop', which lay in the parish of St Magnus near London Bridge, the same area where Sheriff Hugh Pourte and his wife Marjorie Horn had their residence. Mocking's Will describes the different chambers of his 'Castle' and their contents. In the bedchamber were two beds with hangings, chests and counters [tables]. In the Hall two trestle tables, fire-dogs for the hearth, wash-bowls and basins, candelabra and cushions. In the store-rooms stood barrels and vats for ale and wine, jugs, plates, salt cellars, silver cups, mazers (maplewood bowls) and table linen. In the upstairs parlour were dining tables, an accounting table, benches, stools and even chairs. There was a room for workmen and apprentices – suitably furnished and a kitchen with plates, cups, tankards, tripods, spits, pots and cauldrons. This should be compared with the 'shop' of John Le Botonner in Cheapside on the corner of Soper Lane, open on three sides: this was five feet square and six feet high. The contrast in wealth was marked but, what united Mocking and Botonner, was that, rich or poor, they were both citizens of the capital.[3]

London's principal church was the towering mass of St Paul's, its steeple packed with relics to protect it against lightning. The Thames was spanned by a high bridge lined with shops and houses as well as pikes for the severed heads of traitors. The bridge had its own chapel dedicated to St Thomas à Becket, a fitting memorial to a famous Londoner who had dared to withstand the anger of Henry II, Edward I's great-grandfather. Becket paid the price of such resistance with his life for which Thomas was rewarded with sanctity, martyrdom and a religious cult which became the envy of every church in Christendom.

On the northern bank of the Thames stretched the broad quaysides. The river was the principal route through London and constantly thronged with barges, skiffs, boats and wherries. Wharves such as Dowgate, Queenshithe and Billingsgate had developed into busy import and export centres. To the north of these quaysides, entered through needle-thin alley-ways and runnels as well as the occasional broad thoroughfare, stretched the City proper, a bustling trading centre which exported English wool and grain whilst importing cloth, wine and other European luxuries. Foreign merchants flocked to such a booming town. The Hanse of Germany, a powerful merchant syndicate, had their own quarters at the Steel yard in Dowgate, whilst the Lombard Bankers such as Frescobaldi had already made their impact in the City with their loans both to the Crown and the merchant community.

The Church was another powerful corporation. Most of the city land was owned by the Church. Besides St Paul's and 110 parish churches, there were numerous collegiate foundations such as Holy Trinity and Blackfairs, as well as a wide range of elegant nunneries and priories. The city's commercial hub was the great thoroughfare of Cheapside with its shops and stalls, around which clustered the different quarters or centres for the principal crafts: goldsmiths, carpenters, glaziers, pepperers, cordwainers, fishmongers and drapers, each craft struggling to win civic and royal recognition for itself. The City had spilled beyond the walls. These expansions, however, were linked to the quarter enclosed by the city walls. 'Cripplegate Without' is a fine example of London recognizing its geographical limits yet equally determined to control what spread beyond its gates. Due to the great use of timber in housing, fire, as Fitzstephen noted, was a constant hazard. This fear of fire led to a series of injunctions about citizens keeping ladders, vats of water and fire hooks ever ready. Fear of fire in London could also prompt its own black humour. In 1267 the royal army, mopping up the remaining forces loyal to the memory of the dead Simon de Montfort, laid siege to London. The army needed provisions, so the enterprising Sheriff of Essex, Richard de Southcote, plundered the Hundred (a unit of local government) of Chafford and seized 'for the provisioning of the King's host' wheat, oats, cheese, bacon, pheasants, meat and forty live cockerels which Southcote proposed to use as incendiary bombs by tying fire to their feet and send them flying into London so as to burn the city to the ground. The good citizens of London, if not the cockerels, were relieved when Roger decided that all the goods he'd seized would be better used for feeding himself and his extended family than sustaining the royal army or setting London alight.[4]

The mass of buildings clustered around Cheapside, that broad market thoroughfare had its own spacious Conduit, a massive underground water system drawn from Tyburn stream and brought through lead and elm-wood pipes. The Conduit was the glory of the city as well as a famous luxury. Elsewhere public hygiene was a mixture of public proclamation and desperate measures to clear the narrow lanes of refuse heaped round makeshift central gutters, empty the lay stalls (the great rubbish heaps) as well as keep the streets clear of dangerous over-hanging signs, wandering pigs and scavenging dogs. Animals were a constant source of vexation. Pigs, except for those belonging to the hospital of St Anthony and marked by their special bells, could be killed on the spot and their owners fined 4*d.* a day. Horses, too, had to be supervised for there are cases of a horse kicking a man to death or biting off some unfortunate's ear.[5]

Hugh Pourte, Sheriff from 1302 to 1303, had, with his colleague Simon de Paris, the unenviable task of enforcing law and order in London. He was responsible to the council, the mayor and aldermen who represented the twenty-four wards of London, units of government which had grown up and developed around some local landmark or church. The mayor and aldermen were all-powerful, their dignity, processions and rituals are lovingly described in the *Liber Albus*, (*The White Book*), drawn up in the fourteenth century to consolidate and publicize the organization of the City. Each alderman ruled his ward like any modern gangster would his 'patch', being responsible for law and order, fire regulations and even the appointment of four scavengers to keep the streets clean. The ward was a tightly knit organization: strangers were recognized, the King's peace maintained, the hue and cry raised, felons pursued, public hygiene managed, the curfew imposed, lighting at night devised, beggars controlled, orphans looked after and widows cared for.

Even the most superficial survey of the *Liber Albus* reveals an eagerness for organization second to none. There were regulations for corn dealers and porters, masons, carpenters and plasterers, how attorneys and pleaders were to act in the courts, how the water from the Thames should be supervised, how each ward council must be elected. Indeed, every aspect of life was regulated, from ordinances against usurers to the sale of lampreys. Each ward was under its alderman and 'moot', or council, with an executive staff of serjeants, bailiffs, clerks and scavengers. The alderman was given the title of *Dominus* [Lord]. He wore robes of office, supervised the assize of arms (the deployment of weapons), and, when the military contingent of the ward assembled under its banners, the alderman would lead them out to the great mustering place near St Paul's. These aldermen patronized the local churches, endowing them with chantries where Masses would be sung for their dead. They administered their own poor relief and, as a group, they even had their own festival 'La Fête du Puy' dedicated to music and singing which met in their private Chapel of St Mary at their headquarters in the Guildhall.[6]

When an Alderman was robbed in 1304, the court roll gave a minute description of the contents of his ward chest. It was crammed full with letters and documents, charters and indentures covering every aspect of ward life. Indeed, woe betide anyone who brought the office of alderman into disrepute. In 1298 Adam de Rokesle, a member of one of London's most patrician families, intervened in a fracas in Thames Street. One of those involved turned on him, cursing and vilifying him then, horror upon horror, actually struck the alderman in the face. This miscreant was condemned to walk barefoot, clad only in a tunic from Thames Street to the Guildhall carrying an axe in the offending hand, the loss of which was the ancient penalty for such a heinous felony.[7] The wards therefore were cells of government within the city, self-enclosed units where it was the duty of one's neighbour to keep an eye on everything that happened. The Crown would exploit such organization in its investigation into the robbery at Westminster in summer 1303.

Towards the end of June 1303, Hugh Pourte, along with the mayor and aldermen, would have met in the Guildhall with its upper chamber, offices, gardens and courtyard on what used to be called Cat's Street. They assembled to discuss the crisis. Hugh Pourte, a fishmonger, must have recognized the dangers posed by both the robbery of the treasure and the arrival in London of royal ministers such as John de Drokensford. Edward I's intervention usually spelled trouble for the kingdom's premier city. Forty years earlier, when the Londoners had supported the rebel Simon de Montfort, they had pelted refuse from London Bridge at the queen-mother and fielded their ward levies to help defeat the Crown at Lewes in 1258. Edward I was deeply suspicious about both the aldermen and the unruly gangs which roamed London. The King was ever eager to exploit the issue of lawlessness to exercise royal authority over his boisterous capital.

London, however, was a community of individuals who knew their rights, so eccentricity and bizarre behaviour were commonplace. In 1300 the Rector of St Margaret's Lothbury had imported the rotting corpses of four wolves in an attempt to cure a mysterious disease call 'Loup'. London was the place where jousts were very popular being held on land, water and even ice, such tourneys could bring all work in London to a halt for an entire week. Above all the City refused to be disciplined. John Le Furder used church towers for target practice with bow and arrows. At Clerkenwell a wrestling match brought down the friary wall. Passionate public disputations took place in the schools; cock fights, bear and bull baiting were highly popular. All this frenetic activity was fuelled by the 360 taverns and 1,400 beer and ale shops which served the capital during the first decade of the fourteenth century. Alcohol, as in any age, fed the fires of lawlessness. Bellatores (battle-men), rifflers and brawlers, organized gangs, roamed the streets after curfew looking for trouble. Time and again Royal Justices were sent in to sort the problem out. Time and again their cry was: '*Nulla inquisicio recte facta est in civitate Londoniarum* – It is not possible for an inquisition to be made correctly in the city of London.' In 1281 an investigation into such lawlessness led to sixty-nine men being accused of a wide series of crimes from mayhem to murder. However, the majority walked scot-free but the interesting aspect of this investigation was how many of those indicted were the sons of noble families, apparently on very good terms with the professional rifflers and gangsters whose daggers could be bought for a pot of ale. The Crown responded with stringent proclamations such as the following, issued by Edward I, sometime between 1285 and 1298.

These are the articles of which our Lord the King has proclaimed in his city of London for the preservation of its peace. Whereas many murders, robberies and homicides have, in times past, been committed in the city by day and night, it is now forbidden that anyone walk the streets, with sword or other weapon, after the curfew bell is tolled at St Martin le Grand, unless he be a great Lord, a respectable person of note or an acknowledged servant. They must bear a light and, if any be found doing to the contrary, they are to be committed to the tun [a huge prison cage kept on top the Great Conduit in Cheapside]. On the next day such criminals must be brought before the Warden or Mayor and punished accordingly. No taverner is to keep his tavern open for wine and beer, nor to admit anyone into his tavern, or into his house, unless he be willing to answer for the King's peace under the penalties named [these penalties can be found in the *Liber Albus*]. No one is to keep a fencing school by night or day under imprisonment for forty days. Whereas malefactors, who have been arrested are often treated far too leniently to the encouragement of others, it is proclaimed that no prisoner shall be released by the Sheriff, or his officer, without the permission of the Warden, Mayor or one of the Alderman and that each Aldermen must make diligent search in his Ward for misdoers. If any be found, he must bring them before the Mayor and the Alderman for due punishment if he is proved guilty of the charge brought against him. No foreigner or stranger is to keep a hostel in the city, only those who are free men of the city or can produce a good character reference from the place from which they have come and are ready to find surety for their good behaviour. No broker is to be allowed in the city, except those who are sworn before the Mayor and Aldermen and, if any broker or hostler be found in contravention of these ordinances, after one month of publication, they are to be arrested and punished. The King, who desires that his peace in the city be well kept amongst all folk, has heard that the above articles are not observed, and cannot be observed, because his own ministers often incur and provoke displeasure and punishment for having imprisoned and punished misdoers, for which reasons his ministers are reluctant to punish evil doers and suspect persons, and so such evil doers are becoming more bold in their evil ways. The King therefore commands that his ministers be no longer sued for punishing offenders unless it be shown that they have acted through malice. The King demands that the above-mentioned ordinances be kept for preserving the peace, together with any other injunction it may please him to make, for the benefit of the city.[8]

The *Liber Albus*, in page after page, lists the punishments for any infringement of the King's peace in the City. Nevertheless, it all made little difference. Ale, beer and wine were plentiful. The narrow streets were dark and fetid. Every man carried his dagger or club and was ready to use them, as a contemporary entry from the Coronor's roll testifies:

On Friday, before the Feast of the Purification [2 February 1301], information was given to the Coroner and Sheriff of London that a certain Copyn le King lay dead, other than from his rightful death, in the house that he hired of Robert de Rokesley in Dowgate Ward in the parish of St. Laurence, Candlewick Street. Accordingly, they proceeded there and, having summoned the good men of the Ward and the other three nearest Wards, namely Candlewick Street, Langeborne and Bridge, they diligently examined how his death had occurred. It appeared that, on Thursday before the Feast of the Conversion of St Paul at the hour of curfew, a certain trader carrying apples for sale came before the building of Master Gilbert the Marshal at the top of the street near Grace

Church crying 'Apples for sale'. The said Copyn le King and a certain William Osborne bargained for some of these apples and wished to take five of them against the will of the trader who raised a hue and cry. Along came a certain Thomas le Brewer who reprimanded the said Copyn and William for taking the apples against the wishes of the trader. Angry words rose between them and the aforesaid Copyn and William assaulted Thomas le Brewer following him with abuses as far as Fenchurch where, at the top of the street, the said Thomas turned back and struck the said Copyn on the left side of his head with a staff. He inflicted a wound an inch long and two inches deep and another wound on the right of the head of the same length and breadth. So, wounded, Copyn lingered until the Thursday before the Purification and then died of his injuries at the hour of prime. Nevertheless, the Jurors say, Thomas acted in self-defence. Asked what became of the said Thomas, the jurors replied that he had been taken and committed to prison at Kingston where he was living before being moved to Newgate. The corpse was viewed on which the wounds appeared. Afterwards, the said Thomas appeared before the Justices of Newgate on which day came Christiana wife of the said Copyn ready to prosecute her appeal against Thomas. However, the King allowed the said Thomas into his peace and the writ remains in the hands of Hugh Pourte Sheriff in the thirty-first year of the King's reign [1302–3].[9]

This fascinating incident demonstrates how tightly the wards were organized, the role the jury played as well as the sudden violence of London's streets where a war of words could soon be drowned by the clash of weapons. However, what concerned Edward and his ministers, and would have some bearing on the investigation of the robbery, was the way this violence could be stirred by the very class supposed to suppress it. The aldermen, the *domini* of London, could rouse the mob as they did in 1272 when, for two weeks, the mob besieged the Palace of Westminster where the old King Henry the III lay dying, Edward his heir being absent on Crusade. The crowds demonstrated shouting its refrain over a period of fourteen days: 'We are the Commons of the City, we have the right to elect our own mayor.' From the very beginning of his reign Edward, tired of such insults to both his family and Crown, waited for his revenge.

Nothing exemplifies better the ties between the alderman class of London and the City's squalid underworld than the case of Ralph Crepyn, Clerk to the Aldermen's Council. Crepyn was a money-lender, a loan shark with a mistress Alice Atte Bowe who kept a tavern in Mark Lane not far from St Paul's. Crepyn, by day, was a public official, a leading clerk, an important man in London. By night he was a criminal who used his office to protect his own nefarious activities. Crepyn became involved in a feud with a goldsmith, Lawrence Duket, who was as big a rogue as Crepyn. In 1276 Lawrence Duket killed a physician, William le Frenoud, but walked scot-free when he produced a royal pardon obtained for him by no less a person than Ralph Crepyn to whom Duket became indebted. This debt was never resolved. Both men, former friends and allies, now became inveterate enemies and hired gangs of riflers to pursue their own vicious vendetta. On 26 July 1284, both gangs met in Cheapside and, in the sword fight which followed, Duket wounded Crepyn, so he fled for sanctuary to the church of St Mary le Bow. Duket stayed there five nights and, on the fifth night of sanctuary, he apparently took his own life by hanging himself from a bracket on the wall. However, a young page boy staying with Duket, who was sleeping in the church, revealed that a gang organized by Crepyn's mistress, Alice Atte Bowe, had broken into St Mary's and hanged Duket but made it look like suicide. The King was furious. Crepyn was arrested and sent to the Tower. At least six others were hanged whilst Alice Atte Bowe was burned alive. The Crown and its ministers held the City aldermen responsible for this vicious, squalid crisis.[10]

Matters were not helped by gaol breaks from the Tower, the fugitives being pursued into St Paul's churchyard where they were captured and beheaded, their heads taken back to the Tower for display. At the same time four men and a woman escaped from Newgate Prison and staged a demonstration on the roof – all five were dragged down and hanged out of hand. There were other concerns. The area around St Paul's, the very place where the City wards would muster, was becoming the haunt of felons, thieves and vagabonds. Edward, determined to bring such lawlessness to an end, sent one of his ministers, Roger de Kirkby, and a panel of judges into the city. The leading Londoners were furious. They controlled the gangs as they controlled the wards. They objected to Kirkby's interference and publicly hectored him. Edward's reaction was violent. Some aldermen were banished, others imprisoned and the running of the City was taken into the King's hands. Edward I had made his point, proving the words of Andrew Horn the Chronicler who wrote the *Annales Londonienses* – The Annals of London. '*Malum est incidere in manus Regis et ideo, Cavete!* – It is an evil thing to fall into the hands of the King so, therefore, beware.'[11]

By 1299 the Londoners had their liberties restored and these were developed further, even the carpenters' guild held its own 'parliament' at Mile End. However, the great robbery at Westminster now threatened all this. Were Londoners involved? Had its leading aldermen and merchants been accessories before, as well as after the fact? Pourte, along with his colleagues Simon of Paris and John le Blund, were party to the proclamation of Sunday 16 June 1303. They had witnessed William of the Palace's confession and, above all, realized how the Treasury had been plundered. Pourte had good reason to be anxious as would his colleagues. Would this be a repeat of 1284 when the City was blamed for lawlessness? He and others would be interrogated on what had happened and what they had done about it, all played out against a background of increasing tension between the Crown and the City over the question of a fresh tax, the New Customs.

5

The Justices' Tale

'Sunt Justiciarii
Quos favour et denarii
Alliciunt at jure.
Hii sunt nam bene recolo
Quod censum dant diabolo
Et serviunt hii pure'

'There are justices whom favour and money entice from
what is right. These are they, and I recall them well,
who pay dues to Satan and serve only him.'
Contemporary ballad

John de Bakewell was an uncommonly fortunate man. He was
owner of Bakewell Hall in London, former residence of the great
noble Roger de Clifford. The hall enjoyed a prime location near
the Guildhall. The aldermen of the City had tried to buy it for the
Commune but royal pressure led to Bakewell's purchase of the
mansion. Bakewell was always fortunate. When Ralph Crepyn,
the City clerk, was indicted in the famous scandal surrounding

83

Laurence Duket's murder, Crepyn had to give up his distinguished post as clerk to the mayor and sheriffs (or Clerk of London) and Bakewell, a royal nominee, succeeded him, a great achievement for the son of leather-workers, tanners and skinners. Bakewell had risen due to his loans and gifts and, above all, his marriage to Cecily de Ludlow, sister of one of the great wool merchants of England. Bakewell also became a court favourite. In 1286 he was, due to Crown pressure, made an alderman as well as Custodian of the Merchant Seal, an important office under the Statute of Merchants, one of the King's legislative measures to regulate and control commerce, especially the wool trade.

Bakewell was fiercely resented by Londoners so, when Bakewell Hall was given to him, two powerful aldermen, though heavily indebted to Bakewell, organized a revolt. However, Bakewell, being also Deputy Royal Warden of the city, was in a position of power and King Edward was determined to break opposition to the Crown in London. In the short term, the King won. He held out for five years, the dispute with his capital rumbling on over the question of taxes and the way the City was organized. Nevertheless, the citizens of London were determined on the restoration of their rights and, in 1298–9, they managed to reach a rapprochement with the Crown, but they had further demands, too – Bakewell's removal being one of them. Bakewell did surrender the clerkship of the City, although he was instructed to be one of those who would observe that the 'ordinances of the King be strictly observed.' Bakewell continued to hold a series of high offices and was involved in the negotiations for a Peace Treaty with France whilst, in 1296, he was sent to Scotland as an escort to Cardinal Sabina, a papal envoy.

The citizens of London persisted in their dislike of Bakewell. In 1303, Edward I, in the throes of a new dispute with the City over the question of customs and other issues, gave vent to his anger: Bakewell would be of one of the justices appointed to inquire into the robbery at Westminster. This was a shrewd move betraying the King's suspicions about the City's involvement in the robbery. Since Bakewell had been the City Clerk, he would know of the Londoners' secret dealings and take no nonsense from former opponents on the Council.[1] He was joined on the bench by the Constable of the Tower, Ralph de Sandwich, another of the King's bully boys, a royal henchman who would brook no insolence and insist that London fully comply with royal demands.

By Saturday, 29 June 1303, the Royal Justices were ready to act. They would operate like any important assize court, moving round the city from one place to another, taking the depositions of the juries summoned from different wards. The itinerant nature of the inquiry was to ensure that no one place became the focal point and so allow crowds to gather or the alderman of any particular ward to exert undue pressure. The court would sit, the justices enthroned behind a long bench table with their clerks and officials ranged on either side. The judges would be accompanied by guards, criers and servants. The jury of each ward, already convoked by the sheriff and alderman with the help of the Ward Council, would assemble. In number the jury could range from twelve to twenty-four male citizens.

Citizenship of London was a great prize, it was all-important in public life, with duties as well as cherished and hard-fought privileges and liberties, which had been gained over the last hundred years. The key to citizenship was trade. Only Londoners could possess shops and do business with 'aliens' or 'foreigners', the term used to describe people who were strangers to the city. At first, such a right came only through inheritance. However, as trade expanded, the different crafts flexed their muscles. Apprenticeship became another route, apprenticeship contracts being enrolled on the City records for 3s. 4d. By the last quarter of the thirteenth century, the three main routes to citizenship had been clearly defined: inheritance from a citizen's father by a legitimate son born within the boundaries of the City; service as an apprentice of a legitimate citizen trading for seven years; and, finally, purchase of the freedom of the City from the Chamberlain of London before the Mayor and aldermen. In such a process money would be paid, the oath taken and the roll of loyal citizens in both the City and a particular ward would be expanded.

In each ward a citizen had a range of duties from law enforcement to fire fighting; jury service was one of them. Once empanelled, the jurors would elect a foreman or speaker and take the oath before Bakewell and the rest to deliver their evidence in accordance with the truth. It is interesting that the King decided on this format of inquiry, bearing in mind that, by the end of June 1303, Drokensford and the rest had already made significant arrests, including Richard de Puddlicott – the Benedictine monks, along with goldsmiths who had acted as fences, such as the Barber sisters and John of Newmarket. Edward I apparently wanted more. Indeed, the suspicion that permeated this investigation suggests that the King and his ministers were hunting for bigger quarry, people of rank in the City. The appointment of judges hostile to London, such as John de Bakewell and Ralph de Sandwich, prove this, as do the questions posed by the King in his letter of 6 June 1303, from Linlithgow:

- Who are the malefactors?
- Who was consenting and gave them counsel and assistance in the robbery?
- Who knowingly sheltered and received the robbers?
- In whose hands is the said treasure now?
- How was the treasure taken away and what were other circumstances surrounding the said robbery?

The King's fury at the robbery of his Treasury must have been made all the more bitter by the possibility of leading citizens in London being involved, as well as the grim reality that many such good citizens, so hostile to the King, might, according to their disposition, be laughing behind their hands or crying through their fingers.

86

At first glance it would seem that Bakewell and his colleagues were following the set pattern of judicial investigations throughout the kingdom. The justices would move into a specific area and ask the jury summoned to make either a general presentation or specifically investigate a certain incident. A good example of how the system operated is provided by the Assize Roll of Lincolnshire in 1298 and the dispute between Simon de Worth, a canon of Lincoln Cathedral, and Ralph Notebrouen, chief bailiff in the West Riding of the shire. The case was presented as follows:

> Simon de Worth complains of Ralph Notebrouen, that, he, on the Wednesday next after the Feast of the Translation of St Martin, in the twenty-fifth reign of Kind Edward [10 July 1297], against the protection of the Lord King, took from Simon at Nessingham in his common pasture, one ox at the price of sixteen shillings and drove it to Lincoln and caused damage of half a mark [a mark was 13*s*.4*d*. sterling]. Ralph came into the court and acknowledged that he took the aforesaid ox to the Lord King's larder by order of the Sheriff but, that he knew nothing of the Lord King's protection [for Simon against such appropriation] and, as to this, he puts himself upon the country. The Jury, on oath, replied that the aforesaid Ralph did take the aforesaid ox from Simon, that it was put to the King's use. The jury declared that the aforesaid Ralph however did not know that the aforesaid Simon had the Lord King's protection [against such levying] but they do add that such protection was proclaimed throughout the district. Therefore, it is awarded that the aforesaid Ralph do restore the said Simon, three shillings for his damages, and not more because the King shall answer concerning the ox, and let Ralph be committed to gaol.[2]

This is a birds-eye view of the medieval system. Someone lays a charge, the defendant answers, the jury give their verdict and the conclusion is reached. The same system was followed by the inquiry into the robbery at Westminster during the summer of 1303, but the scope of this inquiry was very wide-ranging. The investigation, led by Bakewell and others and scrupulously watched by royal officials such as Drokensford, cast its net as far as it could, despite the fact that the principal malefactors had already been captured and the crime had been committed 'beyond the bar of London' in the town of Westminster. The City as a whole was under suspicion, so the different wards must know something. Such an ebullient attitude by the Crown would be resented: there is an implication of the City's guilt. It is not surprising that the jury of Bishopgate Ward gave the abrupt and stinging reply: 'The jurors say that they know nothing about the "articles" under which they are being questioned.' These articles, the principal headings of the investigation, were the questions contained in the royal letter of 6 June. These questions, as did the proclamation of Sunday, 16 June, threatened anyone who refused to help with dire penalties. The ward system lent itself to collective security: these juries had to go on oath to vouch for what was said. Perjury before Royal Justices was a heinous matter, the King hoped that Londoners would be cowed into telling what they might know. In the main this held true. Nevertheless, throughout the investigation runs a vein of surly, latent opposition: the jurors do not know anything, or they know people were involved but have no names, or they have had insufficient time to make proper inquiry. John de Bakewell and Drokensford would take careful note of this.

John de Bakewell and his associates opened proceedings with the London wards at the Bishop of London's Palace near St Paul's on Wednesday, 3 July.[3] The jurors of Farringdon Ward were the first to appear. They named those whom they considered to be the ring leaders: Richard de Puddlicott, William of the Palace, with Adam de Warfeld the Sacristan as receiver. They also named two London goldsmiths as buying some of the stolen jewellery, although they add the caveat, 'They did not know that a felony had taken place.' The goldsmiths named were the master craftsmen William Torel and John de Bridgeford. The jurors were playing a very cunning game. William of the Palace and Richard de Puddlicott, not to mention Adam de Warfeld, were already under suspicion. The news of Drokensford's visit to Westminster and the raid on Puddlicott's and John of Newmarket's house must have swept the City. The sale of stolen jewellery was also common knowledge throughout London. The jurors had no choice but to name two leading merchants, then immediately offer them protection: 'they did not know they were buying stolen goods'. The King, Drokensford and the Royal Justices would have to decide whether this was either an acceptable explanation or a valid excuse.[4] The jury of Cripplegate sang the same hymn: Puddlicott, William Palmer and Adam de Warfeld were guilty; they, too, named prominent goldsmiths, this time, Geoffery de Bradley and Thomas Frowick, Adam le Orfevre, along with John de Bridgeford but, 'all these, too, were not knowing that felony had been committed'. Bradley was a leading girdler, Frowick belonged to a powerful family of goldsmiths – his father the redoubtable Henry had virtually established a trading dynasty within the City.[5] The other juries summoned added to or developed what had already been said. Puddlicott and William Palmer of the Palace were responsible, as was Adam the Sacristan. One jury pointed out that Puddlicott had also taken stolen treasure to goldsmiths (of course they did not know any names) at Northampton and Colchester. The jury of Bread Street, in particular were able to give a fuller picture of the villains of the piece, their evidence reflects the quality of all the presentments offered before Bakewell and his associates. It reads in translation, as follows:

> The jury of the ward of Bread Street declare that the above-mentioned Richard de Puddlicott is guilty of breaking into the Treasury and that the Sacristan and William of the Palace were consenting to it and helped him. The said

Sacristan offered the daughter of William Russell, procurator of the London Arches, a brooch and a gold ring from the jewels of the said Treasury so that she might become his friend. The jurors also say that John of Newmarket, goldsmith, bought jewels from the said Richard [de Puddlicott] knowing it is a felony but they do not know what quantity he bought. James the taverner was frequently in the company of the said Richard at taverns, that Joanne, daughter of Richard Picard, was concubine of the said Richard de Puddlicott and that James the Horner, staying in Candlewick, was a friend of Richard but, if he knew of the felony, they have no knowledge. Nevertheless, they believe evil of all these. They [the jurors of Bread Street] also say that Castanea Barber and Alice her sister were receivers for the above-mentioned felons and that Peter of Spain, staying near the church of the Blessed Augustine in London, had food and dress which they do not believe he could afford, consequently they believe evil of him.[6]

This verdict is interesting because it illustrates how the wards worked and how everyone else's business becomes their own. The good citizens of Bread Street all knew about Adam de Warfeld offering stolen jewels to a young lady so that she could become 'his friend', of John of Newmarket the 'fence', of Joanne Picard being Richard de Puddlicott's mistress, of the Barber sisters being the shelterers of felons, whilst Peter of Spain, a foreigner, was able to eat and dress in a manner well above his obvious means, a crime in itself to the xenophobic Londoners, consequently they believe evil of him!

John de Bakewell and Drokensford knew the ward system lent itself to collecting such information, since it was highly organized under its alderman, council and secretariat. They must have wondered why Bread Street knew so much, yet Bishopsgate so little. Unlike modern jurors, who must be impartially objective and not party in any way to the matters before them, medieval juries were summoned to declare exactly what they knew. More importantly, if juries like that of Bread Street were so suspicious of 'foreigners' such as Peter of Spain or Richard de Puddlicott, why had the City authorities not done something before? Why hadn't the sheriffs, Hugh Pourte and Simon de Paris been alerted? Royal officials, lawyers like Drokensford, would want answers to that. The ward of Cordwainstreet named the usual suspects but also included the Sacristan's servants. The same jurors also refer to Puddlicott's trip to Northampton and elsewhere, whilst the jurors of Queenshithe emphasize the role of John St Albans, the mason.[7] The rest of the wards repeat the same story and continue to highlight the guilt of one particular goldsmith, John of Newmarket, who emerges as the principal 'fence' or receiver of stolen goods.[8]

On Thursday 4 July, the justices moved deeper into the City to receive the depositions of the juries of Cornhill, Walbrook, Candlewick Street, Bridge Ward, Billingsgate, Castle Baynard and Alegate. In all, seven juries delivered their verdicts that day and the evidence against the usual suspects mounted. Richard de Puddlicott received six indictments. Williams of the Palace seven, Adam de Warfeld six, certain monks are mentioned at least four times, John of Newmarket is mentioned by at least five of the wards. John of St Albans the mason, Alexander de Pershore, sub-prior of Westminster, and the servants of the Sacristan also figure prominently.[9]

A number of interesting facts emerged from the proceedings of Thursday, 4 July. First, as shall be shown, the London wards have their own idea about the robbers not being Londoners. Secondly, the jurors of Alegate, following Bishopsgate, are extremely uncooperative, they do not know about anyone who robbed the Treasury but, whoever it was, must have had the support of William of the Palace and certain people from the Abbey must have been consenting to it. Finally, Bridge Ward mentions the role of the City law officers, specifically the alderman and sheriff, Hugh Pourte.

They point out that Puddlicott was captured and led to the house of Hugh Pourte where he was imprisoned for five days. He had then escaped from there to sanctuary in the Church of St Michael Candlewick with the connivance of a certain Richard, valet of Gaucelyn le Servient. Puddlicott had then been plucked from sanctuary, whilst Hugh Pourte had called guarantors to swear on oath that he had not been party to Puddlicott's escape.[10] This statement is cold: it doesn't exactly exonerate the sheriff and clashes with later evidence which depicts the sheriff in a more pro-active role. Perhaps some of the good citizens of Bridge Ward were not happy with Alderman Pourte.

Nevertheless, all these London juries had followed the lead set the previous day. Apart from the Barber sisters and some lesser, minor figures, the jurors are keen to depict the malefactors as non-Londoners. Puddlicott, as shall be shown, came from Oxford, William from Westminster Palace whilst many of the Abbey monks came from western parts of England. John the Mason came from St Albans whilst the only truly guilty goldsmith was from Newmarket. If an important Londoner is named, the phrase is always added, 'They did not know a felony had taken place', a refrain Bakewell and his associates would hear repeated *ad nauseam*.

Later, that Thursday, the justices arrived at the Guildhall to receive the testimony of the goldsmiths, not yet a guild in the city but still very powerful men. Their admission in Norman French is breathtaking in its insolence.

William of the Palace, Richard Puddlicott, and John of St Albans the mason, arrested at Chertsey, were all guilty. Adam the Sacristan and Adam [the Skinner] his servant, and other monks and servants of the Abbey, whose names they did not know, were consenting to the robbery. John de Newmarket bought jewels and precious goods knowing it was a crime. Walter de Walpole, goldsmith, bought three gold rings from Richard [de Puddlicott] and sold the same to Robert Pipehurst, but he did not know it was a crime. William Torel bought from Richard de Puddlicott two gold rings with rubies and sold the ring to Nicholas de Saint Botulpho and William de Beaupho and he sold two rubies to Richard le Breun [all of these were goldsmiths]. John de Bridgeford bought from the said Richard de Puddlicott a brooch, and a bracelet not knowing it was a crime; Thomas de Frowick bought from a certain Imania la Porteresse five rubies and four emeralds. The same Thomas bought from the same Imania, nine rubies and twelve emeralds and the said Imania had five rubies and four emeralds from John de Newmarket, now in Newgate prison, and the aforesaid nine rubies and twelve emeralds came from Nicholas de Saint Botulpho who bought such precious stuff from John de Newmarket together with a ruby which he sold to John le Peret. William, valet of William Keles, bought from the said Richard de Puddlicott gold from broken rings and sold them to Adam de Bentley who did not know it was a felony. John Bonaventure bought from Richard de Puddlicott twenty-eight precious plates but did not know these were from a felony. William of York bought from John de Newmarket gold and jewels but did not know it was a felony. John de Bridgeport bought gold from Richard de Puddlicott and sold it to Robert Pipehurst but did not know it was a felony. The aforesaid John de Bridgeford also bought from the aforesaid Richard de Puddlicott, fifteen small plates and sixteen great plates which he sold to Robert le Convers and the said Robert then sold the same to Adam Bentley the goldsmith but they did not know it was a felony. The aforesaid John de Bridgeford also bought a brooch and bracelet from Richard de Puddlicott but did not know it was a felony. Geoffrey de Bradley bought from the same Richard de Puddlicott a silver plate but did not know it was a felony.

The conclusion reached here was that these goldsmiths had

brought into safe custody the aforesaid pearls, emeralds, rubies stolen from the Royal Treasury.

[However,] because the said goldsmiths had bought in the aforesaid gold, jewellery and precious goods and did not know of any felony they were released on bail.[11]

The goldsmiths had responded to the general proclamation of Sunday, 16 June, flocking to the Guildhall to hand in their ill-gotten gains to the sheriff, yet their stance of wide-eyed innocence is extremely difficult to accept. The names of some of these goldsmiths, and those who stood bail for them, are leading figures of the City: Torel, Walpole, Box, Bonaventure, Beaupho figure prominently in the Letter Books A-D of the City. They were leading merchants, prominent citizens, and their involvement in the purchase of ill-gotten gains from the robbery is highly suspect. According to the evidence delivered at the Guildhall, which is based on their own admissions, some twenty-four transactions took place involving at least a dozen goldsmiths whilst over a hundred different items including plates, rings, jewels and other precious goods exchanged hands.

The royal ministers would find it difficult to understand that these goldsmiths had no suspicions of this sudden influx of precious plate and jewels, at a time when such goods were rare, and the Crown itself had desperately tried to stabilize the market in precious metals by issuing the 'Statute on False Money' in May 1299.[12] Puddlicott and John of Newmarket were not *London* merchants. The robbery had taken place at the beginning of May 1303. Yet, within six weeks of that robbery, these leading merchants, prominent citizens, were virtually queuing up to buy goods from this precious pair and never asked any questions. The goldsmiths must have been suspicious yet they looked after their own. They don't even mention the goldsmith Roger of Westminster who was later indicted and released on bail.[13] Nor do the goldsmiths of London explain why they took such goods so readily from the likes of John of Newmarket, Richard de Puddlicott or that mysterious Imania la Porteresse. They offer no explanation of why they expressed no surprise at this sudden influx of precious goods or, more importantly, why they only came forward when the alarm was raised. They adopted the stance that they were merchants involved in legal trade who, by mistake, had come into possession of stolen goods. So, in the last analysis, they were innocent of any crime.

On Friday 5 July, John de Bakewell and his associates arrived at the Great Hall of Westminster within walking distance of both the Abbey and the Palace to receive the indictments of the different juries from the shire of Middlesex. On the following day, Saturday, they moved across to Southwark to meet the juries from the hundreds of Surrey. All these juries name the usual suspects once again, Richard de Puddlicott, William of the Palace and Adam the Sacristan. They also provide new evidence about goods being found in the cemetery of St Margaret, of the old woman (Isabella/Mathilda Lovett/Lovit) finding precious items and handing them over to Adam the Sacristan, who kept them for himself.

They also mention three carpenters, probably working for the Abbey and the Palace, who gave help to the robbers by wandering the cemetery at night armed with bow and arrows. The jurors refer to stolen treasure being moved hastily to Kentish Town and, for the first time, Edelina, the daughter of Nicholas the Cook, is named as William of the Palace's concubine, as well as two other characters who played a prominent part in the robbery: John de Lenton and a man known as John le Riche, servant of the Abbey who liked to be called John Ramage. The jurors describe John le Riche being poor yet suddenly acquiring the means to buy a horse and armour so as to join the King's army in Scotland.

The jury of Suffolk corroborate this. John de Lenton is also named whilst there are more references to treasure being found here and there before being handed over to the Sacristan. John de Bakewell and his associates would also reflect on testimony given later about the Barber sisters and their gang who moved from Fleet Prison to Westminster. They had been drinking heavily and helped themselves to so much treasure that precious items were dropped all over the place to be found by other people. One declaration however would have puzzled the justices: according to the evidence of the river boatmen, Geoffrey Atte Stigle a fisherman had, while working on the Thames, brought up in his net a precious cup and, not knowing it was stolen, had sold it on. The date given for this was most interesting. The Treasury burglary had taken place between 30 April and 3 May, yet the boatman had made his lucky catch before Christmas 1302. So how many raids on the Treasury had been made? How many burglaries? Did the robbery take place before Christmas 1302 or, as all the evidence indicates, at the beginning of May 1303?[14]

On Saturday 29 July the justices took the evidence of leading aldermen from the twenty-four wards of the City, these, including Hugh Pourte the Sheriff, went on oath at the Guildhall, their testimony reads as follows:

They say that Adam de Warfeld, Sacristan of Westminster, Alexander de Pershore and Thomas de Dene, monks of the said church, were ordainers and contrivers in the burglary of the Treasury of the Lord King and that John of St Albans mason, and a certain John servant of the aforesaid mason and Richard de Puddlicott broke into the Treasury and entered it and carried away the treasure and jewels found therein. They also say that Roger de Prestok, cellarer of the Abbey, Robert de Cherring, John de Noteley, John de Prescot, Thomas de Lichfield, Walter valet of St Arnold, William valet of John Shenche, Keeper of the King's Palace, Roger and Adam pages of the aforesaid Sacristan of Westminster, were aiders and abetters in the aforesaid robbery. They also say that the aforesaid Richard de Puddlicott, when arrested, was found in the possession of part of the treasure, including coronets, gold girdles, cups and dishes of silver to the value of £2,200. They also claimed that the aforesaid Adam the Sacristan was seen with a bowl and cup of silver, the value of which they do not know. They also say that John of Newmarket, a goldsmith residing in Billingsgate, was arrested in possession of gold weighing six shillings and three precious stones so they hold him suspect. They say that Walter de Walpole bought, in good faith, from the aforesaid Richard de Puddlicott three gold rings and William Torel two gold rings. Geoffrey de Bradley [girdler], in like manner bought from Puddlicott a plate of silver weighing fourteen pounds and fifteen shillings and that John de Bridgeford [goldsmith] likewise bought gold and oriental pearls to the value of seventy shillings. Thomas Frowick, goldsmith, in like manner bought from Imania La Porteresse precious stones to the value of forty-two shillings. Nicholas de Saint Botulpho bought stones from her to the value of twenty shillings, which stones the said Imania received from John of Newmarket. They also say that around about the Feast of the Finding of the Holy Cross [3 May 1303], John de Uggele, William de Kynebaston and John his brother and Castanea Barber and Alice her sister met in a certain house within the precinct of Fleet Prison, together with a horseman and four other ribalds whose names they do not know. They stayed there for two nights and spent their time until midnight eating and drinking before advancing with arms towards Westminster. In the morning they returned, they did this for two nights but, after that, they never returned to the prison and because this happened at the same time the treasury was broken into, they are held suspect of the robbery and the aforesaid felony.

Such testimony from the most powerful men in London is interesting. They named the main perpetrators: first, the Abbey monks, Adam de Warfeld, Alexander de Pershore, and Thomas de Dene were the moving spirits, 'the ordainers and contrivers'. The blame for the robbery is placed squarely on these three monks. The message is very clear, the origins of the robbery lay with the Abbey, not the City. The aldermen then move to naming the actual burglars, they had no doubt that three men were responsible: John of St Albans the mason, Richard de Puddlicott and William of the Palace. They then named the accessories, the valets, and servants of the Abbey. They refer to Puddlicott's arrest and the nefarious work of John of Newmarket the receiver of stolen goods. However, all the London goldsmiths are innocent, purchasing in good faith, the spoils of these felons. The alderman, however, added a surprising postscript. They accuse a specific gang of thieves, who acted suspiciously in May 1303, led by the Barber sisters. They actually describe them gathering 'in the precincts or close of Fleet prison' and, over a succession of days, moving backwards and forwards to Westminster at the very time the robbery occurred. Bearing in mind that William Palmer, Deputy Keeper of the Palace, was also Acting Keeper of the Fleet Prison, there can be no doubt that he also was a prime mover in all of this. The overall conclusion reached by the aldermen is that the break-in was organized by the monks and carried through by Puddlicott and John of St Albans, whilst a gang, gathered at the Fleet Prison, waited for the signal to move down to help themselves to the plunder.[15]

This part of the investigation should have ended on Saturday 6 July. However on that same Saturday, the justices had a surprise visitor: William Palmer, Deputy Keeper of the Palace. William must have realized that, despite his earlier declaration of 17 June, the week beginning 1 July 1303 had proved to be most damaging to him: no less than twenty indictments from the different wards had been brought against him. He had turned King's evidence too late and, even when he made his surprising reappearance before the justices on Saturday 6 July, he simply developed his original story, depicting himself as a victim. The translation of his confession in Latin reads as follows:

On Saturday following the Octave of St John the Baptist [Saturday 6 July], the said William Palmer, Keeper of the Palace, came into the presence of Ralph de Sandwich, John de Bakewell, Roger Southcote and the Mayor and Coroner of London. He said that he had often seen Adam de Warfeld, Alexander de Pershore, Thomas de Dene, monks of Westminster, and the two monks known as the de Bures brothers, enter and leave on the evening and the morning after the burglary of the Treasury, carrying many things towards the church, but he did not know what or in what quantity. He also claimed that Roger de Wenlok and Hamo, the Sacristan's valet, would often accompany the said monks and were present there. He claimed that John of St Albans was the organizer of the tools used for breaking into the said Treasury. He added that Alexander de Pershore had threatened him that he would have him killed if he revealed their plans to anyone. He also says, that on a certain day around Pentecost [that would be in the week beginning 26 May, 1303], Alexander de Pershore, the de Bures brothers, Thomas de Dene, Simon de Henley and Walter de Erskdale, monks of the Abbey, embarked on a certain barge, under its boatman Godde, at King's bridge Westminster, and they carried away with them two great baskets bound by black cord. These baskets were of a great weight but he [William] did not know what was inside. The monks took their baskets with them to London for dispersal but he did not know the details. In the evening they returned on another boat and landed near the Abbey Mill. He also claimed that John de Uggele was a shelterer of those thieves who committed the burglary.

The memorandum then adds that Simon de Henley and Walter de Erskdale as well as the aforesaid Godde, were arrested on suspicion but later released on bail.[16]

William of the Palace's confession is illuminating. Alexander de Pershore is depicted as the principal villain, organizing and transporting stolen goods with that strange-named boatman, Godde, as well as threatening William with murder if he revealed their plans. John de Uggele is portrayed as a shelterer of the felons and John of St Albans the mason as the supplier of the tools necessary for the break-in.

The confession must not have impressed the likes of Drokensford, Ralph de Sandwich and Justice John de Bakewell. William makes no mention of his whore Edelina, daughter of Nicholas the Cook nor, above all, of Richard de Puddlicott. He makes no attempt to refute the evidence of twenty juries but simply hides behind the pretext that he was threatened. William was a rogue and a fool. He had breached the very defence that the robbers had put such faith in, the clerical status of the monks of Westminster and the sanctity of their buildings. William was now blaming them for the robbery, and the monks of Westminster would not forget it. William of the Palace was on his own. The justices gave him a fair and full hearing. Their lack of confidence in his confession is illustrated by the fact that three of the people William indicted, Simon de Henley, Walter de Erskdale and the boatman Godde were arrested but released on bail. William of the Palace did not fare so well. He and his whore Edelina were soon included on the list of prisoners incarcerated in the Tower.

From 6 July 1303 to August 1303 there was a break in the proceedings. The justices were needed for other business whilst the likes of Drokensford had to consolidate what they had done. Jewels and coins continued to be found in the possession of men like Walter Russell, a broker, taken up and imprisoned because he was in the company of Richard de Puddlicott and was found selling florins and other different jewels belonging to the Royal Treasury.[17] The same was true of Roger of Westminster, goldsmith, who was detained because of his links with the Abbey as well as the goldsmith John of Lynn in Norfolk.[18] This Norfolk link was one the Crown would pursue in October, appointing justices to hold an inquiry there regarding certain florins. On 26 October a commission was issued to three different justices:

> Touching the purchase from a stranger who, recently, after the break-in of the treasury at Westminster, went to the town of King's Lynn, County Norfolk, with a hundred florins of gold from that treasure to sell for much less of their value to Walter de Tylneye and John de Elmham goldsmiths of that town, who concealed the stranger and secretly permitted him to escape so he could not be arrested by the bailiffs of that town and take his trial.

This writ proves how the treasure from the Abbey was moved around the country as quickly as possible at a time when precious coinage would be highly prized.[19] In the meantime Drokensford continued to collect such stolen goods. The Keeper of the King's Wardrobe carefully counted and assessed these in the presence of a number of witnesses including the Mayor of London on 23 June. A week later the indenture was re-opened to include stolen items recovered when the formidable Treasurer, Walter Langton, Bishop of Coventry and Lichfield, arrived in London to view for himself the damage caused.[20]

On Wednesday 6 August 1303 the Royal Justices sat again, this time at New Temple.[21] The location was most appropriate. The Templar Order had been founded to protect the Holy Places in Outremer, Palestine. However, the Templars had developed not only as a fighting order but as international bankers throughout Europe. New Temple was the English headquarters of the Order after they had sold their old site in 1161. The justices must have chosen this place especially. First, New Temple was consecrated ground. Secondly, the Templars were soldiers whose loyalty to the Crown was more reliable than that of the City. Thirdly, New Temple was a fortified place, with a church hall, barracks, curtain wall and guarded gates and stood on the edge of the bustling, seething ambitious commune of London: it was well protected and close to both Westminster and the river. The location was also neutral ground and reveals the anxieties of Drokensford and the likes of Bakewell who had to deal with the City and its patrician aldermen who, at the blow of a horn, could summon their wards to arms. The growing suspicion that monks from Westminster, allied to a gang of malefactors, had plundered the Royal Treasury with the help of the great ones of the City such as the goldsmiths, must have left a nasty taste in the mouths of the justices. The defence offered so far only worsened matters. The powerful patrician class had confessed that they knew very little about the robbery, apart from a list of offending monks, whilst the goldsmiths were astonished to learn that jewels and precious items bought from the likes of John of Newmarket and Richard de Puddlicott had been stolen from the Royal Treasury.

If the justices hoped that the jurors of Westminster and Fleet Street were going to be more informative they were bitterly disappointed. The juries concerned did not concentrate on the burglary itself but what happened to certain items afterwards, such as Adam de Warfeld finding a cup and bowl. The jurors used this to name other monks – Raymond de Wenlok, Alexander de Newport, John Wenlok, William de Chalk – these are casually mentioned but depicted as not knowing of the burglary or guilty of carrying away the treasure. Adam the Sacristan is depicted as an innocent who happened to find some precious items, so he approached his colleagues about what to do with them? They replied that he should consult John de Foxley, Steward of the Abbey lands. Warfeld did this together with Richard de Burgh, the Abbey bailiff. They visited John de Foxley at his manor at Bray in Berkshire. Foxley advised them to approach the Abbot, who declared that if the precious items had been found on Abbey land, they belonged to the Abbey. The evidence finishes with that well-repeated phrase Bakewell and his colleagues must have come to detest, that the jurors believe nothing evil of John de Foxley or Richard de Burgh.

In view of a later testimony it is difficult to accept that these jurors, from the very vicinity where the outrage had occurred, knew nothing about strange comings and goings at the dead of night: of gates to the Palace and Abbey being closed off; of undesirables wandering the cemetery with bows and arrows: of hemp being sown to hide the work of the thieves, or the doings of Master William of the Palace and Richard de Puddlicott; of parties and revelries where whores joined the monks in their festivities. Instead, the jurors of Westminster and Fleet recount this wide-eyed tale of the Sacristan finding some precious goods and enquiries being made. In this part of their evidence, no one is guilty of anything. Of course, this is understandable, at least from the viewpoint of the Westminster jurors. They had close business links with the Abbey and the Palace, so Westminster people would look after their own. The introduction of John de Foxley was a perfect pitch by both the thieving monks and the jury. John de Foxley was a man of integrity, later knighted and promoted to be Baron of the Exchequer.[22] Richard de Burgh the bailiff was not so innocent, he was later indicted and certainly removed from his position, but the introduction of Foxley and the Abbot is significant. It reveals the long-term plan of the monks involved in the robbery. They wanted to spread the blame as far as possible, drawing in their steward as well as their abbot. If these were implicated, what could the King do?[23] John de Bakewell and his associates must have been deeply dissatisfied with such evidence.

In the second part of the submission from the jury, the justices concentrated on another servant of the Abbey, Gerin the linen draper, who had moved some of the treasure from the Abbey to his house near St Giles Hospital and from there to a field in Kentish Town where a boy had found it. The justices had learnt about this in earlier testimony and used it to propose two damaging questions:

'Why had the linen draper moved the treasure?'

The answer was surprisingly blunt; 'because he was frightened of his house being searched by ministers of the Crown.'

The second question followed immediately:

'Were the jewels moved by day or night?'

The jurors replied that they did not know.

The last question was more relevant. 'If the jewels were removed in a basket, where did that basket come from?' The jurors, of course, had to tell the truth – the monks of Westminster – but they did not know their names. The inquiry of summer 1303 ends on that sour note.[24]

Edward and his ministers were clearly dissatisfied with the summer inquiry of 1303 and, within months, the Crown launched a second investigation. The source of their dissatisfaction is obvious. Important questions needed to be answered. Were the monks of Westminster the true 'contrivers and ordainers' of the robbery? How had these monks, sworn to chastity and poverty, been allowed to act as they did? What control, if any, did Abbot Wenlok and his Prior William de Huntingdon exert? Was the entire community guilty? Hadn't the Abbot and his priestly brethren learned the lesson after their previous attempt to rob the royal purse? Little wonder that the King lost his temper and later ordered the *entire* monastic community to the Tower in the autumn of 1303.[25]

The juries of London and the adjoining shires had hardly been forthcoming. A few present proper answers whilst the refrains, 'They did not know it was a felony' and 'they know people were involved but can't recall any names', frustrated any proper investigation. How could the juries be so adamant in repeating these refrains yet be so unclear about other information? Was the robbery just the work of some Westminster monks, Puddlicott, John of Newmarket the goldsmith, John of St Albans the mason, William of the Palace and a few rogues from London's underworld? Yet how had 'strangers to the city', 'aliens', 'foreigners' like Puddlicott and John of Newmarket been able to sell precious items to leading goldsmiths and merchants of the City in the space of one month (6 May to 6 June 1303) without questions being asked about the source of such mysterious wealth, especially at a time when the precious metal market had been drained of such commodities?

Why had the City government, its mayor, aldermen and sheriffs not been alerted by the presence of suspicious characters like Puddlicott living in the claustrophobic atmosphere of the ward in his house near Dowgate? After all, Puddlicott had become a well-known figure in the London taverns with his friends and mistress? And why had the City authorities not reacted to the swirl of rumours, as the Coroner of Westminster Henry de Cherring did, about treasure being found in fields or fished from the Thames?

No action had been taken in the City until the King's letter of 6 June became known and the royal ministers arrived there – even then, Sheriff Pourte had bungled and kept Puddlicott in his own house for five days. This was in direct contravention of the King's order, contained in his letter of 6 June, that those implicated in the robbery must be kept '*salvo et secure in prisona nostra –* safe and secure in our prison.'

6

The Constable's Tale

'Iah herde men upo mold, make much mon'

'I heard men on the earth make deep lamentation'
Contemporary ballad

'*Non Placet Nobis* – It does not please us' was Edward I's reaction to the extensive inquiry into the great robbery at Westminster in late summer of 1303. The inquiry ended on or around 7 August when the justices left the New Temple. They immediately reported their findings to Edward and the King's reaction was also immediate. On 14 August 1303 he issued a new writ from Brechin in Scotland re-appointing the same justices under the same terms and emphasizing the important clause 'We, wishing to be more certain about the truth in this matter, order you, as permitted by the above commission, clearly and rightly, to make a return, without delay regarding those matters which must be clarified.'[1]

In other words, the King was not satisfied with the inquiry's conclusions. Now, to a certain extent, Bakewell, Sandwich and the rest had made it perfectly clear who the perpetrators of the robbery were. Sixty-four indictments in all had been presented against both Richard de Puddlicott and William of the Palace [thirty-two each]: ten were levelled against John of Newmarket, six against John of St Albans the stonemason, two against John de Lenton, two against John le Riche [also known as John Ramage], eighteen against Adam de Warfeld, three against Alexander de Pershore and a number against an assortment of servants and retainers of the Abbey such as Gerin the linen draper. Moreover, Drokensford was still pursuing the missing treasure. London goldsmiths were queuing up to return their ill-gotten gains whilst Westminster prison, Newgate and the Tower held an impressive list of those detained. In the Tower were Puddlicott, William of the Palace, John the Mason, Adam de Warfeld, Alexander de Pershore, Ralph de Morton, Thomas de Dene, Robert de Cherring, John de Noteley, John de Prescot, Thomas de Lichfield, Roger de Bures, John de Butterley, all monks of the house of Westminster and six page boys of the said Sacristan namely: Walter de Ecclesford, Roger de Wenlok, Hamo de Wenlok, Adam the Skinner, John de Caumpes and Hugh de Eye. In addition Roger de Prestok, John de Lenton, Adam Crul, John Fitz-Geoffrey of Lalham, Edelina daughter of Nicholas the Cook, Richard of Kent clerk, and Cecily his wife, and Gerin of St Giles. Newgate held John of Newmarket, Castenea Barber and Alice her sister, John de Uggele, John son of the glazier from Southwark, Joanna daughter of Richard Picard the Tailor, concubine of the said Richard de Puddlicott, John de Barreler and Peter of Spain.[2] Also captured and detained in the same place were: Gilbert Wayte from Westminster arrested and detained on the suspicion that he stood guard during the time that the Treasury was robbed. Peter the Server and Nicholas the taverner were both arrested and detained on suspicion because, 'they were often in the company of Richard de Puddlicott and they were in his house when the same Richard was found and captured'. Walter Russell, broker, was also in Newgate because he was 'often in the company of Richard de Puddlicott and sold florins and other diverse jewels'.[3] The gatehouse prison of Westminster was graced by Henry of Sutton and Walter, son of William of Mulhurst – two carpenters.[4] Some, however, had fled the clutches of the law: Richard Gaucelyn Le Servient, who had helped Richard de Puddlicott escape from the Sheriff Hugh Pourte's house, and William of Kynebaston together with his brother John. William was later arrested at York and detained in its prison, and an order would be issued on 14 November to transfer him to Newgate. John le Riche, also known as John Ramage, was also on the run, as was James the Taverner.[5] Not all prisoners were detained. The Abbot of Westminster and certain servants of the Abbey were released on bail, as was Roger, a goldsmith from Westminster. Queen Margaret, busy with diplomatic matters, intervened, possibly under pressure from fellow citizens, to organize the release on bail of the Barber sisters.[6]

So, if most of the robbers were arrested, what other things, '*certiora aliqua*', needed to be made 'clear and more certain'? The pursuit of felons and the constant search for stolen treasure might be factors as was other urgent business of the Crown, the negotiations with France over a proposed marriage alliance between Edward Prince of Wales and Isabella, daughter of the French king; the collection of desperately needed taxes of one sort or the other; the pursuit of William Wallace in Scotland, as well as the need to use valuable justiciars for pressing matters in other places. The commission of 14 August 1303 was never acted upon but that letter, together with Edward I's appointment of his most senior justices in November 1303, to re-open the inquiry reflect his deep anxiety that the full truth was not yet known. Edward wanted his expert senior judges to concentrate on the case but that would take time. Royal Justices of the era were not exclusively judges but responsible for a wide array of duties both at home and abroad. They were close advisers of the King and took a special oath of loyalty to him. They attended his councils and parliaments advising him on matters of law, taxes and any other issue the King might wish to choose. When they were away from the King, they travelled the shires, holding court, delivering gaols, hearing pleas and chairing special investigations. Sometimes they were sent on general circuit to listen to all the grievances and cases in a particular shire or group of shires. They were responsible for the assessment of subsidies and other taxes. They acted as commissioners of array, organizing the levy of men for military duty. They fined those who tried to abscond from such duty, punished officials who raised recruits then pocketed the proceeds themselves. They were often involved in the arduous systems of processing pardons whereby people, guilty of homicide, robbery and other crimes, received a pardon in return for military service either at home or abroad. The justices looked after a host of civil matters, the boundaries between one shire and another, defining what was forest land, even acting as commissioners of the sewers, pathways and roads. They suppressed illegal meetings and became involved in the intensive diplomatic negotiations over Gascony and the re-organization of Scotland during Edward's conquest of that country. As private individuals they acted as '*periti*', men skilled and learned in law, hired by individuals to advise them on certain issues. They wrote pamphlets on the law. The lives of these judges were packed with incident as they moved from place to place, from one commission to another or followed their King on his military campaigns.[7]

Medieval justice, moreover, was extremely complicated and litigious. People knew their rights, eagerly argued them, and often the justices would act not only as judges but as detectives. A case of abduction and rape in Oxford in 1282 exemplifies both the type of case which came before the judges and the action they would have to take. The entry can be found on the Coram Regis Roll of Michaelmas 1282.

Rose, daughter of Nicholas de Savage, appeals John de Clifford of rape and breach of the King's peace. Namely, she was in the peace of God and the peace of the King on the Sunday before the Feast of St Hilary in the eighth year of the present King's reign in the village of Ilchester in the County of Northampton on a certain croft called 'Holm Croft', which belongs to her father Nicholas and lies near her father's house. Rose went into the croft walking west towards the Church just before sunrise when John de Clifford, with other unknown felons, wickedly and maliciously abducted Rose in his two arms, and forcedly against the will of the said Rose, put her on a palfrey and took away from the said croft and brought her to the village of Middleton in the County of Oxford. When they arrived there, de Clifford and other felons took her to his hall. There he made her dismount and, together with his accomplices, took her in his arms and led her to his bed in the same house and stripped her of the miniver robe in which she was dressed. He took her into his arms and made her sleep with him in the same bed and held her there all naked, he slept with her on the right side of the bed. He held Rose's hand with his left hand and raped her virginity so that Rose became all bloody from John's attack. Rose wanted to escape from John but he took her and imprisoned her in a certain upper room and shut her up, securely imprisoned from Sunday after the Feast of St Hilary in the eighth year of the reign of King Edward I until Martinmas in the tenth year of the same King's reign [which means she was imprisoned for almost two years!]. On this day, the Feast of St Martin, she escaped at dawn through a certain stone window from the aforesaid upper room. Rose quickly raised the hue and cry and instantly sued John, by writ of the Lord King, in the Lord King's Court that what he did, he did wickedly and villainously, against the peace of God and the peace of the King as she offered to prove.

John de Clifford came to court and denied the rape, felony, whatever it is, against the peace, crown and dignity of the Lord King. He passed judgement on the appeal of the aforesaid Rose, in so much that she accused him of raping her at Middleton in the County of Oxford. Yet, Rose did not name a definite day, or specific year, or a certain place when he had raped her. Accordingly, it was awarded that the appeal of the aforesaid roll be cancelled as regard John de Clifford whilst Rose was committed to gaol for false accusation. John de Clifford was then asked how he wishes to clear himself at the suit of the Lord King? He replied that he is guilty of nothing and so he puts himself on the country. Accordingly, the Sheriff is instructed to order, before the King, a fortnight after St Hilary next [January 1283], twelve men to make admission regarding this . . . Afterwards, three weeks after Easter in the eleventh year after the present King's reign [1283], Bartholomew of Northampton, the King's attorney, came before the judges and said that John had not come back to court to clear himself. Accordingly, the verdict is against him by default. The jurors say on oath that the aforesaid John de Clifford, and other unknown men, did take Rose wickedly and villainously and assaulted her in the village of Ilchester in the County of Northampton and forced her against her will to Middleton in the County of Oxford and did there rape her of her virginity. John therefore needs to be arrested. Afterwards, John de Clifford came into court and paid the King a fine of ten pounds.[8]

Now the pros and cons of this crime, abduction and rape which lasted over a period of two years do not concern the present study. However, the case of Rose de Savage exemplifies the judicial process which would take place before the Royal Justices in the question of the robbery. It just was not good enough for the jury to name people; detailed proof had to be offered and then the jury would decide. Accordingly, the judges would have to discover from the jury, or elsewhere, proof against those indicted. For example, it wasn't acceptable simply to allege that the Barber sisters had travelled from Fleet prison to Westminster around the night that the robbery took place. The court would have to be presented with proof positive, hard evidence, that the Barber sisters were actually implicated in the robbery itself or received goods from that robbery.

To a certain extent the Royal Judges had their work made easy. Both Puddlicott and John of Newmarket had actually been arrested with plunder found in their house. It would be more difficult to prove the case against the likes of Adam de Warfeld. Drokensford, in his indenture of 20 June 1303, had already signposted this. He lists '*Jocalia*, – jewels,' found in '*custodia* – in the care of' Adam de Warfeld. The Sacristan would certainly plead that he was simply 'holding' these precious items which had been found in the Abbey or its grounds. He would maintain that he had even approached the Abbey steward, John de Foxley, not to mention the Abbot himself, to enquire what should be done with these. The same can be applied to the goldsmiths and merchants of London: as long as they sang from the same hymn sheet professing, that they had bought jewels 'not knowing they were the result of a felony', they were fairly well protected. Edward, however, was determined to ferret out the entire truth as well as use this to exert pressure on the City Council. In the meantime, the justices could obtain results from the other prisoners, particularly the monks at Westminster.

Between August and November 1303, there were further developments. In a letter dated 10 October 1303 from Kinloss in Scotland, the King ordered the principal justices of the kingdom to conduct an inquiry of '*Oyer et Terminer*', that is, to listen and determine over a certain appeal that he had received from the monks of Westminster. The document reads as follows:[9]

Commission of Oyer and Terminer to Roger Brabazon, William de Bereford, Roger de Hegham, Ralph de Sandwich and Walter de Gloucester on petition by the following persons that they are falsely indicted of the breaking of the Treasury at Westminster and of carrying away treasure to the value of a hundred thousand pounds. For which they are in custody in the prison of the Tower of London. Namely, Walter, Abbot of Westminster and the following monks of that house: Alexander de Pershore, Roger de Bures, Ralph de Morton, Thomas de Dene, Adam de Warfeld, John de Butterley, John de Noteley, Robert de Cherring, John de Salopia, Thomas de Lichfield, Simon de Henley, Walter de Erksdale, William de Chalk, Robert de Bures, Richard de Sudbury, Henry Atte Rye, Adam de Lalham, John de London, John de Witney, Robert de Middleton, Richard de Colworth, Roger de Aldenham, John de Wantage, William de Braybook, Robert de Reading, Peter de La Croix, Henry Payne, Henry de Bircheston, Philip de Sutton, Guy de Ashewell, William de Kerthington, Thomas de Woburn, William de Glastonbury, John of Worcester, Robert Beby, William de Almaly, Roger de Ringstead, William de Huntingdon, Lawrence de Beamfleet, Alexander de Newport, John de Wrotting, Reginald de Hadham, Raymond de Wenlok, Richard de Waltham, Richard de Favelore, Henry de Temple, Henry de Wantage, John de Wenlok.

Also the following: Gerin of St Giles, Roger de Prestok, Walter de Ecclesford, Roger de Wenlok, Hamo de Wenlok, Adam the Skinner, John Sharpe, Richard Smart, John of St Albans, John de Lenton, John de Lalham, Henry the Cook [father of Edelina], Richard de Weston, Richard la Brajue, Thomas of Knightsbridge, Geoffrey of the Cellar, Ralph de Ditton, Ralph de Huntingdon, John de Sudbury, Richard de Hurley, Joceus de Cornubia, Jeffrey de Kent, John de Oxford, Richard del Eire, John de Bracyn, John de Beamfleet, Robert le Porter, Peter le Mounier, Roger le Orfevere, Robert Bolthod, Maurice Moell, and Godinus de Lamholt.

This list of appellants must include the entire monastic

community of Westminster, as well as their auxiliaries and servants. This is a significant document in the proceedings. First, according to the opening lines of the commission, the entire community had apparently been taken up during the early autumn of 1303 and committed to the Tower prison despite earlier proceedings. This must have been the result of the King's letter of 14 August demanding greater clarification. The Westminster Benedictines were lodged in the Tower for further questioning as well as to provide an excellent opportunity for the royal searchers to make a clean sweep of the Abbey buildings and grounds in their hunt for more treasure. Secondly, it shows the Abbey community going on the offensive as a group, guilty or not guilty, indicted or not indicted. In view of the testimony of the juries, the inclusion of names in the royal writ, such as Adam de Warfeld and Alexander de Pershore, and some of the Sacristan's servants all depicting themselves as innocent lambs bleating for justice, is as staggering as the arrogance of Adam de Warfeld and others who argued that they had simply been 'holding' certain items stolen from the Treasury which had been handed to them.

Naturally, the monks would challenge the veracity of London jurors, who had good reason to dislike them, whilst the good brothers had yet to play the ace in their pack, that they were clergy and, consequently, not subject to secular law – such a ploy would come later. The Abbot and his company would have also been advised on the law and its proceedings. Their stance, as described in the King's letter of October 1303 is very clear: they had been falsely accused and they wanted their innocence vindicated.

Walter de Wenlok had access to a wide range of legal advice. No less a person than Justice William Bereford, who'd been assigned to hear this particular case, was on the Abbey books as a legal 'consultant'. In 1298 Bereford had been awarded a retainer of three marks a year, half by the Abbot and half by the monastic community. True, this lapsed that same year, yet, curiously enough in 1305, when the case against the Abbey and its monks ended, the pension was renewed with all arrears owing. Other leading judges and attorneys including Roger de Hegham [again one of the justices assigned to hear this case but who didn't actually attend the proceedings] were on the Abbey's books. There was apparently no conflict of interest between the likes of Bereford and the Abbey: such men of law must have advised Wenlok that such an appeal was viable.[10] In addition, the petition of the Abbot and his community to be cleared of any charges illustrates their true situation. Time and again the Benedictines had been blamed for the robbery, not only by the London juries, but also by their confidant and ally, that purveyor of fine parties and ladies of ill repute, William of the Palace.

The Westminster petition makes no reference to anyone else being innocent except themselves. The first part of the list includes monks, the second their servants and retainers, many of them sharing the same surnames as their monastic brethren. The list also includes the likes of Gerin [or Gerinus] the linen draper of St Giles. Little wonder he was accused of carrying treasure here and there as he was often used as a messenger of the Abbey.[11] The list also includes the Abbey mason, John of St Albans. However, by mixing the guilty and innocent together, the Westminster Abbey petition simply confused matters and helped concentrate the King's mind on deciding to hold a fresh investigation.

Finally, the petition of the Westminster Benedictines does provoke speculation about what had been truly happening in that great Abbey. At no time did any indictment blame, either obliquely or indirectly, Abbot Walter de Wenlok – or, indeed, many of the monks mentioned in the King's letter of 10 October 1303. Yet, in all the Westminster Abbey records, there is not a scrap of evidence that the Lord Abbot and others tried to distance themselves from monks such as Adam de Warfeld, against whom the evidence was so damning. Why not? Surely Abbot Wenlok could argue his own innocence and that of others? True, the

King, in his exasperation, might have held all the monks, especially Wenlok, guilty by default, however, the Abbot doesn't even offer token resistance or objection to this. He virtually sides with the guilty and raises the very strong possibility, as shall be discussed later, that he was blackmailed first into allowing the likes of Pershore to do what they wanted in the Abbey and, when they were caught out, provide unconditional support for his criminal brethren. The rest of the monastic community had no choice but to follow suit.

Another cause for further investigation was London, and Edward's deep antagonism towards his capital city. The King must have been concerned at the number of goldsmiths implicated, as well as why nothing had been done about the scandalous robbery, despite popular rumour, until his ministers had intervened almost six weeks later. If Londoners were implicated, Edward would certainly use this against them in his struggle to levy the New Customs tax. The King would have also recognized weaknesses of the inquiry held during July and August 1303. The juries had been summoned rather quickly whilst the justices had moved swiftly around London. Perhaps more time and mature reflection would help elucidate the truth.

Undoubtedly, the petition of Wenlok and his community was listened to very carefully, and, once the royal searchers had finished their hunt through the Abbey, many of the monks were released on bail. The King, however, was not going to give up. On 14 November 1303 from Kinloss in Scotland, Edward I issued a new commission of inquiry, similar to the one of 6 June, but with three significant changes.[12] First, the personnel of the commission reflected the royal concern. Walter of Gloucester was retained, as was Ralph de Sandwich, Constable of the Tower. Walter of Gloucester is a rather shadowy figure but Ralph de Sandwich, one of the King's well-known 'bully boys', enjoyed quite an extraordinary career.[13] During the civil war he had, for a while, fought for Simon de Montfort and actually been King [then Prince] Edward's gaoler. Nonetheless, Ralph de Sandwich so impressed the future king that, after the civil war, Ralph was pardoned and retained by the King as his personal adviser and councillor. Ralph de Sandwich became essentially the King's 'trouble-shooter', someone whom Londoners hated. After the crisis of 1284, when the city was taken into the King's hands, Sandwich was made warden of the City, and given the disgraced Ralph de Crepyn's houses. He was also military supremo, being appointed Constable of the Tower, an office he held for the rest of Edward I's reign. Ralph de Sandwich had considerable judicial experience, being made temporary Chief Justice of the Bench when the disgraced Thomas de Weyland was removed. The Constable was a man who would take no nonsense from Londoners or the prisoners he housed during their trial.

Ralph de Sandwich's forceful personality comes through in two well-known incidents. During the investigation of the great robbery, Ralph was seconded for a short while to deal with a fresh crisis. A collector of papal taxes had arrived in England and was busy interfering with the King's rights: Ralph de Sandwich was ordered to summon the papal collector to the Tower, take him aside, well out of earshot of his household with no lawyer present. The Constable was to give the papal collector the King's curse. He was then to seize any monies the papal official may have collected and expel him from the kingdom. Secondly, in 1303 after the liberties of the city had been restored, a London grandee, Peter Bernevale, frustrated at the length of time business was taking, openly prayed in the mayor's court for the return of the rule of Ralph de Sandwich, 'as business was done speedily under him', Bernevale was summarily punished![14]

The Constable of the Tower was a character who would have no truck with the likes of Pourte or other Londoners, a justice who voiced his concerns to the King that the inquiry of summer 1303 had not clarified matters satisfactorily. It is no coincidence that the new investigation would not take place in London but in Ralph de Sandwich's territory, that hard, close fortress of the Tower, a narrow, forbidding place, with its walls, turrets and fortified gatehouses, where the influence of both the City and Westminster could not be felt. It was also the prison which housed the principal malefactors, as well as most of the recovered loot listed in Drokensford's indentures of June 1303. If the different aldermen had their wards, the Tower was Ralph de Sandwich's personal fief. He virtually ran it from his own pocket, be it the care of prisoners or his passion for the little tower chapel of St Peter ad Vincula which he lovingly restored. The Constable would have been a resolute prosecutor of the Crown's case. Later on, when matters were settled, there is no record either of the City or the Abbey fêting the Constable or hiring him as a 'consultant'. Ralph de Sandwich probably dragged his feet over the eventual release of the ten indicted monks in 1304.[15] He could not be bought; he would also be the main link between the first inquiry of summer 1303 and the second which met in the Tower.

The remaining judges Roger Brabazon the Chief Justice, and William Bereford, were again King's men in both heart and soul. Like Ralph de Sandwich they would have taken the special oath of loyalty to the King devised in 1290, to be incorruptible and take no presents except meat and drink.[16] However, in the end, the fate of many of those imprisoned in the Tower would not be settled in court but at the dining board.

The second feature of this commission of 10 November 1303 is that ominous phrase, '*Ad negocium illud audiendum et terminandum secundum legem et consuetudinem nostri regni* – That they should hear and bring to an end that business [the robbery] according to the law and custom of our kingdom.' The Royal Justices were given the power of '*Oyer et Terminer*' to conduct a hearing then move to trial and punish all according to the law.

The justices were undoubtedly busy in the short time before Christmas 1303 as well as after the New Year. It would take time for them to assemble and other preparations had to be made. The Hilary Law term for the year 1304 began on Friday, 23 January. The likes of Bereford and Brabazon would have other business to attend to, so they sat two weeks before the beginning of the official law term on Friday after the Feast of the Epiphany [6 January], that is 9 January 1304. The different juries had been summoned to the Tower, empanelled and sworn, supervised by the clerks and other royal officials. This time the juries would be closely inspected, not hastily assembled as they had been in the previous summer. The Second Statute of Westminster, Chapter 38, had vehemently inveighed against the practice of City and Shire sheriffs of packing juries with the old and infirm, in fact, who could be easily persuaded to follow a certain line of argument. The Statute listed the abuses as follows:[17]

> Sheriffs and other have been accustomed to burden those under their jurisdiction, putting on assizes and juries, men sick and decrepit, ill or with temporary infirmity, men also not living in the locality at the time of their summons, also by summoning an unreasonable number of jurors so as to extort monies from them to let them go in peace. Consequently juries are often made up of the poor whilst the rich, through their bribery, remain at home. It is ordained, therefore, that no more than twenty-four should be summoned for one trial. Old men, moreover, above seventy years, chronically ill or infirm at the time of summons, or not living in the locality, shall not be put upon juries, nor shall anyone be put upon juries, even though they ought to be taken in their Shire, whose property is of less value than twenty shillings per year [this was later raised to forty shillings].

Edward's letter of 10 November 1303 specifically demanded that the verdict of the juries be by, 'the Knights and other upright and lawful men of London and the counties of Middlesex and Surrey'. This time each team would have a leader, a well-known figure, to make a return, leading London merchants, such as Richer de Refham. There would be no repetition of June, July and August when some wards simply refused to answer whilst many had recorded their verdicts anonymously. Others, for example the jury of Kingston, reported that they were scarce in a position to answer about who robbed the Treasury or about who had received the plunder: they simply had not had enough time. Brixton simply named Richard de Puddlicott and William of the Palace; Alegate and Langebourne were equally nonplussed, claiming they had had insufficient time to reflect.[18] Before seasoned justices like Brabazon, Bereford and Sandwich in the Tower and, given the fact that the juries had enjoyed more time, their members would have to act properly. In the end, the evidence indicates that they all made a full return, though, where they could, they presented their evidence to blame some and exculpate others. The justices sat on Friday 9 January, Tuesday 13 January and Wednesday 14 January 1304. A summary and analysis of the findings of the different juries from Westminster, London and the Shires is as follows:[19]

The main characters involved in the robbery of the royal treasure at Westminster

- *Richard de Puddlicott* He is indicted time and again. He is accused of breaking into the Crypt and taking treasure away. He is described as one of the, '*Principales ordinatores et malefactores* – the principal organizers and malefactors'. He was found with some of the treasure on him in his house near Dowgate and he was often seen consorting with others implicated in the robbery. He was also guilty of robbing the Abbey refectory, being found with 32 silver spoons emblazoned with the Abbey arms. He is described as the leader of his gang and the indictments talk of '*Ses compaygnons et sa compaynie* – his companions and his company'.
- *William of the Palace* He is indicted time and again. He received and sheltered the burglars in the King's Palace, allowing them in whatever the hour and letting them wander wherever they wished. He had a bad reputation, having left his wife in their

lodgings at Fleet Prison and openly consorted with his whore Edelina. He received part of the stolen treasure, particularly the Cross of Neath and the Unicorn Horn which held sacred oil for anointing, these were found under his bed. William had openly boasted about being involved in the robbery.

- *John de Rippinghale* He is described as 'the Chaplain' or 'Priest'. He had raided other churches particularly St Mary's Woolnoth and when he was arrested at Westminster, a chisel and hammer were found on him. He was often in the company of Richard de Puddlicott. The juries knew that he had turned King's approver but they did not put much weight on his evidence.

- *Edelina daughter of Henry the Cook* She is described as a '*Puteyne* – a whore'. Edelina advised and helped the burglars. She sheltered William of the Palace and knew of his wickedness.

- *John de Lenton* He advised and helped the burglars. He too was one of the principal organizers and malefactors. He was the one who sowed the hemp seed where and when it should not have been sown. He was also involved in moving the stolen treasure to a field near St Pancras. He was a companion of Richard de Puddlicott and, when he was arrested, the key to the Abbey refectory was found on him.

- *Roger de Wenlock, Hamo de Wenlock, Walter de Ecclesford* These were servants of Adam the Sacristan, accustomed to sleep in the abbey church. They held keys to the church and sacristy which stand near the monks' cemetery where the hemp seed was sown. They were responsible for closing doors and gates as well as for ringing the bells of the Abbey [The bell stood in its own building, a tower in the abbey grounds], so the robbery could not have taken place without their knowledge and support.

- *Adam the Skinner* – He was Adam de Warfeld's chief assistant and what the above-mentioned three were accused of certainly applied to him. He is described as '*Custos ecclesiae*, Keeper of the Church' – he was more active than his companions in the matter of the burglary, carrying stolen goods to the house of Philip the Carpenter and giving a pot of silver to a valet of the King's yeoman, John le Convers. Adam also hid treasure in a field near the royal mews. He is described as one of the principal organizers and malefactors in the business of the robbery.

- *John of St Albans* He was a mason, captured at Chertsey. He gave advice and help regarding the burglary. He provided the tools used in the breaking 'of the wall' of the Treasury. These tools, along with jewels, were found on him when he was arrested. He had been poor but, since the robbery, had suddenly found the means to make expensive purchases.

- *John le Riche, alias John Ramage* He had been born in Westminster and was a servant of the monks, his mother lived near St Giles, Cripplegate. John had a very bad reputation and had been indicted for other crimes. Around the time of the robbery he was seen coming and going to the Abbey. He suddenly had new-found wealth, being able to equip himself like a knight with horses and arms. He even had the impunity to dress himself up as a soldier to join the King's army in the north. However, discretion is the better part of valour, 'Ramage' had returned to Westminster where he had been sheltered by the monks. He had even boasted that he had enough money to buy a town! He had kept some of the stolen treasure at his mother's house before moving it so as to escape the royal searchers. He should have been arrested but had fled.

- *Gerin the linen draper* He was a receiver: some of the treasure was hidden in his house for at least fifteen days, moved there by the monks, principally Alexander de Newport. Gerin was responsible for taking some of the treasure to a field near St Pancras.

- *John of Newmarket* As a goldsmith, he had bought jewels knowing they were stolen. He had made a profit from such sales and hidden part of the treasure in the house of a washerwoman in Southwark. Sheriff Hugh Pourte had discovered this, and John of Newmarket had been caught red-handed with some of the treasure. Under interrogation he broke down and informed Sheriff Pourte where Richard de Puddlicott lived.

- *The Barber Sisters* Around the time of the robbery, these, together with six men and a horseman, had gathered in the close of Fleet Prison in the company of John de Uggele and others. They had then moved down to Westminster and stayed there at least two nights.

- *Richard the Bailiff* He had been present when Walter de Gloucester, on the day the search was made at Westminster, discovered some of the treasure in the Abbey cemetery. The jury believed that Richard himself had put it there. The jurors also believed that Richard was party to the deliberations of the monks because his sister was married to one of the monks involved, William de Chalk.

Minor characters
- *The valet of John de Convers* He was found in possession of a precious cup.
- *Robert le Barber of Candlewick Street* He was a friend of Richard de Puddlicott.
- *Philip the Carpenter* He helped John of St Albans.

The monks
- *Adam de Warfeld* One of the leading figures in the robbery, he received stolen property in the Abbey. Precious items, found in the grounds of the Abbey by two carpenters and an old woman, were appropriated by him. He paid the old woman four pence not to reveal her find to anyone else. When the Coroner and the bailiffs of Westminster came to the Abbey regarding such items, Adam refused to surrender them. He was seen handling stolen goods on and around the Feast of St Barnabas [11 June]. He was in charge of the sacristy servants who were also involved in the robbery. The Sacristan held keys to the Abbey doors and gates. At the time of the robbery he closed the gates

when he should not have, so as to protect those trying to break into the Treasury. He even refused access to a farmer who had bought grazing rights in the Abbey wastelands and would not allow others to use the latrines there. Finally, on the day of the search, Adam had tried to conceal some of the King's treasure he was holding from royal ministers.

- *Alexander de Pershore, Ralph de Morton, Robert de Cherring, John de Noteley, John de Prescot, Thomas de Lichfield, Roger de Bures, John de Butterley, Thomas de Dene*
  - All these above-mentioned monks are described as consorting with William of the Palace, meeting him in the royal gardens and revelling there ['eating, drinking and playing with women of ill repute'], even though they were often reproved about this by their own Prior, William de Huntingdon.
  - These monks are all mentioned with reference to an attempt to steal the royal treasure four years earlier.
  - The above-mentioned monks are all mentioned in connection with £100's worth of silver, stolen from the casket containing money sent to the Abbey by the King, for Masses to be sung for the repose of the soul of his dead wife Eleanor.
  - All these monks are mentioned in close reference to the theft of precious goods from the Abbey refectory.
  - Thomas de Dene was certainly involved with the stolen treasure hidden in the house of Gerin the linen draper which was later moved elsewhere.
  - Roger de Bures, John de Butterley and Thomas de Lichfield were often seen in the company of William of the Palace. They used the Abbey cart to go back and forwards between the Abbey and the Palace.
  - Ralph de Morton is specifically mentioned as receiving stolen treasure in the Abbey.
  - John de Witney also held keys to the Abbey and must have known what was going on.
  - Alexander de Newport too was involved in the movement of

the stolen treasure to the house of Gerin the linen draper, before it was taken elsewhere. Moreover, Alexander's bedroom overlooked the monks' cemetery, so he must have heard the noise of those who perpetrated the robbery. Alexander de Newport, together with William de Chalk, also took stolen items to his Abbot at Pershore, attempting to depict them as treasure trove. The Lord Abbot, however, was not convinced.

To a certain extent these indictments of January 1304 simply reflect and develop some of the information given earlier. Richard de Puddlicott and William of the Palace are indicted eight times, as is Adam de Warfeld. 'John the Priest', the Chaplain who was captured at Westminster is indicted six times. John of St Albans, who provided the tools and actually assisted in the break-in, emerges prominently, being indicted seven times. John le Riche [John Ramage] is indicted six times, John de Lenton, who sowed the hemp, five times, Edelina, daughter of Henry [Nicholas] the Cook, three times, whilst the monks Thomas de Dene, Alexander de Pershore, and Alexander de Newport were named at least three times along with Adam the Skinner, the Sacristan's boy who, with other companions, played a major role in the robbery. John of Newmarket is twice described as a receiver or 'fence', knowing it was a crime. There is a passing reference to the Barber sisters and City jewellers but, in the main, the robbery is put down to certain monks who aided and abetted the burglars by closing gates and doors to prevent access. The jurors paint a picture of Westminster out of control with Henry de Cherring, Coroner of Westminster, being rebuffed in his inquiries; William Palmer having the run of the Palace and its grounds, whilst the Abbey was under the control of the monks, who not only closed gates and doors but allowed the likes of professional robbers such as John le Riche and John de Rippinghale to wander their cloisters.

According to the King's letter of 10 October 1303, these

monks had protested their innocence. In truth, they come across as hardened criminals and their house no more than a robber's den. The indictments list at least ten monks, certain names such as Alexander de Pershore, being repeated time and again. Moreover, the juries were quick to pile agony upon agony as regards the Benedictines. The robbery of 1303 was not their first felony. They refer to an attempted robbery which had taken place four years earlier in 1300 and had been hushed up by the Abbot while the juries make explicit reference to the disgraceful plundering of a royal coffer of £100's worth of silver. London, however, is hardly mentioned – the goldsmiths are referred to but, in the main, responsibility for the robbery rested with the above-mentioned characters. It is really quite remarkable how the City of London emerges unscathed from this investigation, especially their Sheriff Hugh Pourte, who is depicted as the hero of the hour.

Now the juries, led by the likes of Richer de Refham, could have been deliberately picked, eager to exculpate London citizens but the likes of Sandwich were not to be hindered in their questions. They could have concentrated on the involvement of the goldsmiths but ten of these (Adam le Orfevre, Thomas Frowick, William of York, Walter de Walpole, John de Bridgeford, John Bonaventure, William Torel, William de Keles' valet; Nicholas de St Botulpo) are simply named as '*Aurifabri*' who '*emerunt de dicto thesauro* – bought from the said treasure'.[20] Nothing more clearly demonstrates a change in emphasis than these few simple words: there is no reference to that famous excuse or explanation given in the earlier inquiry 'that they bought, not knowing it was a felony,' a phrase which infuriated the King and his justices: it was not the role of juries to decide that but the judges. Nor is there any reference from whom they bought their plunder: that, too, is quietly omitted. Finally, what is most surprising is the way the goldsmiths' actions are so briefly and quickly mentioned, they are summarized in six words, 'they bought from the said treasury', so brief and succinct that this must be compared to a later entry about John le Riche's movements, which amounts to about forty words. If they so wished, the justices could have pursued the matter.

The inquiry at New Temple in August 1303 had illustrated how the King's men could fasten on items such as the ownership of the basket used to move the treasure or whether that basket was moved at day or night. In the trials of January 1304, they chose not to. Undoubtedly the leader of that particular jury, John le Cofferer, had been briefed on how to act. The court did not want to hear any insolence or insult: the goldsmiths were not to depict themselves as innocent, well-meaning merchants; it would go easier for them in court. The goldsmiths apparently heeded this advice. However, the Crown was not just interested in rebuking open contempt but reserving its case vis-à-vis the goldsmiths. The latter were powerful merchants, they had great influence in the City and the King would need them in forcing the City Council to accede to his request for the New Customs. It was the mailed fist-in-the-velvet-glove approach: the goldsmiths could, as could Sheriff Pourte, be called to account for their actions on a different day in a different place, if the King did not have his way in certain matters.

The indictments depict three distinct groups operating. The first were the monks themselves, about ten in number, together with six servants of Adam the Sacristan and a number of officials attached to the Abbey such as Roger the Bailiff. The second group include William of the Palace with his links with the Barber sisters and other characters of ill repute such as John le Riche and John de Rippinghale. Finally there is Richard de Puddlicott, the actual person who led the break-in. However, one thing the jurors do not reveal, as did previous juries, is the actual means of entry. They talk of hemp being sown to shield the area outside the Treasury from watchful eyes, of gates and doors being locked, of people who had every right to go there, such as the farmer who had paid money to graze his cattle, being banned. A professional mason, John of St Albans, together with a carpenter, were brought in to provide tools and technical help whilst a valet of John le Convers, who had paved the floor of the Treasury in the 1290s, was also suborned, perhaps bribed to provide information about what lay within. Yet never once is any specific information given on the actual method of access. The nearest, the indictments come to this are the words: '*John le Mazoun fregit murum thesauri* – John the mason broke the wall of the Treasury.'[21] The justices would now look to the confessions of the three principal malefactors to resolve this and other problems: William of the Palace, John de Rippinghale and, above all, Richard de Puddlicott.

7

The Thieves' Tale

'Ytel devendra Leres que ne fust unque mes'

'He will become a robber who never was before.'
Contemporary ballad

William Palmer's self-serving confessions of June and July 1303, together with the verdicts of the juries, depict the man as a fool. He was one of those royal officials satirized by contemporaries, full of his own importance, venal, corrupt and, worst of all, a man unable to keep his mouth shut. Deputy Keeper of the Palace of Westminster and of the Fleet Prison, William had, in the absence of his masters, inflated his own importance. He had left his wife and moved his mistress Edelina to the Palace where he entertained the monks with illicit revelry in the royal gardens. Controller of the keys, he had allowed whoever he wished to wander the Palace and, like the monks, was consumed by greed for the treasure in the Abbey Crypt. He had openly boasted about his exploits and when the '*Dies Irae* – The Day of Wrath finally arrived, he tried to pass the blame on to the monks, casting himself as the innocent victim forced to cooperate out of fear for his life. The inquiry of January 1304 soon depicted such claims as mendacious, reinforcing the views of the previous summer that William Palmer, Deputy Keeper of the Palace and of the Fleet Prison, was not only involved in the robbery of his own free will but was one of its leaders.[1] William of the Palace's confession is more interesting for what it omits than what it says. He blames the monks, knowing full well that the good citizens of London would only be too eager to rise to such a bait whilst the monks themselves could hide behind their clerical status.

The confession of John de Rippinghale is more complex. During the inquiry of January 1304, Rippinghale's name comes to the fore when the jury of Middlesex called him 'John de Rippinghale known as the Chaplain' and bracket him alongside Puddlicott as one of the principal perpetrators of the robbery. The jury of Westminster claimed that John de Rippinghale was both consenting and participating in the robbery. Elsewhere, he is called 'John the Priest' and is guilty because, when arrested, the plunder of other churches, such as vestments and plate as well as the tools of his illicit trade as a church-breaker, namely an iron chisel and hammer, were found on him. Another jury refers to Rippinghale as a 'Chaplain' and mentions his recent exploits and depredations against the Church of St Mary Woolnoth, pointing out that before such a raid he didn't even have the means to eat and drink, let alone dress, whilst he had been often seen in the company of Richard de Puddlicott.[2] Indeed the juries had no difficulty in delivering indictments against John de Rippinghale because they knew that Rippinghale, imprisoned at Westminster beyond the bar of London, had turned King's evidence. He had, according to the jury, become an approver ['*devout un appelour*']: someone who buys his own life on condition that he turns King's evidence. John de Rippinghale happily obliged and, even before the justices met, on the Feast of St Lucy [3 December 1303], Rippinghale had made what he would regard as a full and frank confession before a Royal Commissioner, Hugh de Veer and Henry Cherring, Coroner of Westminster. The confession, still in manuscript form in the National Archives, is written in a staccato style whilst the phraseology is convoluted. John de Rippinghale's words were probably taken down verbatim by the Coroner's Clerk. The Norman French is translated as follows:[3]

John de Rippinghale of the County of Lincoln, formerly a monk of the Abbey of St Peterborough, confessed before Hugh de Veer on Friday the Feast of St Lucy [3 December] in the year of King's Edward I, 1303, that he had been present at the break-in of the Treasury of Westminster on the Tuesday before the Feast of the Finding of the True Cross. [The Feast of the Finding of the True Cross was, in 1303, Friday 3 May, so Tuesday was 30 April.] They began the actual break-in on the Wednesday night following [1 May], wrenched open the coffers and, during the night of the Thursday [2 May], took away the treasure of the King, his silver and other precious goods and jewels to the amount of four hundred pounds. The said John claims that, at the above-mentioned break-in, there was with him in his company: Ralph de Morton, monk of Westminster, Ralph de Cannes, monk at St Swithun's in Winchester, Simon the old Knight of the County of Somerset; that the above Ralph had companions John Peche, Forester of Selwood, John of Spain, Forester of Chaddre, Robert son of Robert de Chaddre, John de Soonborne of the County of Sussex, Sir John Malmains of the County of Kent, living near a town in Rochester; Robert Romain of Gravesend, William de Val from the County of Kent; Richard de Puddlicott from the County of Essex, then living in London; Nicholas the Jeweller of London, Ralph de Bures, Ralph of St Peterborough, John of St Albans mason, William, Guardian of the Palace of the King at Westminster, and Richard de La Mare of the county of Lincoln.

The aforesaid John de Rippinghale says that Nicholas the jeweller of London brought goods from the said John and separately paid each of their company. John had been given four hundred pounds of jewels which the said Nicholas sold and changed for two hundred pounds and eighty pounds in plate. The said John gave to the Abbey at Peterborough, through Father Kite, monk of the said Abbey, in the chamber of Sir John de Ashewardeby on the third day after the Feast of St Peter and Paul [2 July 1303] thirty-one pounds. The said John delivered to the Abbot of Peterborough, in the presence of William Marewell his Chaplain, in the prison of Bernak, within the octave of the Assumption of Our Lady past [sometime between 15–23 August 1303] fifty pounds in coins and eighty pounds in plate. Of the hundred and twenty pounds of jewels remaining, Nicholas the Jeweller advanced to him thirty pounds. Robert of Ashebridge, Walter de la More, Henry de la Chambre, Bailiffs of the said town then in the Bishopric of Baa, in the town of Ashebridge arrested him with gold and silver plate and rings of gold to the amount of forty pounds which they retained. The said John gave to Nicholas de Langton, Steward of the Bishop, forty shillings in order he might go his own way. The aforesaid John says Ralph de Morton changed some of the jewels which amounted to two hundred pounds and he sent these to Sir John de Ashewardeby, Parson of the Castle in order to save himself. He understands that these are in the coffers of Sir John at the house of the Carmelites in Stamford. On the Saturday following, [4 December 1303] the said John declared he understood all these things written here before Sir Hugh de Veer and Henry de Cherring, Coroner of the Liberty of Westminster, to which the said Henry puts his seal and the aforesaid Hugh puts his seal.

This is the first time this confession has been translated. It has been ignored by both Victorian commentators, as well as Professor Tout in his lecture (1934). The reasons are understandable. Rippinghale's confession is rambling nonsense, most of the names he mentions cannot be traced or referred to in other documentation of this case. True, a few are recognizable, Ralph de Morton the monk, Richard de Puddlicott, William of the Palace. However, even here Rippinghale is wrong in claiming that Puddlicott was from Essex when there is every likelihood that Puddlicott came from Oxfordshire. The reference to the '*Evesque de Baa* – the bishopric of Baa', as it is written in French, is a clue. Rippinghale couldn't remember the bishopric and why should he? He was making it all up. Rippinghale had been in prison for almost six months: a destitute, defrocked priest, who would have few friends. He must have been, both physically and psychologically, in very poor shape and his confession reflects this. He sensed the royal searchers would be looking for stolen items so he rambles on about old knights of Somerset and unknown foresters. Little wonder that those interrogating Rippinghale formally asked him if he understood what had been taken down. Of course, Rippinghale provides a few accurate details, particularly the date of the robbery, the Tuesday just before the Feast of the Finding of the True Cross – in 1303 Friday 3 May. So, according to Rippinghale, they began the robbery on 30 April. They entered the Treasury by Wednesday 1 May and moved the treasure by the following Thursday night. This agrees with the aldermen's evidence. They claim that, around the Feast of the Finding of the True Cross, the Barber sisters, gathered in the close of Fleet Prison, had proceeded towards Westminster Abbey with other members of their gang. For the rest, however, Rippinghale is simply lying to save his own life. He was not a monk at Peterborough. 'John the Priest' or 'John the Chaplain' came from Rippinghale in Lincolnshire. A former secular priest, he'd been excommunicated and outlawed in 1296 for refusing to pay a royal tax. He and others had been given forty days to comply and, when Rippinghale failed to do so, the bishop asked the Crown to arrest him. John de Rippinghale, therefore, was a defrocked priest, an outlaw on the run.[4] Like many of his kind he had drifted into London. By 1303 he was a professional church-breaker. The jury of Westminster accused him of other such robberies and, when arrested, he had been found with the necessary implements for church-breaking. Rippinghale had been arrested and imprisoned in the Gatehouse at Westminster. He'd been kept separate from the rest but his previous depredations against churches like St Mary Woolnoth were well known, as was his apparent poverty before such robberies, when he lacked the 'means to eat, drink, let alone dress'.

John de Rippinghale had turned King's approver, a kind of state evidence which was often used by the Crown during the medieval period.[5] A felon would confess and appeal [that is accuse] his accomplices. If this proved successful in securing a conviction, the approver was to be released and exiled from the kingdom. If, however, he turned approver and was unsuccessful he was hanged out of hand. A man could not be an approver if he had been outlawed or convicted of a felony. This explains why Rippinghale depicts himself as a monk of Peterborough, he does not wish to reveal his murky past; it also explains why the juries were quick to report Rippinghale's more recent depredations. Rippinghale had offered his services to the Crown who, of course, would accept him to be what he claimed to be, until proved otherwise.

Approvers could be highly dangerous, vicious men. Some made a living out of it because they often challenged those they appealed to trial by battle. Approvers were sometimes professional swordsmen, skilled killers, who would make short work of some hapless citizen. Rippinghale, however, was pathetic: he had to tell the Crown something they didn't know, hence the fabrication about fictitious people and places. The King's 'bully boys', Bereford, Brabazon and Ralph de Sandwich, would make light work of his evidence.

The jury of Walbrook were certainly suspicious of

Rippinghale's confession which must have been shown to them. Approvers were intensely disliked and juries usually declared against them. Walbrook specifically rejected the allegation that any 'stranger' or 'foreigner', be he squire or knight, was present at the robbery, an allusion to Rippinghale's fictitious confession about the old Knight of Somerset and foresters from areas beyond London, as well as his assertion that he had not really profited from the robbery of the Treasury.[6] Rippinghale's veracity is, of course, highly suspect: he was an outlaw, a defrocked priest, guilty of sacrilegious robbery. Benefit of Clergy would not help him, he would hang unless he turned approver. The only way he could save his neck was by casting his net as far as possible and accusing others. What else could he do? If he confessed the truth, Rippinghale would only be telling the Crown what they already knew. He could have supplied names but the juries had already done that. Rippinghale was a minor member of the gang: he enjoyed no privileges or protection except to lie and play for time. Secure in Westminster prison, away from the other principal malefactors, he concocted a story which he knew the Crown would spend a great deal of time investigating. He deliberately created a 'paper trail' of where the treasure had gone, so that the Crown could pursue it; whilst they did, there was time, life, and the opportunities which a pragmatist like John de Rippinghale might grasp. Like any professional liar Rippinghale threw in a few facts to spice the story, the date of the robbery, the names of his principal accomplices, the rest he left to chance. In the end, however, it would not save him: the juries rejected his evidence and Rippinghale's fate, a degraded cleric and a lying approver, would be sealed.

Richard de Puddlicott's confession, also in Norman French in manuscript form, is attached to Rippinghale's. It has the title:[7] '*Le dit Richard de Podelecote*' and was transcribed by a high-ranking King's clerk. The Norman French is easy to understand, its letters and words are, in the main, very well formed. There are phrases added: for example, the confession ends, 'He took the plunder outside the gate near the church of St Margaret.' The clerk then adds a phrase, probably at Puddlicott's insistence when he read it through, 'and the cemetery of the Church of St Margaret', so it reads 'the Church of St Margaret's and the Cemetery at the Church of St Margaret'. It is, therefore, a thoughtful, precise piece of work, yet, this too, is a work of fiction. It translates as follows:

'The confession of Richard de Puddlicott: he claims he was an itinerant trader in wool, cheese and butter who was arrested in Flanders for the King's debt in the city of Bruges where he lost fourteen pounds and seventeen shillings because of the King. He sued for this in the court of the King at Westminster around the beginning of August, the thirty-first year of Edward I [1302]. Whilst at Westminster he studied the situation of the refectory of the Abbey, he noticed how its servants carried in and out hampers of silver, dishes and mazers and he thought how he might acquire such goods, for he was poor due to the losses he had sustained in Flanders. So he closely studied the precincts of the Abbey and the area around it. About the same time the King departed towards Barnes, the night following, the said Richard acted on what he had learned. He found a ladder standing against a house which was being roofed, close to the Palace gate over against the Abbey. He placed this ladder against a window of the Chapter House, which was opened and shut by a cord. He forced this window open and entered, swinging himself down by the same cord. He went to the door of the refectory but found it locked, so he opened it with his knife and entered. Inside he found six hampers of silver in a cupboard behind the doors and thirty or more dishes of silver in another cupboard. Underneath a bench, were baskets containing drinking cups all packed together. He carried these off, closing the doors behind him though he did not lock them. He then sold the feet [base] of the cups, the

136

dishes and hampers of silver before Christmas so, when his money failed, he thought, he might return to break into the King's Treasury. By now he knew his way around the precincts of the Abbey and where the Treasury was and he wished to get at it. He began his work eight days before Christmas [17 December 1302] in order to make a breach and took the following implements with him, that is two tarriers, one large and the other small, knives and many other engines of iron. He grew busy, trying to break in under the cover of night, whenever he could plan it, from eight days before Christmas to the Quinzaine [fifteen days after the Feast] of Easter following, [Easter was 7 April 1303 so that would mean the 22 April]. He entered the Treasury for the first time on Wednesday, 24 April, the eve of the feast of St Mark and for the whole of St Mark's day [25 April] remained inside arranging what he planned to carry off. He took away the following night what he wanted and left this outside the breach until the following night, when he carried it with him as far as the gate behind the Church of St Margaret. He placed this beneath the wall outside the gate and covered it with a heap of earth: it included twelve jugs and, in every jug, he put some jewels and cups, standing and covered. Beside these he put a great jug full of precious stones and a cup in a wooden shrine together with three sacks of jewels and vessels. One sack was full of cups, whole as well as broken, in the other a great crucifix [the Cross of Neath], jewels, a case of silver and some gold dishes. In the third sack, cups, plates, nine saucers and a silver-gilt image of Our Lady and two little silver jugs. He also carried to a ditch near the Royal Mews, a pot and cup of silver. He also took with him dishes, plates and saucers for spices, a crown cut up, a ring, clasps, precious stones, crowns, belts and other jewels which were found in his possession. The same Richard says he took all these out of the Treasury and carried them straight away outside the gate close to the church of St Margaret, and the Cemetery of the

church of St Margaret's, without leaving anything behind
him within that gate.

The confession is delivered in that sharp staccato tone of
Rippinghale's, the clerk taking down Puddlicott's words
verbatim.

Now Puddlicott may well have been a wandering merchant in
lambs' wool, butter and cheese. He could have been arrested in
Flanders when the Flemings' quarrelled with the English King
and decided to call in their debts. However, the rest is a delib-
erate attempt to mislead. First, Puddlicott claims he arrived at
Westminster hoping to sue the King because of his losses in
Flanders. Puddlicott is mixing fiction and fact. Edward I did
return to Westminster in the summer of 1302, he was definitely
there at the beginning of August but the Court of King's Bench
and all the great offices of state remained in the north at York.
Puddlicott virtually describes himself as a tourist who notices the
Abbey's silver and decides to rob it. He waits until the King
leaves London, a rather strange remark depicting the King as a
security guard for the Abbey silver. It is a slip, a tacit confession
of the truth. What Puddlicott is really saying is, of course, that he
was waiting for the King to desert the Palace so as to prepare for
his great assault on the Treasury. However, in his story about the
refectory, he is apparently lucky enough to find the ladder which
provides access to the Abbey refectory and, once in, he steals the
silver. He does not explain how he got so much silver out, or how
he carried it away nor does he mention John de Lenton who was
found in possession of the refectory key, or the fact that some of
the monks, according to the indictments, also participated in that
robbery.[8] They certainly never raised the hue and cry. Nor does
Puddlicott explain how the good brothers let him wander their
Abbey, even entering their refectory.

Puddlicott also claims to have spent most of his ill-gotten gains
by 17 December 1302, a remarkable feat for a burglar to dissi-
pate so much wealth in scarcely a month. Accordingly, he returns

to Westminster 'as he understands the ways of the Abbey' and, a
week before Christmas with 'engines of iron', begins the assault
on the wall of the Treasury. He then breaks through on 24 April,
stays there virtually two days before carrying the goods away on
the nights of 25 and 26 April.

If a comparison is made between Puddlicott's confession and
the indictments of the jury, not to mention Rippinghale's confession, a number of serious contradictions emerge. Puddlicott's lies
are obvious. First, who was he? A lone thief? The 'man of Kent'
as described by Rippinghale? The truth is hidden away. Richard
de Puddlicott may have been a travelling merchant in wool,
cheese and butter which could explain his links with the mercantile class of Colchester, Northampton and Kings Lynn, towns
closely associated with the wool trade, as well as the likes of John
de Newmarket, his means of introduction to the goldsmiths of
London. Puddlicott, however, is not a Kentish name but an
Oxford one. It is small village in the hundred of Charlbury, a
parish of the rural deanery of Chipping Norton owing dues to the
Benedictine Abbey of Peterborough in Lincolnshire, a possible
connection with the defrocked priest John de Rippinghale.

The Puddlicotts were landowners in Oxford as far back as
the twelfth century with links to the Benedictine monasteries in
the area at Abingdon, Evesham and Waverley. In May 1301 a
Henry de Puddlicott, described as 'Kitchener' of Abingdon
Abbey, an important post, disbursed monies regarding land
deals in a charter witnessed by very important people including
the Mayor of Oxford. Henry witnessed another one on 25
August 1309 along with certain knights. A Hugh de Puddlicott
was also a charter witness to an agreement between the Abbots
of Abingdon and Waverley on 8 September 1310 whilst a John
de Puddlicott witnessed a similar charter in August 1338.
Undoubtedly, these must have been members of Puddlicott's
family, the names John and Richard being commonly used. In
fact, our felon may have been a married man. Some twelve
years later, a Richard and Joan de Puddlicott attended the

courts at Westminster in January 1315 and, again, the following June because they were involved in complicated negotiations over certain land. It is rather ironic that one of the justices involved was William de Bereford who had tried the burglar Richard de Puddlicott [possibly the father of Joan's husband] during the robbery crisis of 1303 to 1305.[9]

Accordingly, we have Richard Puddlicott a wool merchant, who claims he was so desperate for money, that he was prepared to hang round Westminster to sue the King for just over fourteen pounds. However, that same Richard had a house in London down near Dowgate[10] where he stored the plunder from both the Abbey refectory and the Royal Treasury. He also had a mistress, Joanne or Joanna Picard, daughter of a tailor. Moreover, Puddlicott was regularly seen in the taverns with the likes of James the Taverner, whilst some of the plunder taken from the refectory in November 1302 was still in his hands some seven months later.[11] Puddlicott apparently enjoyed high enough status to negotiate with merchants in Northampton and Colchester, not to mention at least six leading London goldsmiths.

In truth Richard de Puddlicott emerges as a man of some breeding and background: the son of an Oxford land-owning family which had strong links with the Benedictine communities of Evesham, Abingdon and Waverley, not to mention the monks of Westminster who owned land in Oxfordshire, having a country seat at Islip. Puddlicott may have tried his luck at trading, hence his move to London, the purchase of a house, the retention of a mistress, moving easily amongst the mercantile class. Being a foreigner, however, a merchant outsider, he would also be known and watched in the closely packed ward of Dowgate. Certainly his status with London's merchants must have been fairly considerable. The robbery took place at the beginning of May 1303. Puddlicott enjoyed so much confidence that he was able to set up negotiations with the goldsmiths and sell them jewels, gold and plate within at least four weeks of the robbery. He is also well known at the Abbey. He himself admits in his confession 'that he knew all its ways'. He may have even traded with the Abbey itself through family links in Oxfordshire.

Puddlicott's confession betrays nothing of this and begs several questions:

- Why was he so eager to cast himself as the sole thief, admitting to plundering the Treasury, carrying it away and even being found with it when arrested?
- Why does he lie about the robbery of the refectory – depicting himself as solely responsible when he would have needed help to carry away so much plunder? Why does he say had spent all his ill-gotten gains for such a crime when, four years later, the goods of the Abbey refectory were still in the hands of Hugh Pourte, the former sheriff?[12]
- Why does he refuse to name one accomplice either in the Abbey, the City or anywhere else?
- Why does he lie about the date, placing it around 25 April, a week earlier than that provided by all the other evidence?
- Who was he protecting and why? A brave man who wanted to be the hero of the hour? Or a born gambler making his last desperate throw – but for what?

In turn these questions prompt one overall conclusion about the inquisition before Ralph de Sandwich and the rest at the Tower during those January days of 1304. The juries had delivered fuller, more detailed replies than those of the summer of 1303 yet, in the end, there was nothing substantially new: certain monks and members of the Abbey community, together with the likes of Puddlicott, William of the Palace, John of Newmarket, John de Lenton, John of St Albans, John de Rippinghale, John Ramage and an assortment of minor characters had been involved in the robbery. If anything, the role of Londoners had been played down. So what or when had the King been hunting? What was the truth behind the great robbery of May 1303 and the investigation which ensued?

Part Two

8

The Tangled Web

'Quy Le mieux puet eslyre, foe est ge ne velt choyser'

'He who has the chance to choose what is better,
is a fool if he does not make that choice.'
Contemporary ballad

The robbery of the Royal Treasury at Westminster in May 1303 was the result of many factors coming together. Medieval astrologers would have put it down to the malign influence of certain planets clustering together 'a multitude of clouds and severe cold in winter with an excess of heat in the summer which led to disputes over produce. Tiredness and thickness of the eyes whilst robberies and highwaymen will multiply in the streets'.[1]

Certainly in 1303 times were harsh and money scarce:

There is a scarcity of money amongst the people, although they may possess cloth or corn, pig or sheep, the people can do very little with them. There are so few buyers in the market. In truth, there are so many needy people; when money is so scarce that the people are not joyful.

So the prophets of doom lashed the Kingdom of England as it moved from one century to another. 'False and wicked is such a land, as every day reveals, riven by both hate and conflict. I think it will always be so. Covetousness has the law fast in its hand.'[2] The object of this covetousness in 1302/1303 in the thirty-first year of Edward I's reign, as far as his capital city of London and the royal village of Westminster were concerned, was the King's treasure buried deep in the Crypt beneath the Chapter House of St Peter's Abbey, where the monks of St Benedict were vowed, at least in theory, to the glory of God and the salvation of souls. The treasure had been moved there from the Tower for a variety of reasons. Parish churches were commonly used to house money and valuables, stored carefully in wooden, iron-bound chests. Westminster Abbey was the King's own chapel, his personal shrine, the glorious mausoleum of his family, sacred ground blessed by the bones of the Confessor and centuries of holy ritual. The Tower had its dungeons and strong rooms but it was cut off from the City and, above all, the Royal Palace of Westminster where the Exchequer and Chancery offices executed their business; the Tower was too far from the King's chamber and the workings of his great household. The Abbey was an ideal place, the hallowed heart of the royal Plantagenet line, a short walk from the gardens of the Palace; it was also secure. The Chapel of the Pyx in the south cloister served as a store-room for documents, but the Crypt beneath the Chapter House was an excellent strong room. It was sealed off by stout doors, and a booby-trapped winding staircase. Inside, its central pillar, ingeniously carved out to form secret recesses, served as a strong room within a strong room. True, in 1296, John the Cook had attempted to violate the Treasury but he had been caught. The cook's nefarious attempt must have prompted the work of the royal official, the mason John le Convers, to make the Crypt even

146

stronger. Nevertheless as the contemporaneous satire laments, 'Pride and covetousness were the masters', in the end greed would have its way: the guardians of the Westminster shrine, the Black Monks, had become corrupted by the times.

> The Black Monks love drinking. Indeed they are drunk every day because they do not know any other way of living, yet they claim they do it for the sake of society not at all out of gluttony. It is ordained that each brother drink before dinner and after. Moreover, if it happens that a friend visits a brother (and such should always be at hand to comfort a brother), they shall play until late in the evening. I tell you this for certain they will all sleep late in the morning!

So writes the anonymous author of the libel, 'The Order of Fair-Ease', a bitter attack upon the laxity of the religious orders of the times.[3] For the Black Monks of Westminster the harvest time for their greed came to fruition in the early summer of 1303. Corrupt and venal, they found themselves cheek by jowl with a royal ransom belonging to a King, who had left Westminster to wage bloody war hundreds of miles to the north. His palace lay forsaken and had become a breeding ground for lawlessness and ribaldry. The place and time were set. However, the 'fount and origin' of the robbery of the Treasury at Westminster was Lord Walter de Wenlok, Abbot since 1283. Wenlok was an absentee lord, in that alone he seriously violated the rule of St Benedict, but there was worse. Wenlok was a shepherd more interested in the fleece than the flock, grasping and greedy, who feasted at his estates on wine and beer, twelve geese, 200 eggs, twelve partridges, not to mention the larks and plovers.[4] Of course, similar allegations of self-indulgence could be levelled against many of the great and good in Church and State at the time. However, Wenlok comes across as a true mystery. He acts as the great lord and man of his times. His epitaph in the *Flowers of History* is more of a eulogy than an obituary. The chronicler, writing of Wenlok's death on 25 December 1307, piously intones:

> The Supreme Wisdom who orders all things and, now and
> again mixes laughter with tears, gave the monks of
> Westminster a chalice of bitterness by taking from this light
> [*Ab hac luce*] their venerable father Walter de Wenlok, a holy
> shepherd of that church, a zealous defender of the rule of St
> Benedict, who secured many benefits and bestowed them
> liberally on his church and his brethren.[5]

Nonetheless, this was the same abbot who, after his twenty-
four year rule, had left a community bitterly divided, so riven
with scandal that, on 14 July 1308, the new king, Edward II, not
exactly a mirror of virtue himself, took the extraordinary step of
ordering his Chief Justices Roger Brabazon, William Bereford
and others to intervene. Two years later in 1310, the same king
had to write to the new abbot about the continuing problems of
discipline at the Abbey,[6] whilst amongst the Abbey muniments is
a document dating from the same time which refers to 'assaults,
fights, abuse and scandalized talk amongst the monks'.[7]

Now, undoubtedly, Wenlok had his virtues but he was an
abbot who spent lavishly, and borrowed just as much, patronized
his own family and was often absent. Nevertheless, Wenlok had
more secret and serious vices than this. The Abbot of
Westminster enjoyed the full authority of the papacy, the backing
of the King and the power vested in him by the rule of St
Benedict. All these were reinforced by the *Customary of the Abbey of
St Peter*, a long and complex document which provided a detailed
description of how the monastic life at Westminster was to be
lived. Wenlok himself was a stickler for order and propriety as the
publication of the ordinances for his own household bear witness.
Nevertheless, he was also an abbot who allowed his friends and
lieutenants, led by Alexander de Pershore, William de Chalk and
Ralph de Morton, free rein in the Abbey. They had definitely
tried to perpetrate their own robbery in 1300. They certainly

stole at least a £100's worth of silver from a casket intended for Masses for the soul of the late Queen Eleanor, yet all Wenlok does is hush it up. The brothers hire as servants the likes of John le Riche [Ramage], and Adam the Skinner, professional thugs, outlaws and thieves who can wander the Abbey and hide there, yet Wenlok does nothing about it. On the other hand, when it comes to his own household, the Abbot proclaimed the strictest rules against intrusion by such disreputable men, whilst even the honest washerwoman had to wait by the door.

Worse still, Wenlok's leading monks, at least ten of them, broke every single axiom of a priest and monk. They shattered their vows of poverty, chastity and obedience by consorting with libertines such as William of the Palace. They joined the latter in the gardens of Westminster Palace, a mere walk away from the Abbey, to indulge in frequent orgies, playing, eating and drinking with women of bad reputation. This was not just an exception but a common occurrence and, when the same monks were repri-manded by their prior for such conduct, Alexander de Pershore and the rest simply defied William de Huntingdon.[8] The latter must have appealed to Wenlok but, again, the Abbot did nothing, the likes of Pershore must have had his Abbot's tacit approval for such nefarious activities. True, Adam de Warfeld was not included in that list of revelling monks (Pershore, Morton, Cherring, Noteley, Prescot, Lichfield, Bures, Butterley and Dene), but he was busy trying to seduce the daughter of Walter Russell, Procurator of the Arches in London, with precious items stolen from the King's treasure. Nor is William de Chalk mentioned in the above list. However, according to an Abbey document from 1308 entitled *Forma Pacis*, which was a blueprint for imposing order on the warring monastic community of Westminster, there was scandalous talk about William de Chalk's liaison with a French lady Roesia de Gisors. The same document also reveals that, by 1308, Alexander de Pershore had certainly not changed his lifestyle, as his name is also linked to two ladies, Matilda of Durham and Beatrice of Baldok.[9] Despite all this scandal, or because of it, Alexander de Pershore remained as Wenlok's lieutenant from the day Wenlok was elected abbot in 1283 to Wenlok's death on Christmas day 1307. Indeed, Alexander de Pershore's influence over the Abbot provoked a fresh crisis in the Abbey between 1305 and 1307. In the former year, after the death of William de Huntingdon, Reginald de Hadham was elected prior. Wenlok tried to overturn this, so it led to civil war within the Abbey. The reason behind Wenlok's decision was that the Abbot probably wanted Alexander de Pershore in that important post. He certainly used Alexander as his confidant and counsellor during the vicious in-fighting with Hadham and his opponents, appointing him as his Deputy and Attorney.[10]

Why did Wenlok place such trust in a man like Alexander de Pershore, even as late as a few months before his death, bearing in mind that Alexander de Pershore had been named time and again by the juries of 1303 and 1304 in the matter of the robbery of the King's treasury at Westminster? Moreover, every account of Abbot Wenlok's role in that robbery depicts him as guiltless. That being the case, why didn't the Lord Abbot distance himself from these errant monks? Yet there is no record of this. The Crown certainly regarded Wenlok as involved. He was lodged in the Tower and had to pay bail before he was released. The mystery is deepened by the fact that there were two robberies at Westminster in 1302 and 1303. The plunder of the royal treasure and the theft of precious items from the Abbey refectory (sometime in November 1302) had the full connivance of some of the monks, who must have provided John de Lenton, Puddlicott's friend, with a key to the refectory. According to the *Customary* of Westminster, the refectory silver was stowed away and only brought out for display on great feast days.[11] Wenlok must have noticed such valuable items were missing when he visited the Abbey, as was customary for the great feasts of Christmas 1302, the Epiphany (6 January 1303), Easter, Ascension Day and Pentecost (15 and 25 May 1303). Yet, Wenlok apparently never noticed the Abbey treasure was missing. The Prior had a duty to bring such a matter to his superior's attention. The Refectorian certainly would. (From February 1303, this was Reginald de Hadham, who would become Prior and Wenlok's inveterate adversary a few years later.) Hadham and his lieutenant Roger de Aldenham were certainly 'whistle-blowers' in the Abbey, alerting the Crown to the robbery – 'the faithful and worthy men', mentioned by Edward I in his letter of 6 June 1303, who later cooperated with the Crown in providing names. Wenlok obliquely refers to this in a document of September 1307, in which he launched a vicious attack on Hadham. Wenlok accused his Prior: 'You falsely and maliciously caused your Lord Abbot to be summoned to the King's Exchequer in the matter of the robbery and the break-in of the Prior's Chamber.'

Now the dissension at Westminster from 1305 to 1308 was bitter, the different factions eager to attack each other without making their accusations and counter-accusations too public, as they all had a great deal to hide. However, the documentation does touch on sensitive issues. Wenlok's above-mentioned allegation against Hadham accused the Prior of 'maliciously slandering' him. Hadham and his party replied in kind. Muniment 5460 at Westminster Abbey contains a schedule of letters and documents dating from around midsummer 1308. In one of these Roger de Aldenham, Haddam's lieutenant, begs the Prior to seek the influence of Henry de Lacey, Earl of Lincoln, and uncle to the new king, Edward II. Aldenham points out that their opponents had approached the royal favourite Peter Gaveston (whom de Lacey hated). Aldenham advises, 'Tell him [i.e. Henry de Lacey] how our late Abbot [Wenlok], knowing he would be discredited, *if his conduct became known*, went over to Gaveston's party and gave the favourite £200 along with innumerable other presents.' Aldenham then adds how Wenlok 'oppressed and destroyed the entire status of our monastery'. Wenlok undeniably gave gifts, even bribes to powerful men of the kingdom but, so did others. The Abbot treated his own mother like a queen but, so did others and, in the spirit of the age, he looked after his kith and kin. But, all this was done in the light of public scrutiny. Wenlok was undoubtedly lavish to himself and his circle.

However, what had Wenlock done so wrong ('if his conduct became known') that his enemies could hint at a great scandal? Whilst friends and allies, such as Alexander de Pershore, could do what they liked in the Abbey, be it theft, sacrilege, the violation of their vows, leaving the Abbey, consorting with felons, relaxing with prostitutes and allowing a wandering merchant of wool and milk to steal the Abbey's own silver in a long-term project to fund an even greater crime, it must have been more than financial irregularity in Wenlok's case unacceptable patronage or even sexual peccadilloes. Wenlock's self-indulgence is a matter of public record. Aldenham is hinting at something that very few people knew about, not an incident, but something long-term which defines 'his conduct'. Wenlok had done something which could not be undone, removed or forgotten. The evidence would seem to indicate that Lord Walter de Wenlok, Abbot of St Peter Abbey at Westminster, had a common-law wife/mistress by whom he had had at least one child.

Wenlok lavished wealth on his mother Agnes, widow of an apothecary in Wenlok. He bought her land in Shropshire, sent her money, decorated her house in Wenlok, the list of such gifts is lengthy. When his mother, the Lady Agnes died, sister Edith comes to the fore, travelling up to Westminster until her own death in the summer of 1307. Of course, this is all commendable but, as soon as sister Edith dies, a young lady abruptly emerges for the first time on the good Abbot's expense list, a 'niece', Alice. In the last quarter of 1307, considerable sums were paid out for Alice's clothing, almost £9 on coloured cloths and linen, as well as three months' lodgings with Agnes of Wickham. Such entries are tucked away, only two slips denote her sex, as *Nepte* could mean nephew. First, the Latin '*pro eadem*' (the feminine for 'the same') and, later in the same document, a reference to lodgings where '*Nepte*' is named as Alice. The Abbot even arranged a suitable marriage for this Alice: 'Item, paid to Thomas of Amersham, 20 Florins in full payment for the marriage of the Lord Abbot's niece.' This entry, however, was only written up after Wenlok's death. Moreover, the original had been written '*in preparatione* – in preparation' for the marriage but, later charged to the actual marriage itself. These entries seemed to have caused the Treasurer, Henry Payn, some difficulty, first concealing them, then not writing them up until after the Abbot's death. Only then does information surface about the expenses of this 'niece' who never stepped from the shadows until Wenlok's sister dies. The entries themselves are elliptical and hastily crossed out and rewritten. Why such subterfuge? Was Alice Abbot Wenlok's niece or really his daughter, first entrusted to his mother Lady Agnes, then to his sister Edith? It would appear so and, once the latter died, Wenlok had no choice but to take over the care of this young woman directly, feed her, lodge her and marry her off in considerable haste and subterfuge. Of course, it could be argued that Alice was Edith's daughter but there's not a shred of evidence before 1307 to substantiate this, in fact to the contrary.[12]

The Domesday Cartulary of Westminster contains a memorandum signed by ten Italian bishops granting forty days' indulgence (remission of time in purgatory) to anyone who made pilgrimage to Westminster or St Milburg's in Wenlok to pray for the soul of the Lord Abbot and members of his family. The document is dated 1298. However, in the Year Book of 21 Edward I for the year 1293, there is a reference to a 'sister' of Abbot Wenlok called Cecile (or Cecily) who apparently lived in Westminster and died there in about 1292–3.[13] This is the only reference to that sister living or dead. Cecile is not mentioned in the above-mentioned prayer list and the omission is quite remarkable for Abbot Wenlok who took so much care of his family. He never mentions this Cecile anywhere else, nor is any reason given why she was at Westminster or died there. (The *Customary* of Westminster quite categorically excludes the presence of women from the Abbey.) Wenlock's own household ordinances (issued before 1293) were translated and quoted as they repeat, time and time again, who can go where and when. Cecile appears to be a remarkable exception to this. Now Walter de Wenlok was a priest of the Church, he obtained indulgences for those who prayed for his family, living and dead, including his own father, but never this Cecile.

In my view Cecile was Wenlok's dark secret brought into Westminster between 1291 and 1293, who died, perhaps, giving birth to Alice who was entrusted to Wenlok's mother and sister to rear, the lavish generosity accorded them being part payment for the expenses of raising that child. Once both were dead, Wenlok moved swiftly to care for Alice himself with presents, lodgings and a suitable husband. Little wonder that when sister Edith stayed as a house guest of one Gunhilda Lawes, the Abbot became very concerned when he heard that the landlady had not been paid. He ordered his Sub-prior to summon those responsible for paying the bills so that he would find out exactly what happened. 'Lest', Wenlock urgently adds, 'after my sister's leaving, there should be grumbling and disturbance amongst the neighbours about her stay, oh heaven forbid that!'[14]

Wenlok's agitation is most understandable: he would not want people making enquiries about his sister and her household [including Alice], staying in a house in London and leaving without payment. It might have caused all sorts of comments and scurrilous gossip. The truth of the situation would be very damaging, the potential for scandal immense. A Benedictine abbot, Lord of Westminster, the Royal Chapel and Mausoleum, maintaining his own concubine within its sacred walls where she gave birth to a child was serious enough. If it was also discovered that for years afterwards Wenlok had diverted Abbey funds for her sustenance, he would have been destroyed: this is what Aldenham was referring to with that cryptic phrase, 'if his conduct became known'.

The existence of this Cecile surfaces in a rather extraordinary way. The Year Book of 21 Edward I (1293) contains a very strange law case brought against the Abbot by one 'Henry the son of Nicholas' in the court of Common pleas:

that the Abbot of Westminster and Richard his monk, who are there, tortuously detain and do not render to him [Henry] ninety marks [about £60 sterling] which Henry bailed to one Cecily his grandmother and sister of the said Abbot. The Abbot and his monk waged their law that they did not receive from Henry any moneys which one Cecily ought to have paid them and had not any of his moneys and had detained none of his moneys.

The case apparently revolved around a minor [Henry] son of Nicholas [who was dead] being looked after by a nameless 'Guardian' who is claiming that his ward is owed sixty pounds, a sum lent to Cecile in Henry's name. Wenlok and 'his monk', Richard, probably Richard Fanelore, Abbey Treasurer in 1293, stoutly resisted such a claim. It is possible that Cecile was a widow who had children by a former marriage before becoming involved with Wenlok. Isabella, wife of Edward II, was twelve when she married and was barely fifteen when she first became pregnant. 'Henry' and his 'Guardian' could have been suing for part of Cecile's estate or, in their own way, trying to extract money from the Abbot by threats and menaces for they mention that they had '*sovant* – often' come to the Abbot for that amount. Wenlok's reply is even more significant. He doesn't refer to Cecile as his sister but, '*de une Cecile* – of one Cecile' as if trying to distance himself from her. Wenlok would be confident that 'Henry' and 'his guardian' did not have the full truth about his relationship with Cecile, he was prepared to defend himself publicly and meet any threat head-on. The existence of this 'Cecile' is certainly mysterious as she is never mentioned in any of Wenlok's accounts or lists, the Domesday Cartulary of Westminster or any Abbey Muniment. 'Henry' and his anonymous 'guardian' would be very careful not to state the true nature of Cecile's relationship with Wenlok which would have left them vulnerable to counter-allegations of blackmail and extortion, hanging offences in themselves. Wenlock was able to face them down.

Alexander de Pershore, however (who had accompanied Wenlok to Rome in 1284 for his confirmation as abbot and was raising loans for his master in that same year), was a different matter. Little wonder that Walter de Wenlok who, in 1287, could insist that monks who nodded or talked in choir be rigorously punished, did, by 1303, turn a blind eye to the most serious violations of monastic life and discipline. In short he was being blackmailed by Alexander de Pershore who knew his dark secret. Pershore comes across as a tough, unscrupulous man, not above browbeating Abbey tenants.[15] It is significant that William of the Palace, self-serving liar though he be, named Alexander de Pershore as the one who threatened to kill him if he revealed their plans. Such a threat from Alexander de Pershore would be very much in character.

This is the background to the robbery of the Royal Treasury 1303. Had Wenlok been a more disciplined master, it would never have occurred, yet he had no choice but to surrender his Abbey to Alexander de Pershore who had his own agenda. Alexander was definitely a man who loved the ladies and such a lifestyle demanded a constant flow of silver.

The Abbey became a robbers' den, for the presence of the Royal Treasury so close was the height of temptation. In 1296 John the Cook, a common name in the Domesday Cartulary of Westminster, was implicated in an attempt on the treasury. It failed.[16] However, the fact that Edelina, daughter of Nicholas the Cook, was also involved in the 1303 scandal raises the strong possibility that monks might have been involved in that escapade. There is certainly a triangle involving the Abbey, the Cook family and attempts to rob the Royal Treasury. In the attempt of 1300 the monks were definitely involved. This too failed, and led to Ralph de Manton's formal audit of the treasure in that same year.[17] The good brothers were more successful in stealing £100's worth of silver, sent to the Abbey for the dead queen's Requiem Masses to be sung. Wenlok had no choice but to hush these matters up and buy off the King who could at least take consolation that the Crypt had proved impregnable.

Alexander de Pershore and his confederates waited. In the late 1290s Edward became an absent ruler, campaigning in Scotland; the Palace was deserted, its keeper John de Shenche left everything to his Deputy William Palmer, with whom the community forged closer links. Abbot Wenlok, sharply checkmated, became a mere observer, whilst his Prior, William de Huntingdon, was an old man more interested in Abbey lands in the Honour of Eye than anything else.[18] The monks had all the time in the world to study the outside of the Crypt, search for its weaknesses, and plan. Due to their lifestyle, William of the Palace's keepership of the Fleet Prison and their own Sanctuary Men, the monks also cemented relationships with the underworld of both London and Westminster, drawing in the likes of John le Riche (Ramage), a servant of the Abbey with a bad reputation and a history of felony in the county of Bedfordshire.[19] Others too became members of the gang. John of Rippinghale, the defrocked priest and John de Uggele. The latter managed to survive the débâcle of 1303 but, two years later in 1305, he was back to form, the Crown being informed,

> John de Uggele has been taken because he was indicted before the Mayor of London, for being involved in a certain robbery against Ivo de Fitchingfield who was robbed of goods amounting to 20 marks. He was also indicted for another robbery at Barking Church because he, along with others, was accustomed to enter houses of different people at twilight and plunder them.[20]

The monks attracted such twilight figures as they planned their robbery. They needed money to finance their lifestyle, and were dismissive of their superiors. Perhaps the Brothers found consolation in the fact that they were paying the King back in kind.

Edward I's hunger for money had led to many extraordinary measures, not the least being the plundering of parish chests during the summer of 1294 when sixteen commissioners were appointed to scrutinize all deposits in parish churches and religious houses. The pretext was to hunt for debased coinage which the Crown wished to destroy. In fact, the King was looking for money. At the beginning of July 1294 the commissioners began seizing parish chests, smashing them open when keys were not produced and taking their contents.[21] The monks of Westminster must have heard about this. They came from different villages in the Midlands and the west of England. Families and relatives must have been hit by the royal seizure, perhaps even themselves. It was not a great logical leap to decide that what the King could do, they would copy. If the Crown could steal from the Holy Mother Church, then the King's treasure buried in the Crypt was also vulnerable. By the summer of 1302 what the monks still needed was a middle man who could, after the robbery, break up the treasure and sell it on the London markets. In Richard de Puddlicott, the Oxford man, the merchant from a family with close connections with the Benedictine community, they found their 'broker'.

One of the indictments describes Puddlicott as a very close friend of one of the monks in the Abbey but 'they don't know whom'.[22] There is every likelihood that this was Alexander de Pershore. When Pershore was in Rome in 1298 he obtained a papal indulgence for those who prayed for his soul and that of his good friend Thomas de Lenton, buried in the cemetery at Westminster.[23] It is probably through John de Lenton, a kinsman, that Puddlicott and Alexander de Pershore became close friends. John de Lenton is also described as a friend and associate of Puddlicott and was involved with him in the robbery of the Abbey refectory, John de Lenton had a key to that place given undoubtedly by his good friend Alexander de Pershore. Now John de Lenton was a Westminster man: he and his wife Gillelma owned land in nearby Long Ditch[24] so, when Puddlicott arrived in London, he was not the lonely merchant he describes himself but someone well received by both the City community and that of Westminster. Friendships were forged, alliances entered into, plans laid. The gang had already chosen their means of access so the ground around the Crypt windows was sown with hemp. Hemp was a common crop in medieval England, sown in late spring and fast growing, it would reach its fullness in mid-August so, by the following April, the crop would be quite thick and tangled and provoke little interest as it had been growing there for some time. During the Middle Ages it was essential in the making of rope and cord which the abbey of St Peter's, not to mention the Palace, would need. Moreover, as any modern farmer knows, hemp is a tough plant, very similar to a weed, and would soon spread even beyond its prescribed area. Accordingly, the seed would be scattered across God's Acre, the monks' cemetery, as well as the adjoining wasteland, and would serve as an excellent screen for the actual robbery. Its appearance could be easily explained away. More importantly, it would be used to hide their handiwork once it was finished, and so provide further protection and, above all, precious time to move and sell their ill-gotten gains.

The monks and Puddlicott also needed to finance their operation: there would be other monks to bribe, even City officials, so the refectory was burgled. This was not some daring night raid by one thief, as described by Puddlicott, but a careful, measured task, where Puddlicott and Lenton used the keys to the refectory given to them by the monks. The raid took place sometime between November and December 1302 after the King and Court had left Westminster. The doors and gates to the Abbey were unlocked and the refectory entered. Baskets of jewelled cups and plate were removed through the Abbey grounds into those of the Palace, where of course they would receive the help of William of the Palace, then down across the quayside to King's steps on the river. The plunder was bundled aboard, heaped in sacks, some of it fell overboard and the fisherman, Geoffrey Atte

Stigle, caught one of these precious items in his nets just before Christmas 1302.[25]

Puddlicott used some of this plunder to finance his lifestyle, the rest to bribe and buy, it proved a key to introducing himself to City merchants and goldsmiths. In doing so Puddlicott became a well-known figure on the London scene. People knew where he lived, in a house near Dowgate, as well as his friends, John de Lenton, James Horner and Robert Barber (undoubtedly a relative of Castenea and Alice) who lived in Candlewick Street. Puddlicott had gathered this gang around him, '*sa compagnie* – his company'. John the mason from St Albans and Philip the carpenter were hired for their technical expertize.

The remaining problem was access to the Abbey and nearby grounds of the Palace. The latter was easily resolved by William Palmer, whilst Abbey security was taken care of by the judicious appointment early in 1303, probably at Alexander de Pershore's behest, of Adam de Warfeld as Sacristan of Westminster. The *Customary* of that Abbey devotes entire sections to the work of the Sacristan and his helpers, who were in charge of lighting and security. The Sacristan's duties are covered by no less than twenty-six pages in the *Customary*. He was responsible for placing lights, candles and lamps around the Abbey: 'the lighting of the church must be procured and honourably abundant', as well as custody of the keys. Adam de Warfeld would have exploited this both before and during the robbery as did his pages led by Adam the Skinner, 'who were used to, according to custom, sleep in the church'. They helped the Sacristan with security and rang the bells.[26] Little wonder that the London juries, one after another, pointed out how the Sacristy was near the cemetery where the hemp was sown and the burglary had taken place, so Adam and his '*garciones*' must have known what was happening. Indeed, the juries add, the robbery could not have happened without their full consent.

The sown hemp sprouted tall and thick, the technical help was available and, by the end of April 1303, Puddlicott and his company were ready.[27] The Barber sisters accompanied by John de Uggele, William and John Kynebaston and the rest gathered with William of the Palace in the close of Fleet Prison on Tuesday before the Feast of the Finding of the True Cross (Friday 3 May 1303). They stayed there for two days' feasting and revelling, before moving down to Westminster where gates and doors had been closed, sealed and guarded by the likes of Gilbert le Wayte who stood on watch. According to the indictments, the Barber gang moved down towards Westminster at midnight and returned at dawn and did this for two successive nights. This agrees with both Rippinghale's and Puddlicott's confession that the robbery was spread over three days. Puddlicott's confession places the robbery around the Feast of St Mark (24/25 April), but this was simply his ploy to depict himself as the sole thief. The actual robbery took place between Tuesday 30 April and Friday 3 May (The Finding of the True Cross) when the Palace, Abbey and the surrounding grounds were put off-limits by their gang to anyone else. This, in turn, provides an insight into how they gained access to the Crypt.

Drokensford's indenture of 20–22 June 1303 demonstrates that the keys to all doors leading to the Crypt, as well as to the Crypt itself, were kept by a high-ranking Wardrobe clerk in a sealed pouch which had never been broken. Moreover, as we have already mentioned, there was the gap in the steps leading down to the Crypt which, even today, still has to be bridged by a wooden staircase. Consequently, entry into the Crypt through the usual route would be virtually impossible without the keys and use of a portable bridge. As for robbers burrowing beneath the foundations, it is difficult to imagine even with the help of John the mason, such an operation going either under, or through, walls which, in places, are at least seventeen feet thick.

A study of the Abbey shows the Chapter House, and the Crypt windows beneath, spread out like the fingers of a hand. These were the gap in the Treasury's security. On one of the windows nearest the monastic infirmary, traces of the break-in still remain.

Every other window to the Crypt has a stone sill but this sixth one, removed from any real observation outside, has no sill at all. All the indictments and Puddlicott's confession mention tools, 'engines of iron', used at the break-in. The windows are narrow but wide enough for a man to squeeze through; they would be barred with shutters behind them. The bars were embedded in sills of hard stone about ten inches wide, stretching up into the brickwork above the window. John the Mason attacked the sill of the sixth window, removed it and was able to prise the bars out of the brickwork above. This would take hours of work and be noisy hence the security measures around the Abbey and Palace as well as the declaration by the juries that the likes of Adam de Warfeld and others must have heard the commotion. Puddlicott and John the mason had discovered this one weakness of the Crypt which could be exploited as long as those inside both Abbey and Palace were prepared to cooperate which, of course, they were. Indeed the window in question was not only the sole way through literally metres of hard stone, it was also the one method of entry which could be covered up afterwards. A hole in the wall is difficult to hide but a forced sill and removed bars could be loosely repositioned, so only close scrutiny would reveal something untoward had happened, an unlikely occurrence in such a desolate, hemp-infested part of the Abbey grounds as well as one closely observed by Puddlicott's allies at Westminster. Puddlicott and his gang needed time: the robbery would eventually be detected but, the longer this took, the better.

Once the sill and bars were loosened and the shutters beyond removed, Puddlicott went through the window down into the Treasury proper, details of which he had learned from a member of John le Convers' household. Convers had been responsible for work in the Crypt and perhaps even carved out those recesses in the central pillars. Convers' valet certainly fell under suspicion of receiving stolen goods.[28]

Once in the Crypt Puddlicott could help himself, opening chests and coffers, breaking up precious goods and passing them out to his confederates – the Barber sisters and their companions from the close of Fleet Prison. The robbery took place over successive nights: lamps, candles and cresset torches would have to be lit; locks prised open; bricks in the central pillar forced loose. The window embrasures into the Crypt are long and narrow, rope ladders had to be fixed and a system established to pass the goods out. Gold, silver and precious stone weigh a lot. Many items had to be broken up before they were taken away after nightfall. These were loaded into sacks and baskets, and placed on the monks' cart which the juries mention as going backwards and forwards between the Abbey and the royal enclosure.[29] The spoils were then divided; one indictment actually refers to a three-way split – Puddlicott, the Palace and the Abbey. Individuals would also help themselves and, in the jostling hurry, little wonder that precious items fell out and were found in the Abbey grounds, or individual felons hid their part of the plunder around the church and Palace. Puddlicott apparently chose the smaller items – coins, jewels and broken-up silver and gold plate for his goldsmith colleagues. Larger items, such as the Cross of Neath and the Unicorn Horn used for anointing, were given to William of the Palace who, the fool he was, simply hid them under his bed.[30] In the end Puddlicott and his accomplices considered themselves safe, at least for a while. The plunder had been removed, the window resealed, the King was hundreds of miles to the north, whilst the monks felt protected by their own status and clerical privilege.

The entire gang thought they had enough time for the next stage of their operation: the sale and distribution of their ill-gotten gains. Here, they made one mistake: not all the Westminster community would keep silent and, bearing in mind Wenlok's outburst against Hadham later in 1307, some of the monks must have notified the authorities. Edward I's letter of 6 June specifically mentions: 'we accepted the testimony of faithful and worthy men'. The King keeps his source anonymous. He does not talk of royal or city officials but men who, by their very

163

status, are to be believed. This first breakthrough by the Crown led to the robbers' first mistake, they underestimated the old King. In his youth, Edward I had been called the 'leopard' noted not only for its courage but its speed.

The King retaliated swiftly, ordering Drokensford and other justices into London. These arrived by the middle of June and some of the robbers panicked. Time and again the different juries fastened on to the hapless Gerin the linen draper of St Giles. He had often been employed by the monks as a messenger and they did so again in this crisis, using him to move treasure from the Abbey to the fields around St Pancras. At the hearing at New Temple in August 1303 the justices seized on this. If it could be proved that Gerin had acted on behalf of the monks, their guilt would be established. The Crown intervened long before the robbers had expected. Adam de Warfeld the Sacristan, on the Feast of St Barnabas (11 June), was also moving stolen goods, whilst others were busy transporting items to the fields and ditches between the Abbey and the Royal Mews. Naturally such activity became common knowledge. Drokensford increased the pressure by demanding a proclamation be issued, declaring that anyone who knew anything about the robbery must present themselves at the Guildhall. This was issued on Sunday 16 June and the robbers made their truly fatal mistake – they had placed too much confidence in William of the Palace who, according to one jury, was already openly boasting about his involvement in the plundering of the Royal Treasury.[31]

William hoped to turn King's evidence. The names he gave allowed Drokensford to swoop on the Abbey and, with the help of monks like Reginald de Hadham, discovered the names of the principal malefactors. Further house-raids were organized. The authorities caught Puddlicott with the jewels red-handed, John the mason with his stone-breaking tools, John de Lenton with the key to the Abbey refectory, John de Rippinghale with his mallet and chisel and John de Newmarket with some of his plunder. The word 'captured' is used about all of them. They received no warning and were caught 'red-handed', which provokes the suspicion that the protection the robbers had trusted in had been abruptly withdrawn.

The arrogance of the monks is understandable: they were clerics on holy soil, guardians of the Royal Chapel of Westminster beyond 'the bar' of London or any type of secular authority. Puddlicott, on the other hand, was a 'foreigner' in the city, a man with no reputation, he was trading where he had no right, selling precious plate at a time when this was scarce. Rumours were already circulating about treasure being found at Westminster and of monks rebuffing the local coroner and his bailiffs. Puddlicott's assurance must have sprung from protection he had in the City. The Royal Commissioners' suspicions must have hardened when, after his arrest, Puddlicott was not lodged, as the King's letter of 6 June had ordered, 'in our prison, safely and securely' but in Sheriff Pourte's house, where he stayed for five days before escaping to take sanctuary at St Michael's in Candlewick. On the balance of probabilities, as well as available evidence, there can be no doubt that Puddlicott hoped the City Fathers would protect him, and one in particular: Sheriff Hugh Pourte.

Hugh Pourte belonged to one of the old families of London, a fishmonger, an alderman of this and that ward, who invested in loans and the export of wool, he'd even bought land at Boston in Lincolnshire.[32] Pourte, like other merchants, must have been hit by royal intervention in the wool market. In June 1294 the King published a scheme whereby all wool would be exported by the Crown. This would boost profits, and payments would eventually be made to those who raised the wool. Edward's threat to implement this was eventually withdrawn and replaced by another customs duty imposed at the rate of five marks or £3 3s. 4d. for each sack. This tax lasted for three years until November 1297 when it was abolished.[33] Pourte must be seen against this background, a merchant-alderman in the City of London where the King's constant interference in both that city's trade and internal politics was clearly resented.

Pourte's involvement, or lack of it, in any attempt to detain Puddlicott securely is mysterious. Puddlicott had raided the Abbey refectory before Christmas 1302. Items had been fished out of the Thames, new gold and jewels sold on the markets but nothing was done. Puddlicott robbed the Royal Treasury at the beginning of May 1303 yet, between that date and 16 June, only six weeks in all, this 'foreigner' from Oxford had set himself up as a trader passing on the precious items through the likes of John of Newmarket.

Puddlicott's actions violated every ordinance in the *Liber Albus* – Hugh Pourte and others still did nothing. However, when the Crown did intervene and Drokensford and his colleagues arrived in London, Pourte, according to one of the jury presentments of January 1304, suddenly becomes the hero of the hour. According to this, Pourte had apparently learned how a washer-woman in Southwark was holding some of the plunder from the Royal Treasury, hidden in her house by John of Newmarket. Through that woman Pourte arrested John of Newmarket and interrogated him as to the whereabouts of Richard de Puddlicott, 'who was then arrested through the good offices of the sheriff and, with him, all the aforesaid treasure'.[34] Here Pourte is seen as the hero of the hour. In a different, earlier indictment, Pourte is named by the jury of Bridge Ward: 'They say that the above Richard de Puddlicott was captured and led to the house of Hugh Pourte, Sheriff of London, and impris-oned there for five days.'[35] Here, Pourte is not seen as so active but merely the passive gaoler and, indeed, not a very vigilant or honest one. It is interesting that Pourte's actions are praised as 'the good offices of the Sheriff' by the jury led by Richer de Refham, foreman of the jurors of Walbrook near Ludgate. Refham was a rising star in the City firmament who had married his son John to the daughter of Mayor John le Blund. Refham was a fishmonger, the same trade as Pourte's. De Refham, of course, was looking after his own, because Pourte's conduct is highly suspect.[36] Furthermore, Edward I was talking of £100,000 having been taken. Refham and his fellow jurors were being economical with the truth. They must have known of the evidence given by the aldermen on oath earlier in June that year that the plunder seized with Puddlicott amounted to about £2,200. One of those aldermen had been Richer de Refham. In January 1304 Refham was deliberately trying to depict his friend and colleague Hugh Pourte in the best possible light. No explanation is given why £2,200 suddenly acquires an extra £97,800 or, how it was that the Sheriff of London stumbled by chance on a washerwoman in Southwark, well beyond the authority of a London sheriff, who happened to be the owner of the very house where John of Newmarket, the principal receiver in the great robbery, had concealed his ill-gotten gains. Again, according to Refham, Pourte had seized John of Newmarket for interrogation and, through him, discovered the whereabouts of Puddlicott in his house near Dowgate. Pourte had then organized a raid and managed to seize Puddlicott with all his treasure.

Such a tale becomes all the more remarkable when the times and dates are studied more closely. Puddlicott had, by his own admission, been in London since the early autumn of 1302. He organized the robbery at the beginning of May 1303. The King issued his proclamation ordering the investigation on 6 June. The robbery, therefore, was at least six weeks old before the first obvious royal intervention, yet the City authorities had done nothing, despite silver, gold and precious jewels being found in fields and ditches, not to mention its appearance on the precious metal markets of London, Northampton and Colchester. Moreover, William Palmer of the Palace and others of the gang like le Riche had not been above boasting of their exploits, whilst John the Mason, Rippinghale and le Riche were not at all shy about showing a marked difference in their standard of living, Puddlicott had been seen around London, negotiating with this merchant and that, but nothing was done until Pourte abruptly emerges as the hero of the hour between 16 and 19 June 1303.

According to that well-informed source, *The Annales Londonienses* Puddlicott's arrest, subsequent flight and recapture happened as follows:[37]

> In the same year 1303, on the morrow of the Feast of the Birth of St John the Baptist (Tuesday 25 June), a certain individual, Richard de Puddlicott, was seized violently from the Church of St Michael in Candlewick Street. He had been captured for the theft of the King's treasure and placed in the custody of Hugh Pourte, then sheriff and he [Puddlicott] was seized by Gaucelin and Thomas Attewell, common bailiffs of the city and other unknowns.

This entry must be compared with the above-mentioned indictment presented by the jury of Bridge Ward who had declared that Puddlicott was brought to Hugh Pourte's house

> and imprisoned there for five days. Afterwards he escaped to the Church of St Michael with the counsel and help of Richard, the valet and 'Gaucelin le Servient' but was later recaptured. Therefore, the aforesaid Hugh Pourte was bailed on account of suspicions against him regarding the above escape.[38]

The truth about this rather clumsy sheriff is being deliberately clouded. Richer de Refham's testimony, and that of his colleagues of the jury of Walbrook near Ludgate, depict a vigilant, efficient and able law officer who, through his skill, hunts down and captures not only John of Newmarket, the principal fence, but the chief villain of the piece, Richard de Puddlicott. On the other hand, Andrew Horn, the author of the *Annals of London*, does not depict Pourte as the hero, he just obfuscates the incident. If his entry in the *Annals* is studied more closely, it is difficult to determine whether Puddlicott fled to St Michael's in Candlewick Street and was then dragged out and placed in Pourte's custody, or that he had escaped from Pourte's custody to St Michael's. Andrew Horn, in fact, is a very biased source. He was a colleague of Pourte's, an alderman of the City and, more importantly, like Pourte, a member of the Fishmongers Guild. Pourte was also married to Margaret Horn, a member of Andrew's powerful family.[39]

Dates provide another insight. According to the *Annals of London*, Puddlicott was dragged from sanctuary on Friday 25 June 1303; before that he'd been in the Sheriff's house for five days, which means that his arrest must have taken place in or around 19 June – the week of the general proclamation, when Drokensford stormed into Westminster. After what the royal clerk and his associates discovered there, as well as what they learned from William of the Palace, it was they who ordered the Mayor and sheriffs to carry out raids in certain houses in London and elsewhere, Puddlicott's near Dowgate being one of them. This was done without warning. Not only were Puddlicott and others caught red-handed but some of the treasure was still with them. Pourte may have made the actual arrest but the true credit for the capture of the malefactors should go to the Royal Commissioners.

Hugh Pourte's actions were certainly questionable. They were glossed over by his friends and colleagues, Richer de Refham and Andrew Horn, but the indictment of Bridge Ward clearly indicates that Sheriff Pourte fell under some suspicion. He had to go on oath to purge himself and find supporters who would guarantee that he had not been involved in Puddlicott's escape. This is understandable. Drokensford and the others would consider Puddlicott safe in the hands of the London's sheriff. The *Liber Albus* did allow the Sheriff to detain prisoners in his own house. Nevertheless, why did the Sheriff keep such a notorious criminal like Puddlicott in his house, and for so long, when the King's letter of 6 June 1303 specifically ordered prisoners to be kept 'safely and securely lodged in our prison'? Why hadn't Puddlicott been sent to Newgate or the Tower? The royal ministers would certainly be furious at Puddlicott's escape. The names of those who assisted Puddlicott cannot be traced but the Royal Commissioners' suspicions about the Sheriff must have been so intense that he had to purge himself on oath.

Pourte's actions could be viewed as those of an insolent City officer determined to do what he wanted in defiance of royal authority, but his treatment of Puddlicott during those five days is more than that. By not placing Puddlicott in prison, Pourte was not only providing him with the means of escape, in fact, two other factors come into play. First, Newgate was a foulsome, heinous place, the escape mentioned above and the demonstration on the roof of the prison shows how desperate prisoners could become in a place which reeked of dirt, infection and downright corruption. Secondly, Pourte was keeping Puddlicott out of the clutches of the King's man, Sir Ralph de Sandwich. In view of William Palmer being acting Keeper of the Fleet prison, that left two other places for confining Puddlicott: the Tower – under Ralph de Sandwich – or Newgate, not only a foulsome place, but also under Ralph de Sandwich's authority: according to the *Liber Albus*, Sandwich was Newgate's justice for gaol delivery. If placed there, Puddlicott would have been under the complete power of one of Edward I's most loyal supporters who had little love for the City of London.[40]

Puddlicott indeed was very fortunate. He had not been hauled off to some filthy dungeon but merely placed under house arrest at Hugh Pourte's. From there he managed to escape and reach St Michael's in Candlewick Street, an area which housed two of his accomplices or friends, Robert Barber and James le Horner. It was also the Candle-makers' quarter which did considerable business with the Sacristan of Westminster Abbey responsible for the purchase of so many candles and oil lamps for his house and community. Puddlicott's confidence in the City was certainly strong. He had been lodged in Pourte's house which stood in the Parish of St Magnus near London Bridge. Once he had escaped, Puddlicott could have fled across the Thames into Southwark or east into the wilds of Essex. He does not do this but heads north-west into the heart of the City. He certainly avoided his own house in Dowgate near the river, and was undoubtedly hoping to lodge with friends and protectors who would later smuggle him out. However, Puddlicott was now a 'marked man': the ward system which once offered protection now became a threat. He failed to reach his true destination so he sought sanctuary.

Once inside St Michael's, Puddlicott must have considered himself safe. He was a clerk, or so he later claimed, and he had also sought sanctuary. Puddlicott was, therefore, free from the secular law for forty days. He would be permitted to receive food as well as sufficient liberty to answer calls of nature. Puddlicott's chances of full escape were greatly enhanced because, as he and Pourte would have known, some years earlier the City Council on 'Thursday before the Feast of St Dunstan's [19 May 1298]' had ordered that 'no robber, homicide or any other fugitive in the Churches should, in future, be kept under close guard'.[41] Puddlicott, in other words, wasn't to be hounded or harassed. Moreover, he was in an area of the City where he had friends and support. If Puddlicott decided to stay in sanctuary, he could negotiate with his former gaoler, Sheriff Hugh Pourte, and abjure the realm. Many of the City Fathers, particularly the goldsmiths, would only be too delighted to see the back of Puddlicott on board some ship heading for France or the Low Countries. Most felons elected to abjure the realm. Puddlicott would take the necessary oath, administered to him by the Sheriff, swearing that he would hurry, by the most direct route, to the nearest port, either one he chose, or one chosen for him, and take the first ship abroad. The abjured felon could not return to the realm without royal permission. If he dilly-dallied along the way, or left the highway, he would be captured and killed.[42]

The question of sanctuary was not only sacred but a very delicate one. The Crown was most reluctant to allow sanctuary to the likes of Puddlicott, simply because many malefactors often tried to escape from the shelter of the Church and slink back into society, only to re-emerge to carry out further mischief.

Moreover, as far as Edward I was concerned, if he wanted someone pursued and captured, he would get his man. In 1289, when Edward I ordered a royal investigation into the wrong doing of high-ranking officials, his corrupt chief justice, Thomas de Weyland, fled to Babwell, a house belonging to the Friars Minor near Bury St Edmunds. Once there, Weyland assumed the Friars' habit, declaring had once been ordained a sub-deacon, a clerk, in the years before his marriage. Soldiers under the King's man, Sir Robert Malet, surrounded the buildings, they prevented the Friars from buying food for their sanctuary seeker, allowing the Brothers to leave but not re-enter their house. Weyland was eventually starved into surrender.[43]

Puddlicott was ranked as important as Weyland, the King's men definitely wanted him for questioning. At St Michael's Candlewick speed became the order of the day. It was all very well for irate ministers of the Crown to tax Hugh Pourte with his slackness and question him on why Puddlicott had not been transferred to a more secure place. More pressing, was that they did not wish to make a bad situation worse and allow Puddlicott to escape into the City. Andrew Horn in his *Annales*, describes the seizure of Puddlicott as the work of Thomas Attewell and 'other common bailiffs in the city'. He should have known better. Horn creates the impression that City officials were responsible when he must have known that Attewell was no common bailiff but the King's Serjeant in the City.[44] He carried out the raid to seize Puddlicott, certainly at the behest of officers of the Crown, being quietly rewarded and promised that whatever sanctions the Church did impose, he and his companions would still be protected. The deed was done and Puddlicott was captured. Someone high in the City council must have vehemently protested at this violation of sanctuary, for later that year, in August 1303, no less a person than Robert de Winchlesea, Archbishop of Canterbury, ordered Attewell and his companions to do penance by walking barefoot, clad only in shirt and breeches and carrying a wax candle, from Bow Church to

Newgate and from Newgate to St Michael's, whilst the following day they had to make a pilgrimage to Canterbury walking 'without girdle or hood'.[45] Nevertheless, the Crown had its man and Puddlicott was removed to the Tower.

Pourte was a shadowy, sinister figure. He was a loan-merchant doing brisk business during this period.[46] He also mixed with London's underworld. This was not exceptional. Medieval sheriffs were not noted for their public probity or personal integrity. The legends of Robin Hood contain more than a grain of truth: sheriffs were corrupt. Indeed, the impression created is that in the choice of individuals for such important office, the principle that 'former poachers make good game keepers' held sway. One example will suffice: the enterprising Richard de Southcote of Essex, that expert in flying fire-bombs and the appropriation of other people's livestock, was a professional racketeer, another string to his bow being the arrest of innocents on the false accusation that they had broken the King's peace. The *Rotuli Hundredorum* record the day of judgement against Southcote. On one of Southcote's hapless victims, arrested for so-called 'breaking the peace', the jury replied that 'he had never in his life trespassed against the King's peace as much as Richard Southcote did in one day'. On another of Southcote's 'prisoners', 'we [the jurors] do not know why the sheriff arrested him unless he wanted his money'. Hugh Pourte was no different. In 1305 Pourte led an attack on a royal manor belonging to the King's daughter Elizabeth and her husband Henry de Bohun, Earl of Hereford, in Middlesex. Attacks on royal manors by men 'hooded and visored', were commonplace at the time. Such violence was often to loot treasure. Hereford's manor would be a prime choice: wealthy, not far from London and made even more attractive by the fact that the Earl was absent in Scotland. That the manor belonged to the King's daughter illustrates Pourte's scant regard for the Crown. This would sit easily with a man who had defied the King's direct order about an important state prisoner.[47] Pourte's name is first on the list of those mentioned in the attack on the royal manor, which denotes that he was the leader – the rest of the names are also given which indicates that someone turned King's evidence. What is interesting about the incident is a connection with the robbery of the treasure at Westminster. Pourte's second-in-command in the assault on the royal manor was Richard de Caumpes – also a former sheriff of London.

Now Caumpes is not too common a name in the letter books of London or the rolls of its Court of Hustings. The name Caumpes surfaces in one piece of evidence on the robbery. In the list of prisoners placed in the Tower at the end of the royal investigation during the summer of 1303, are the names of '*sex garciones*' – six pages of Sacristan Adam de Warfeld. One of these is John de Caumpes. He is placed squarely amongst the guilty members of Warfeld's gang imprisoned in the Tower, yet that is the last we hear of him in this matter.[48] In the list of Westminster prisoners in the Tower (October 1303) or as a member of Warfeld's coven mentioned in any indictment, John de Caumpes disappears, as if he and his name were plucked out of the proceedings by some invisible hand. Nevertheless, Warfeld's group of '*garciones*' were well known, indeed, to be a member of that group was synonymous with participation in the robbery. The only conclusion to be reached is that John de Caumpes was a member of a family very friendly to Sheriff Hugh Pourte who was skilled and powerful enough to make his influence felt: any indictment or allegation against John de Caumpes was quickly forgotten.

Suspicions deepen over Pourte when his appointment as sheriff in September 1302 is examined. Pourte was most reluctant to assume office. He actually refused to accept the task, as the records attest:

On Friday the eve of St Michael, 30th year of King Edward I 1302 [28 September], John le Blund and twelve men from each ward were summoned to receive their sheriffs, Simon de Paris and Hugh de Pourte. These Aldermen were elected as

Sheriffs of London. Simon came forward and took the oath but Hugh did not come, he was therefore fined and afterwards he was bailed by Adam de Fulham, Alderman, to come on the morrow of St Michael's [30 September] to do and receive what the Mayor and Aldermen of the city should impose upon him. Hugh did not come and it was only when the said Hugh came on the 30 September, the morrow of St Michael, that he was sworn to office and presented by the Mayor and Aldermen and Commons of the city to Ralph de Sandwich, Constable of the Tower of London, who admitted them in the outer gate of the aforesaid Tower, according to the terms of the Charters and Liberties of the city.[49]

So here is Hugh de Pourte, whose behaviour is so suspicious during the time of the robbery, being most reluctant to become sheriff at the time Puddlicott and his gang were planning to raid both the Abbey refectory and, in the following spring, the Royal Treasury.

Pourte was certainly dishonest. He not only attacked manor houses but, in 1307, the Crown had to write to him about the treasure of the Abbey refectory: this had been stolen by Puddlicott, recovered by royal ministers and entrusted to Pourte, but Pourte had failed to return it to the Abbey. Though Pourte ceased to be sheriff in September 1303, he apparently held on to the treasure for another four years. There is yet another connection between Puddlicott and Pourte. In his confession Puddlicott declares that he was an itinerant merchant in lamb's wool, butter and cheese who had been bankrupted by the Flemings when they seized him because of certain debts owing to them by the English King. No evidence exists one way or the other to prove this. Puddlicott may have been one of the 'small fry' snapped up by the Flemish authorities in their conflict with the English Crown. However, Puddlicott's fate was also shared by Hugh Pourte. In a royal writ of 10 August 1302 to the Mayor of Ghent, Edward I requested the release, amongst others, of Hugh Pourte and other merchants of London who had been arrested together with their merchandise [in Pourte's case it would have been wool] as security for the payment of 730 marks due from the mayor, sheriff and commonality of the city of London to certain burgesses of Ghent which money the King had seized and caused to be distributed amongst such English merchants who had lost their goods in Flanders. Dated at Kennington 23 August, Edward I [1302].[50]

Pourte was back in London by September 1302, the same time that Puddlicott was becoming active. True Pourte was arrested in Ghent, Puddlicott in Brussels. However, they had both suffered a common experience: both were merchants in the same trade and both seized by a foreign power for their King's debts. There is every likelihood, in the claustrophobic world of English trade at the end of the thirteenth century, that they knew each other.

On the balance of probabilities there was a connection between Puddlicott and some of the City Fathers who secretly supported and looked the other way when the robbery took place, and that Puddlicott was given protection through Hugh Pourte who, taken by surprise by the royal ministers in the summer 1303, had no choice but to change roles, organize Puddlicott's swift arrest and depict himself as the hero of the hour. Even then Pourte did his best for Puddlicott and, if it had not been for the swift action of royal officers, nearly succeeded in getting Puddlicott out of England. Edward I and his ministers must have suspected the involvement of the City fathers, but establishing the evidence was another matter. Had they done so, the Crown would have definitely used it to force more money out of leading Londoners. The City Fathers, however, closed ranks; the goldsmiths, in the main, were 'not knowing of any crime'. Pourte was cast in the role of a vigilant royal officer. The robbery was the work of certain monks and their confederates from London's underworld and, because he lacked firm proof, the King would have to concede this. Nevertheless, the City Fathers, Hugh Pourte especially, did not have it their own way. Edward used his suspicions of what had happened to force his will in other areas.

In April 1303 Edward I had promulgated the Statute of the New Customs which proclaimed a fresh tax on goods leaving the City.[51] Now foreign merchants gladly accepted this because it went hand-in-hand with better trading privileges in London and other places. Londoners, however, were furious. When the Mayor was instructed on 7 May 1303 to send two or three citizens from London to York to discuss the New Customs, the aldermen rejected it, informing the King that they were totally opposed to any new customs on wool or skins.[52] On 19 November 1303, five days after the King had proclaimed a new inquiry into the robbery under his leading justices Brabazon and the rest, a fresh writ arrived. The Mayor and aldermen were to appoint two collectors of the New Customs and despatch them to York to be presented to the Exchequer. The City Fathers, uneasy at the prospect of a fresh inquiry, twisted and turned. They pleaded that the royal messenger from York had not travelled fast enough, that the King's writ had arrived too late to be implemented, indeed, they added, tongue in cheek, they had arrested the royal messenger for his slowness and dereliction of duty and thrown him into prison.[53] The King waited. In February 1304, when the inquiry in the Tower was moving to a conclusion, the Londoners received another writ about appointing collectors. By then the citizens were growing more nervous at where Brabazon and Beresford might turn next. The goldsmiths had been named but simply as buyers. This time the flippant excuse: 'that they were not knowing of any felony' was not put forward, their involvement was the sword of Damocles hanging over them. The City Council was brought to heel and its reply to the King was much more muted. All the aldermen could plead was that, according to the ancient usages of the City, such officers were appointed by the Crown, not by the City.[54]

It is interesting to reflect on London's attitude. In May 1303, before any news of the robbery had become public knowledge or the King had issued his writ authorizing the investigation, the Mayor and aldermen were utterly hostile to the New Customs. Pourte, being a wool merchant, would have been in the forefront of this. Six months later, however, they have changed their minds and are secretly searching for excuses. By February 1304 the Mayor and aldermen have conceded the fight at the very time when Edward's judges in the Tower were moving to their conclusions about the robbery.

9

Retribution

'Vengeance is mine – I will repay'
Romans: 12.19

In the end five of the malefactors, headed by William of the Palace, were condemned to death whilst ten of the Westminster monks began a long sojourn in the Tower, as they argued with the Crown over whether they should be tried by the secular courts. The City Fathers, Pourte included, realized that they were not out of the woods and so they conceded to the King's will and sent their men to York. The Crown responded in kind: according to all the evidence, the City of London was never taken to task over the robbery of the Royal Treasury at Westminster. Edward I plotted an even sweeter revenge.

Tax collectors are never popular and London's records are full of accounts of attacks on such officials. William of Aldgate, a tax collector, was stabbed. A second, Richard Leving, was thrown to the ground and had his head cracked open, whilst another tax collector, John Fuatard, had his finger almost bitten off by an angry woman.[1] If the King was told he had to appoint tax collectors in London then Edward would have his revenge both on the City and a man whose involvement in the pursuit of Richard de Puddlicott had left so much to be desired. On 1 April 1304, All Fool's Day, Edward appointed that former reluctant sheriff Hugh Pourte as collector of the New Customs in London, whilst his colleague would be that leader of the Walbrook Ward near Ludgate, Pourte's fellow fishmonger and praiser, Richer de Refham.[2] The Crown could not voice, let alone prove its suspicions, but it might keep digging away at the role of the goldsmiths and others in the great robbery, so the City had better comply, Pourte included. On 27 June 1304 the Treasurer, Walter Langton, Bishop of Coventry and Lichfield, issued a formal letter starkly warning London to comply fully with the Collectors of the New Customs or face the consequences.[3] It is surely no coincidence that Pourte, who had spent a great deal of his personal time, energy and possibly money as Sheriff in 1302–3, together with Richer de Refham, leader of the Walbrook jury, were both saddled with that onerous, dangerous and highly unpopular task of collecting a new tax. By the spring of 1304 the Crown had broken up the great conspiracy of silence in London and Westminster over the robbery and swiftly moved to punish each group involved as best it could.

'*Ad audiendum et terminandum negocium*' – the ominous words from the royal letter, 'To hear and finish the business', moved the process in the Tower to its inexorable conclusion. By the spring of 1304 Bereford, Brabazon and de Sandwich had heard enough. They finished the business in hand and moved to judgement. The story is taken up by the *Annales Londonienses*:

> On that day, 13 January 1304, the justices began their deliberations, on Thursday 5 March they delivered their judgement on one group of robbers: William of the Palace and four others were sentenced to be dragged through the city and hanged on the elms at Smithfield.[4]

We do not know who the other four were but, given the number of indictments, William of the Palace must have been joined on the scaffold by John de Lenton, John de Rippinghale, John of St Albans and John of Newmarket. Sentence was carried out immediately. A Tower Chaplain would have shriven the condemned men, they would have been stripped, apart from their tunics, tied to hurdles lashed to horses and, accompanied by guards and grotesque figures wearing masks, dragged through the mud and dirt of the City along Cheapside, past Newgate and out, as the Chroniclers put it, '*usque elmes* – to the elms', that sinister clump of trees near the Priory of St Bartholomew at Smithfield where executions were carried out until the beginning of the reign of Edward III (1330), when the famous gallows were first built at Tyburn for Roger Mortimer. We do not know what happened to the rest of the gang. According to the *Gesta Edwardi Primi – The Deeds of Edward I* written by the chronicler Rishanger, 'Many were captured and hanged' – but there is no evidence of this in other chronicles or the documents of the time.[5]

The fate of Puddlicott and other monks was a different matter. All the chroniclers talk of ten monks. These must have included the usual suspects listed by the different juries of London and elsewhere: Alexander de Pershore, Ralph de Morton, Alexander of Newport, John de Noteley, William de Chalk, Thomas of Lichfield, Roger de Bures, John de Butterley, Thomas de Dene and, of course, Adam de Warfeld. These had been kept separate from the rest, which is understandable but, surprisingly, they were joined by Richard de Puddlicott, who now declared himself a clerk, and so could not be tried by the secular arm. The *Annales Londonienses* describe the scene when the justices sat once more at the Tower on Saturday 14 March 1304.[6]

Ten monks of Westminster and one clerk, because of the said robbery, were led into the presence of the justices and accused. They replied saying 'that, in no way did they wish to withdraw from the liberty, that is the privilege of the

181

Church, nor would they, without the advice of their ordinaries [Ecclesiastical superiors], submit themselves to secular judges'. Hearing this, the said judges moved to a solemn inquisition. The inquiry condemned [there is a gap in the Chronicle] the sacristan of Westminster for receiving and concealing jewels of the Lord King and the said ten monks were sent to the Tower until the King's pleasure was known.

The chronicler Rishanger tells a similar story,

> many monks of Westminster were placed in custody and, although ignorant of such a great and terrible crime, they were detained. Indeed, it was alleged that several of them had taken treasure from the thieves or that they had known about the robbery and had to satisfy the King concerning that.[7]

It is obvious from the Chronicle statements that Wenlok and others were released, but the ten detained monks played their ace card: they were monks, clerics, and so were not subject to secular judges. The move was a classical one, emphasizing a long-held right vindicated by the martyr Thomas à Becket that clerics were to be tried by the church courts whose sentences were always much more lenient. Technically, according to the law, the trial should have ended there and then but the justices' fury at the obvious guilt of the monks and anger at their arrogance are obvious, they publicly condemned Adam de Warfeld as the person who had received and concealed stolen goods. The justices were on safe ground here. They were not challenging Adam de Warfeld's clerical status, simply recording his dishonesty. Puddlicott was a different matter. He may have been an itinerant merchant, a married man, but that did not preclude the fact that he may have been a clerk, that is someone who had received minor orders but did not progress forward to ordination

182

as a priest. There can be no doubt of this: when the *Annales Londonienses* talk of ten monks '*et unus clericus*' they are, doubtless, describing Puddlicott as, a few pages further on, the same source refers to Puddlicott as '*Clericus* – Clerk'.[8]

Benefit of Clergy depended on the individual's ability to read and write and, most importantly, the tonsure, the cutting of hair on the crown of the head to denote the ordination of a cleric in minor orders. It was quite common for bishops to use a tonsure plate (the medieval one belonging to St Paul's in London is still kept), and the young man would declare that he intended to take the path to full ordination as a priest. John de Drokensford, when later he became Bishop of Bath and Wells, often conferred minor orders. In August and September 1315 alone, he tonsured no less than six candidates who were given the title '*Coronati* – the Crowned'.[9] Of course, such a system was open to abuse. In 1286, Robert de Neuby claimed that he was a cleric. He was brought before the judges who examined his head and noticed that the tonsure was freshly shaved. They set about investigating when and by whom it was done. It was established that Robert, when he went into prison did not have the tonsure, so the judges ordered the Keeper of the gaol in York, where Robert had been before his transfer to Newgate, to be summoned into court to answer. The fact is that the gaoler himself had conferred it![10]

Thomas de Weyland, Edward I's disgraced chief justice, claimed he had been given the solemn order of the subdeaconate. Most defendants who claimed Benefit of Clergy maintained that they had received the minor order of the tonsure and, therefore, were only subject to church courts. This led to hideous abuses, often challenged by Royal Justices, nevertheless clerical status, (Benefit of Clergy) remained a great privilege. It was, in fact, a natural bolt-hole for villains, yet the Crown was still very wary of it. Woe betide the royal official who ignored such a privilege, the Church could demand that he be punished by the State, as well as face the hideous sentence of excommunication. It did not matter what crime the clerk had committed. In 1293 one of the

King's own judges, Solomon of Rochester, invited Parson
Wynard to dinner on 14 August at his manor of Snodland.
Parson Wynard turned up, only to slip poison in to Solomon's
cup, the poor justice fell violently ill, his death coming almost as
a relief a fortnight later. Of course Wynard was arrested and
brought before a panel of judges. He was asked how he wished to
clear himself and Parson Wynard replied, 'I am a Clerk and
cannot answer to that here.' The matter was closed.[11] A similar
case in the London Eyre of 1276 brings home the same point as
well as emphasizing the violence of London's society.

On the Sunday before the Nativity of Mary [4 September
1261] Richard de Borham with many other people from
London went to a wrestling match at Bermondsey outside
the city and there wrestled with the men of the Prior of
Bermondsey; a quarrel arose among them and Richard and
his companions chased the prior's men into the priory; then
came a monk called Arnulf and other monks from the priory
who entered a solar above the gate and threw stones at
Richard and his companions; Arnulf the monk threw a stone
at Richard and crushed him so that he quickly died. It is
testified that Arnulf is still alive and living in the priory, so let
him be arrested. Likewise the Prior of Bermondsey is to be
distrained of all his lands. The Mayor and Aldermen are told
to enquire about the names of those who were present at the
fight and death. Afterwards Arnulf comes and, asked how he
wishes to clear himself of the death, he replies that he is a
clerk and is not bound to answer here. Thereupon Richard
de Harwes, minor canon of St Paul's London, comes and
claims him [Arnulf] as a clerk by virtue of letters of the
Bishop of London which he proffers, testifying that the
bishop entrusted to him his authority for claiming clergy: so
that it may be known for what he is.[12]

It is interesting how this extract shows that no matter what had happened, to whom, in what circumstances, if the defendant pleaded his clergy status – the trial had to stop forthwith. In Puddlicott's case the judges had to be particularly careful. He had already had his rights violated, being plucked illegally from sanctuary in St Michael's Candlewick. On that occasion the Archbishop of Canterbury had intervened and punished the offending parties. Further encroachment of Puddlicott's rights had to be avoided. The Crown had only one choice, it could challenge Puddlicott's clerical status and wait. In the fourteenth century there was no 'Habeas Corpus', no writ had to be produced demanding that people be either charged or released from custody. The chroniclers reflect this, they say that the monks were detained until the King decided, and Edward I apparently took his time. The monks were to be detained at the royal pleasure whilst Crown officials investigated Puddlicott's claims.

In the end Puddlicott was executed, which means that the Crown must have proved he was not truly a clerk by closely questioning the *bona fide* nature of such status. This, in turn, could explain Puddlicott's determination not to implicate the monks in his confession about the robbery and why these ten monks were also detained in prison. Puddlicott eventually would have to name the Ordinary that is, the bishop or his equivalent, who had conferred minor orders on him. Now Puddlicott may have studied at Gloucester Hall in Oxford, which had close links with the Benedictine community at Westminster or, he might have put himself forward for the priesthood in some diocese and received minor orders such as the tonsure, then changed his mind. Of course, there is every possibility that Puddlicott was not a true clerk but, when captured, indicted and condemned, Richard de Puddlicott asked his monastic accomplices to vouch for his clerical status to save him from the gallows. In return Puddlicott would depict himself as the '*Unus Latro* – the lone thief' and exculpate the monks of any charges. He would also be very careful not to implicate anyone in the City. Puddlicott had learned from

185

William of the Palace's mistakes. William had tried to share the blame with others and paid the penalty – brutal execution. The Crown, of course, suspected the truth of the situation and literally laid siege to the monks, trying to break their will.

There is some evidence that the monks of Westminster were accustomed to offering Benefit of Clergy to shield friends and allies: their land housed the Sanctuary where outlaws and felons could take refuge; understandably, ties were forged between the two communities. In July 1307, some four years after the robbery, Robert of Godsfield was accused of sheltering a gang of thieves some of whom had been captured and beheaded for their crimes. 'The aforesaid Robert of Godsfield asked how he wished to clear himself of the aforesaid charges.' He replied 'that he is a clerk [cleric].' He was then asked to produce proof and his saviour appears in no less a person than William de Chalk, monk of Westminster, who arrived with letters from the Abbot, the Ordinary of that place, and demanded that Robert of Godsfield as a Clerk, be handed over to him.[13] The same thing happened in 1304–5, Puddlicott claimed he was the sole thief, in return the Abbot and monks at Westminster maintained he was a clerk. Alexander de Pershore and his companions would support this. Puddlicott would confess that he alone was guilty, the monks would then assert he was a clerk and, therefore, not subject to the secular courts. The Crown recognized this and decided to challenge such claims. In the meantime the monks in the Tower, together with Puddlicott, were not deserted: sheep from the Westminster estates at Knightsbridge were sold to help sustain the brothers. A letter was sent to the Sheriff of Surrey to ask for his help, cash payments were made to the prisoners and bribes handed over to guards at the Tower to release the brothers from their chains, which indicates that the monks were under close confinement.[14] Edward wanted to get to the bottom of the affair. Nonetheless, even from prison, Alexander de Pershore continued to wield his malign influence over Wenlok. The Abbot, now freed, was determined not to forsake his allies imprisoned in the

Tower. Wenlok's pension list, those people to whom the Abbot gave money, comprises a considerable number of justices including the very ones who had tried to bring the monks to justice in 1303–4: Thomas Brabazon, William de Bereford, Roger de Hegham, Richard de Southcote and even John de Drokensford, all were recipients, after 1304, of Wenlok's generosity.[15] In other words the Abbot was beginning to soften the harsh temperament of the King's judges. The accounts of 1303–4 record how the justices were entertained for a day, '*Pro deliveracione Fratrum* – for the deliverance of the brothers'. At the same time Wenlok would seek the advice and support of other people at the Court and, of course, in time the King's temper cooled.[16]

The Flowers of History picks up the story. At first Abbot Wenlok was not able to make any progress but, on 25 March 1304, Edward, pleased with his triumphs in Scotland where he had retaken the Castle of Stirling, arrived with his great Magnates at Westminster to give thanks before the tomb of Edward the Confessor. There, according to Westminster's own chronicle, moved by compassion over the unjust incarceration of the monks, the King ordered them to be liberated. Nonetheless, the *Flores* continues,

> because of the great malice of certain perverse judges, the iniquity was continued, they held back the King's order so the monks stayed another eight days in prison. When the King heard this, he ordered his judges that, putting aside all other cares, the imprisoned monks were to be returned immediately to their abbey.

The same story is repeated by Rishanger.[17] Of course, such a tale is not totally accurate; the justices would have long left the Tower. Brabazon and Bereford would not interfere, but Ralph de Sandwich, Constable of the Tower, would. Sandwich was not included in the list of those who received gifts from the Abbot of

Westminster, nor was he entertained at his board. Ralph de Sandwich was no fool, he must have known that the monks were guilty and resented their release. He was Constable and regarded the Tower as his personal fief. He held the keys. The monks would only be released in his own good time. He only did so when he was specifically ordered to do so by the King. Puddlicott, however, remained a prisoner. The monks returned to Westminster and went about their business.

Later in 1304, Ralph de Sandwich had other business to attend to along with John de Bakewell and John le Blund the Mayor: William Wallace the Scottish leader had been captured, he was hurried south for summary trial. Bareheaded, garbed in a filthy garment, riding a bony nag, Wallace was paraded through London and taken down to Westminster Hall. Seated upon a bench in the south end, a laurel wreath was thrust on his head in mockery of Wallace's alleged boast that one day he would wear a crown at Westminster. Wallace realized that before the likes of Ralph de Sandwich he must expect no mercy. When the indictment was read out, Wallace's defence was simple:

> I cannot be a traitor to King Edward while I hold him no allegiance. He is not my God, he never received my homage and whilst I enjoy life in this body he shall never receive it. As governor of my country I have been an enemy to its enemy. I have slain the English. I have manfully opposed the English King.

Wallace was found guilty and the sentence for treason was passed against him. He was to be dragged to the gibbet in Smithfield, be hanged, his body mutilated, his entrails and heart burnt before his face and his body then quartered. Sentence was carried out immediately. Wallace was dragged on a hurdle to the public gallows at the Elms and thrust on to the scaffold in the presence of a great crowd including the King and the Archbishop of Canterbury. Edward I's vindictive determination manifested itself. Wallace asked for a priest so that he might be shriven, Edward refused this but the Archbishop of Canterbury, so moved, rose and went on to the scaffold. Winchelsea heard Wallace's confession himself then left without the King's permission, before the execution took place. Lord Clifford, who had fought against Wallace, also had a streak of mercy, as the unfortunate man was executed, Clifford held up a psalter so that the condemned man could fix his eyes upon it until he died. The horrid punishment was carried out, Wallace's severed head, still circled with its Laurel wreath, being set upon London Bridge.[18]

Edward I had tracked one enemy down and showed him nothing but ruthless determination and vindictiveness. Puddlicott could expect little different. The King had not forgotten him but the monks of Westminster apparently had. In 1303 Richard de Puddlicott had been the man they needed. In 1305 he became their scapegoat.

In August 1305 Prior William de Huntingdon died. Reginald de Hadham was elected as Prior with the unanimous consent of the community. Now Hadham and Wenlok were undoubtedly enemies. Hadham represented those monks at Westminster who were tired and sick at what had happened over the last three to four years. A great quarrel between Hadham and Wenlok broke out which would dominate Abbey affairs for the next few years. Once Hadham was elected prior he was in a position of strength to launch fresh attacks upon Wenlok. The Abbot, with his allies back in Westminster, had secretly determined that, at a given moment, he would overturn Hadham's appointment as prior and instal his own nominee probably Alexander de Pershore. The crisis broke in 1307 but it had been simmering for at least two years. Hadham proved to be an implacable enemy. Pershore and his coven abruptly realized they could no longer support their former comrade in the Tower. The decision was quite callous. Puddlicott had been in prison for over two years. It might only be a matter of time before he changed his tune and issued another confession which fully implicated Alexander de Pershore and other monks. This could be used by Hadham against Wenlok, so it was better if Puddlicott died. After all, to protect himself and win the support of the monks, Puddlicott had claimed to be the only thief – why not let him go to the scaffold protesting this, and the sooner the better, lest he change his mind?

Sometime in the autumn of 1305 the monks withdrew their protection. It would be quite easy. Wenlok reneged on his letters of accreditation. Puddlicott was not really their clerk so he was subject to the secular arm. Sentence immediately followed and Puddlicott was condemned to death. According to the *Annales Londonienses*:

In that year on the fourth Kalends of November, John de Putticott [Puddlicott] 'Clerk' was led in a certain hand cart ['*careta*'] from the Tower of London to Westminster and there judged on the account of his violation of the King's Treasury.[19]

Edward, and perhaps Sandwich, decided that Puddlicott should be humiliated as well as punished, not at Smithfield but the very place where Puddlicott had carried out his daring robbery, an ostentatious rebuke and public warning to the monks of Westminster.

The Fourth Kalends of November was Sunday 28 November 1305. Sunday a day of rest, was chosen particularly, the crowds would be out and busy, especially around the Abbey. Puddlicott is still called a 'clerk'. He is not dragged through the city: he is ridiculed, placed in nothing better than a wheelbarrow and pushed down through the city along the river bank into Westminster itself. We know Puddlicott was hanged from the letter that Edward sent to former Sheriff Pourte in 1307 asking for the return of the refectory silver.[20] Edward was determined that this Oxford man, whatever he may have claimed to be, who had tried to ridicule the Crown, would be mocked in death. There was further humiliation in store. On a door leading to the

Chapter House at Westminster, beneath the hinges, is what anti-quarians have described as human skin. There is every possibility that, once he had been hanged, Puddlicott's body was not gibbeted but skinned, which was dried, cured and hung on that door in the south cloister as a warning to the monks. The existence of this skin was first noted by the antiquarian G.G. Scott in his book, *Gleanings from Westminster Abbey*, published in 1861. On page 40, Scott reports, 'on the inner side of the door I found, hanging from beneath the hinges, some pieces of white leather. They reminded me of the story of the skins of Danes.' One theory was that the Marauding Danes in the eighth and ninth centuries had been captured and skinned. However, it is highly unlikely that the monks would have allowed this. Another theory was that the 'Skins' were hides used as draught-excluders but Scott continues: 'A friend, to whom I showed them, sent them to Mr Quekett of the College of Surgeons who, I regret to say, pronounced them to be human. It is clear that the entire door was covered with them both within and without.' If this is true, the King may have had the corpses of all the robbers skinned and nailed to the door as a warning to the monks, a logical step if Puddlicott was hanged on the Abbot's gallows in Tothill Lane. It might also explain Robert of Reading's dramatic 'Passion of the Monks', it would serve as an antidote to the grisly warning and macabre royal humour on display on a door near the Chapter House of Westminster.

There is no evidence that Puddlicott changed his confession. Perhaps of all those who were involved in the robbery: thuggish monks, violent outlaws, corrupt officials and greedy goldsmiths, Puddlicott does emerge with some amount of honour, a gambler who played for the highest stakes, lost and went bravely to his death. The callousness of the monks and their arrogance are truly breathtaking. They had betrayed their colleague, companion and associate and, once he was dead, they continued to fashion the legend. As we saw earlier in the *Flores Historiarum*, Westminster's own chronicle, 'The Passion of the Monks of Westminster' links the robbery and the false allegations against ten monks with recent violations against Pope Boniface VIII and even the betrayal of Christ by Judas. Time and again the Chronicler denounces the wickedness of the age which could spit out such dreadful allegations against saintly members of their Christ-like community.[21] It is a farrago of nonsense but what the Chronicle declared is what Wenlok and his party would insist was the accepted story, the official version. Puddlicott had confessed, Puddlicott had gone to the scaffold, he alone was responsible. They, the monks of Westminster, had been unjustly imprisoned, persecuted, made to suffer, yet they were innocent. Alexander de Pershore and the rest had withdrawn their protection just in time. Reginald de Hadham and his associates would not be able to use the matter of the robbery in the great quarrel brewing in their Abbey.

10

The Aftermath

'Nou hath prude the pris in everuche plawe'

'Now Pride wins the prize in every play'
Contemporary ballad

In the end all the actors in the Westminster drama of 1303 slipped away. Edward had to face fresh problems not only from Scotland but from his eldest son and heir-apparent, the Prince of Wales. The young prince had also felt the effects of his father's financial and economic policies. Edward junior was charming enough but lazy and feckless. He had spent his early years at Kings Langley in Hertfordshire. Left to his own devices, Prince Edward dug ditches, consorted with rowers, sailors and boatmen. He liked to play games such as pitch and toss, totally absorbed with his camel and greyhounds. Above all, the old king was infuriated at his son's growing friendship with the young Gascon nobleman Peter Gaveston.[1]

The King, however, was distracted by Scotland. If Edward I thought that he had spent all his treasure crushing Wallace's resistance he was sadly mistaken. On 10 February 1306, Edward I's former ally, the Scottish nobleman Robert Bruce, murdered his rival John Comyn at a church in Dumfries and raised the flag of rebellion against Edward I. Bruce emerged as Scotland's new rebel leader in a war to the death against England. Bruce immediately seized royal castles in Scotland and issued his defiance. Edward, now sixty-seven years of age, was sickening. Nevertheless, he was determined to advance north and crush this new threat.[2] He had to receive specialist medical treatment though a commentator declared: 'The King is healthy enough and strong enough considering his age.' In fact, Edward I was a very sick man and his illness did not make him any calmer, it brought to the fore his violent, hideous temper which blazed out in cruelties towards Bruce whom he had always considered to be his man in peace and war. Bruce's brother Neal was captured and barbarously executed at Berwick, whilst Bruce's women were imprisoned in cages. Undeterred, the Scots fought on, Bruce displaying all the cunning and skill of a veteran guerrilla leader. Once again Edward was desperate for money and supplies. More importantly he was still sorely distracted by his heir's continuing friendship with Peter Gaveston. Matters were worsened when the Prince asked that Gaveston be created Earl of Cornwall. In the ensuing quarrel Edward I smashed his elder son's, head against a wall, tore his hair out and kicked him to the ground.

'You base-born whoreson,' the King screamed. 'You want to give my lands away, you who never gained any? I tell you, as the Lord lives, if it were not for fear of breaking up the kingdom you would never enjoy your inheritance.'

Edward's dying days were blighted by this savage quarrel. Gaveston was exiled, the young prince deserting the English forces in Scotland to escort 'his brother' to Dover.[3] Edward I continued with his war. The old King reached Carlisle and intended to cross the Scottish border but was so ill he stayed at Lanercost Priory until 4 March 1307. The royal quarters there were hastily prepared, glass windows fitted, food and provisions brought from Newcastle and York. The royal household, including officials like Drokensford, went searching for medicines for the King. He was fed with cordials made up of amber, musk, pearls, gold and silver sugar rosettes, his skin treated with Damascus rose water, herbal baths and a range of ointments. Edward was having problems with both his neck and an ulcerated leg, and growing weaker due to chronic dysentery.

He managed to review his troops at Carlisle. At the beginning of July he intended to march across the Scottish border. He spent the night of 6 July at Burgh-on-sands. When his servants came to lift him from his bed early the next morning, he gave a loud cry, threw himself back in their arms and died immediately.[4]

According to many legends, Edward I made his son and barons swear that, after his death, they would have his body boiled in a large cauldron until the flesh separated from the bones, they were to bury the flesh and keep the bones. Every time the Scots rebelled against the English Crown, the English must carry these bones before them as Edward believed most firmly that, as long as even his bones were carried against the Scots, the enemy would never be victorious. The story from the fourteenth-century chronicler Froissart is probably not true but it certainly captures Edward's implacable will.[5]

Whatever Edward I wished, in the end his corpse was brought south to Waltham Abbey. It was not moved into London until 18 October 1307, being first placed in the monastery of Holy Trinity, then St Paul's, before being laid to rest on 27 October 1307 in Westminster Abbey under a tomb, both beautiful and severe, fashioned out of Purbeck marble, and unadorned by any sculpture. It became a place of pilgrimage, and between 1300 and 1500, the Exchequer continued to pay for wax candles to be burnt around the royal tomb. The famous inscription, which can still be read, 'Edward I, Hammer of the Scots, *Pactum Serva* – Keep Faith' was probably added some 300 years later. Edward lay in peace until 2 May 1774 when the Dean at Westminster, and a host of learned antiquarians, opened the tomb and found the corpse in excellent condition, the flesh shrunken but intact:

> The corpse was richly dressed in a rich red tunic and an elaborate decorated stole. There was also a mantle of red satin and the lower part of the body was covered with cloth of gold. In the right hand was a sceptre with a cross in the left another surmounted by a dove, on the head an open crown.

The corpse measured just over six feet. There can be no doubt that the antiquarians of 1774, when they viewed the corpse, also touched some of the royal treasure, buried with Edward, which had fallen into the hands of the likes of Richard de Puddlicott before it was retrieved.[6]

Bruce, the future victor against the English at Bannockburn in 1314, realized the importance of Edward I and how his death provided a breathing space for his cause, adding, 'that he feared the dead father more than he did the living son'.

The new King Edward II soon justified Bruce's comment. Within months the Scottish war had been entrusted to others whilst Edward hurried south to join Peter Gaveston who had returned from exile to be made Earl of Cornwall.

In the end Edward II's reign proved to be one disaster after another, both at home and abroad. He had four children by his French wife Isabella until eventually he provoked her into rebellion and exile. She fled across the Narrow Seas, met the Welsh exile Roger Mortimer and, in September 1326, invaded England through Essex – deposing and imprisoning her husband and ruling the kingdom in the name of her eldest son, the future Edward III.[7]

While Edward I lived, he continued to patronize John de Drokensford, giving him prebends in England and Ireland as well as residences in Surrey, Hampshire and Kent, a sixth estate in the Forests of Wiltshire and another grant of land in Windsor Forest.

After Edward's death, the new king decided to settle scores with former enemies. Edward II had not forgotten how the Treasurer Walter Langton, Bishop of Coventry and Lichfield, had attempted to curb his expenditure when he was Prince of Wales. Langton was removed from his post and subjected to legal investigation and public humiliation. In the political storm which ensued, Drokensford gave up his keepership of the King's Wardrobe. Nonetheless, he had won the favour of the new King. On Christmas day 1308 the King nominated him to the vacant bishopric of Bath and Wells. Drokensford received the temporalities of that see on 15 May 1309 and was consecrated Bishop of Bath and Wells at Canterbury on the following 9 November. A year passed before he was enthroned in his bishopric because, as he himself wrote, of 'political troubles', the growing antagonism between Edward II and his barons led by his cousin Thomas of Lancaster.

Drokensford proved to be a worldly but very industrious bishop. By the time Drokensford was appointed bishop, he could draw on the income from the following ecclesiastical sinecures: Chaplaincy to the Pope, the Canonries of Wells, Lichfield and Lincoln Cathedrals, the prebendaries of Masham, Darlington, Oakland, Chesterlea Street in the counties of York and Durham. He was rector of Drokensford in Hampshire; Heminghburgh and Stilling Fleet in Yorkshire as well as Balsham in Cambridgeshire. He continued to enjoy the favour of the Crown and, when Edward II and Queen Isabella crossed to France in 1313, Drokensford was made Regent of the kingdom for a while. However, Drokensford had been Edward I's man and, when the barons assembled in an attempt to bring Edward II to book, Drokensford supported their petition 'that a Committee of Ordainers be set up to help the King rule his kingdom'. In 1321 Drokensford intervened with other bishops in an attempt to reach a peace settlement in London between the king and his dissident baronage. When the barons actually rose in rebellion in 1322, Drokensford ceased to be the professional administrator and civil servant, the objective bishop. He gave tacit support to the rebellion, so much so that, in February 1323, the king wrote to Pope John XXII complaining of Drokensford's conduct and demanding he be transferred to some see outside England.

Drokensford must have been appalled by Edward II's behaviour, not only in domestic and foreign matters, but towards his hapless wife. He tried to mediate between Edward and his exiled queen in 1325. This failed. When the queen carried through her successful revolution, Drokensford (and he must have remembered those hectic days of 1303 when he investigated the robbery at Westminster), actually joined the Londoners in taking their oath at the Guildhall to support Isabella and her son. Drokensford did not live to see Isabella fall from power in 1330. He died in his episcopal manor house at Dogsmersfield, Hampshire, on 9 May 1329, and was buried in St Catherine's Chapel at his cathedral church of Wells where his tomb can still be visited.[8]

Hugh Pourte continued to experience financial problems; on 20 March 1305 a royal commission was issued to Ralph de Sandwich and others on complaint by Humphrey de Bohun, Earl of Hereford and Essex, and Elizabeth his wife, the King's daughter, that Hugh Pourte, together with Richard de Caumpes and at least twenty others,

> came to their Manor in the County of Middlesex while the Earl was in Scotland on the King's service and under royal protection. They broke the gates of the manor and the doors of their houses, carried away their goods and assaulted their men.

Pourte's financial weakness, as well as his dislike of the royal family is clearly illustrated by this document. Ralph de Sandwich would only be too pleased to bring him to book. Perhaps the case never came to court but the Crown still kept its eye on Hugh Pourte. On 10 February 1307 the old King, recuperating at

Lanercost Priory, wrote at the insistence of the Treasurer, to Hugh Pourte, citizen of London:

> Order to be delivered to the Abbot and convent of Westminster all the cups which were lately stolen from their refectory at Westminster by Richard de Puddlicott who was hanged by consideration of the King's court for different robberies committed by him. These treasures were delivered to Hugh when he was sheriff of London by the justices appointed to deliver the gaol of the Tower of Richard and to be kept safely by him until the King should order otherwise.

Reading between the lines, the Crown's anger is obvious. The cups had been entrusted to Hugh Pourte, the King did not wish to make an issue of it, but they were to be given back to Westminster as quickly as possible. Perhaps the Crown had heard that Hugh Pourte was not in the best of health and decided to act. Hugh Pourte, in fact, died later that year, his Will being enrolled at the Court of Hustings in London: 'To John le Blund [former mayor] a house: To Margaret, Hugh's wife, custody of his son William until he becomes of age, to the said William £40.00'. He also bequeathed certain rents to the parish of St Magnus for the maintenance of a Chantry so that a priest could chant Masses for Pourte's soul, as well as 20 shillings 'to maintain the fabric' of London Bridge. There is no evidence that he ever handed the stolen cups back to the monks of Westminster.[9]

Of the principal justices who tried and condemned Puddlicott, William Bereford continued his career as one of the leading judges of the Crown until 'broken by age and infirmity'. He retired in 1316, died in 1317 and was buried in St Paul's. Roger Brabazon lasted well into the reign of Edward II. He died in 1326 and was buried in the house of the Austin Friars in London. The old warhorse, Sir Ralph de Sandwich, was seventy-two when Edward I died in July 1307. Sandwich was the one person Edward I should have paid but had not. In 1306, a few months after Puddlicott was hanged, Sandwich petitioned the Crown for repayment of all the money he had spent out of his own pocket as Constable of the Tower on building work, including the reconstruction of the Chapel of St Peter ad Vincula as well as for the custody of prisoners. Moreover, in the last twenty years he had not even been paid his annual fee of £100. An investigation was held and, eventually in the new reign, Ralph de Sandwich received the extraordinarily large amount (for those days) of £1,750, 'In consideration of his free and praiseworthy service to him [Edward II] and to his father'. The old Constable was summoned to attend the Coronation of Edward II [February 1308]. By then he must have been frail. On 24 March 1308 he surrendered custody of the Tower to John Cromwell. On 20 August 1308 he died but, as in life, so in death. Sandwich had been the terror of medieval London's demi-monde, so it was only appropriate that he was buried in the nave of Greyfriars Church, opposite Newgate Prison, where he had so often held court.

John de Bakewell continued to advance in royal favour. In August 1305 he tried William of Wallace for treason in Westminster Hall. Bakewell was also appointed Baron of the Exchequer. However, on 25 February 1308, John de Bakewell's extraordinary good fortune ran out. He attended the Coronation of Edward and Isabella and was crushed to death when a stone wall collapsed under the weight of the large crowds. Though a tragic accident, according to the Chroniclers, there would be many in London who would quietly rejoice at Bakewell's fate and regard his death as divine justice.[10]

The treasure, the jewels moved by Drokensford to the Tower to be itemized and stored there, remained in the Tower. In the reign of Edward III an official was paid as 'keeper of the jewels, armouries and other things'. By the sixteenth century this official was known as the 'Master and Treasurer of the Jewels House', responsible for the royal regalia.

In 1642 radical parliamentarians under Cromwell seized control of London and the Tower. A great deal of the royal regalia was broken up and sold. When Charles II was restored in 1660 his coronation was delayed for a year because the regalia had to be replaced at a staggering cost of £31,000. In 1668 the Diarist Samuel Pepys, to celebrate St George's Day, took a bevy of lady friends to the Tower and 'showed them all to be seen there and among other things the crown and sceptre and rich plate which I myself never saw before and indeed is noble, and I am mightily pleased with it'.

Three years later, on 9 May 1671, one final attempt was made to steal the Crown Jewels organized and led by the Cromwellian Irish adventurer Colonel Thomas Blood. This seventeenth-century ne'er-do-well managed to insinuate himself into the Jewel House at the Tower, reconnoitred its security then returned with friends to steal the royal regalia. Once again the theft was frustrated; Blood's attempt may well have been secretly patronized by high-ranking politicians. Common opinion expected Blood to pay for such an outrage with his life. In fact, he was pardoned by the king, restored to his estates and rewarded.

The Abbey treasure had a less dramatic history. Understandably the Abbey worked hard to recover everything that Puddlicott had stolen. Two hundred and thirty years later the Abbey ceased to be a monastic community; most of its treasure was seized by the Crown during the Reformation, when it was broken up and sold off. What can still be seen at the Abbey are beautiful pieces of work but dating from the latter half of the sixteenth century. Very little of its medieval treasure remains.

London continued to fight for its liberties. Throughout the reign of Edward II there were demonstrations, the usual 'push and shove' between Crown and City. Matters came to a head when Edward II's wife Isabella invaded in September 1326. All the resentments and frustrations of the City spilled over into chaos, riot and summary execution. The Londoners seized and plundered the hated Tower and hunted royal ministers through the streets, dragging them into Cheapside and cutting off their heads. Walter Stapleton, Bishop of Exeter, Treasurer of England

and Drokensford's colleague, was caught riding through Newgate on his way to lunch. The unfortunate man, accompanied by only two squires, desperately tried to seek sanctuary in St Paul's but the north door was closed against them. He and his companions were cornered and seized by the mob. Stapleton himself was a good administrator, a loyal servant of Crown and Church but he stood for the Exchequer which Londoners had come to hate, with its constant demands for new taxes and levies. A butcher called Hatfield grabbed the bishop, hammered him unconscious, dragged him into a churchyard in Cheapside and hacked off his head with a bread knife. The revolutionaries sent the head to Isabella who, of course, refused to accept it.

The City slipped into chaos. Isabella, who had assumed the reins of power, sent a placatory letter to Londoners asking them to show protection to a certain foreign merchant. They replied with impunity that no enemy of London could really be a true friend of the Crown. Such opposition was not just the matter of street rage and resentment. London's exasperation at the Crown simply found a voice. The City played a prominent role in the deposition of Edward II. On 13 December 1326, once again all the wards were marshalled, this time not because of some royal ordinance but so that every citizen could swear on oath to support the deposition of Edward II, and the restoration in full of their city's liberties. The Londoners now asserted themselves. They became the judges and arbiters of what happened in the kingdom. Between 12 and 16 January 1327 the Mayor and aldermen of London marshalled leading earls, barons, knights, archbishops, other bishops, abbots, priors and clerks to swear an oath to depose Edward II and observe the city liberties. Walter Reynolds, then Archbishop of Canterbury, had to prostrate himself before the citizens, begging for their forgiveness and making reparation with fifty tuns of wine. On 28 February 1327, Edward III recognized London's achievement in his father's deposition and the removal of his hated ministers. On 4 March, he pardoned the citizens for any crimes. On 6 March he released them from all debts and, on 7 March, a charter was issued restoring the city liberties in their entirety, promising, amongst other things, that there would be no more special taxes on London. The Charter of 1327 brought to an end tension between the Crown and City which had lasted for almost 200 years.[11]

The principal actors in the robbery of 1303, the monks of Westminster, individually went their own way. Alexander de Pershore was released and, by 1306–7, was busy on Wenlok's business. In 1311 he became Precentor, leader of the choir and, at the end of the year, Archdeacon. Pershore must have died shortly afterwards as there is no further mention of him in the muniments of Westminster. Alexander of Newport, also released, returned to his duties, but was dead by the end of 1311. Robert de Bures disappears from the Abbey muniments by the end of 1307. Thomas de Butterley survived at least another twenty-three years after he was released from prison. Adam de Warfeld seems to have been released from the Tower as a broken man. The Abbey muniments record him as being ill around September 1305 and he died on Thursday 25 March 1306. Adam de Warfeld had been the ringleader, the 'ordainer and contriver' amongst the monks in the matter of the robbery. The justices in the Tower had totally rejected his claim of Benefit of Clergy. They could not sentence him but they at least named him as being involved. Sandwich's reluctance to release some of the monks may have broken Warfeld physically and psychologically which could explain his early death shortly after his release.[12]

The Abbey of Westminster had not learned its lesson from the events of 1303 – or the long sojourn in the Tower of ten of its monks. Resentment and bitterness soon manifested themselves in the monastic community which was riven by the Wenlok–Hadham dispute. In July 1307 Hadham eventually appealed to Rome and the King. Wenlok's reaction was to suspend Hadham from office and finally excommunicate him. The dispute rumbled on and would have escalated had it not been for Wenlok's sudden death on Christmas Day 1307. On

17 May 1308 the papal judges decided that the case against Hadham was null and void and they revoked all sentences. However, this was not the end of the affair. The election of Richard de Kedington as Wenlok's successor sharply divided the Abbey community – the monks remained at each other's throats for the next two years. Hadham's party viewed Richard de Kedington as Wenlok's candidate and refused to accept him. In 1308 Edward II had to send his justices into the Abbey to try to impose a peace. Two years later, in 1310, he wrote to the Abbot ordering him to put an end to the scandalous goings-on in the monastic community. Eventually death removed the main participants of the dispute, Westminster Abbey came to be ruled by more enlightened dedicated men, and its peace and harmony were no longer shattered by scandal and rumour.[13]

The same can be said for the Royal Palace. On 12 March 1304 John Shenche and Joan his wife were given back the custody of the King's Palace at Westminster, taken into the King's hands during the trial of Richard de Puddlicott and William Deputy Keeper of the Palace. Shenche appointed another deputy but the Crown had not forgotten. On 17 February 1311, this new deputy, Richard Abbot, was formally summoned to the Exchequer and, before the Treasurer, Chancellor, two Barons of the Exchequer and others of the King's Council, he received the most explicit orders on behalf of the Crown for the Palace's safe-keeping. 'It was laid down that Richard Abbot should keep all the doors and other entrances and exits firmly closed at sunset and not have them opened before sunrise the following day.' They also imposed on Richard Abbot a strict duty of care about who came into the palace. It would take some time for the Crown to forget the plundering of its jewels.[14]

With Edward I's death, the royal court and the main offices of state moved back to Westminster. The Crypt and the Chapel of the Pyx were never used again to store royal treasure. They fell into disuse, being used simply as record chambers. In the end Puddlicott and the robbery were forgotten. One can still walk the beaten flagstones of the south cloister. Nothing remains of the robbery except for traces of that skin which can still be found under the hinge of an old door now moved to the right of the passageway leading up to the chapter house.

Notes and Sources

The principal sources are the Abbey of Westminster and the adjoining church of St Margaret of Antioch. Of course some of the Abbey buildings have gone, as has the famous wasteland and the monks' cemetery, now grassed over or cordoned off as part of the Canons' gardens. Nevertheless the Abbey itself, developed since 1303 with buildings such as the Chapel of Henry VII, has not changed too radically. One can still walk the path leading from the south-east door down to the main road across which stands the House of Lords, the site of the medieval Palace, the same route Puddlicott and William of the Palace must have used when they robbed the Royal Treasury. The Abbey also contains the tomb of Walter de Wenlok and, above all, the curious Pyx Chamber and Crypt which, at the present moment, are not open to the public. I am very grateful to Dr Richard Mortimer and Ms Christine Reynolds who allowed me to visit and study the archives in the Westminster Record office as well as Mr Castledine, Verger, who allowed me to make further visits to the Crypt for a more painstaking study of that fascinating chamber.

I have tried, where possible, to allow the original sources tell the story though one has to be vigilant in detecting bias. I have also tried to keep to one version of spelling when it comes to medieval names, e.g. Puddlicott has a number of variables.

The most important document is Kings Remembrance E/101/332/8 (National Archives – Kew), which contains most of the documents available regarding the robbery. These have been sewn hurriedly together by some clerk and vary in quality. Many of these records have been published by F. Palgrave in his *Kalendars and Inventories of the Exchequer* (Records Commission, London 1836) I, pp. 252–9. However, it is important to realize that Palgrave made some omissions particularly Puddlicott's and Rippinghale's confessions. The list of jewels and Drokensford's famous indenture is printed in H. Cole's *Records* (Records Commission, 1844) pp. 277–84. Cottonian Manuscripts, 'Nero', D. II, f. 192d (The British Library) contains the contemporary picture of the 'sole thief' plundering the Crypt. T. H. Rymer's *Feodera, Litterae et Conventiones,* ed. A. Clarke and F. Holbrooke (Record Commission, 1816–18) contains valuable information (Vol. I, pp. 956 and 959) as does the *Calendar of Patent Rolls* (1301–7). Both are published by HMSO, 1902. I also make reference to other Patent and Close Rolls [that is letters 'open or closed'] of this period.

The Westminster records are varied: there are the Westminster Abbey Muniments (WAM): the Domesday Cartulary (WB: Wam Book) these constitute the main manuscript sources. The two volumes of the *Customary of the Benedictine Monasteries of St Augustine Canterbury and St Peter Westminster,* ed E. Maunde Thompson (Henry Bradshawe Society, vols. XXIII and XXIV, London 1902–4) are a rich source of material. (Vol. XXIV of the Society concerns Westminster.) Other documents are printed but not translated in *Documents Illustrating the Rule of Walter de Wenlock, Abbot of Westminster 1283–1307,* ed. Barbara Harvey (Camden Society, 4th Series, II, 1965) and *The Obedientiaries of Westminster Abbey and their Financial Records,* ed. Barbara Harvey (Westminster Abbey Record Series III, the Boydell Press, 1982). Ernest Harold Pearce's *Walter de Wenlock* (London, 1920) is very biased and most sympathetic to the Abbot. Much more valuable is E. H. Pearce, *The Monks of Westminster*, being a register of the Brethren of the convent from the time of the Confessor to the Dissolution (Cambridge, 1916). This provides a 'potted' biography of Wenlok, Pershore and the rest. One version of the Westminster chronicle, *Flowers of History (Flores Historiarum)* is that edited by H. R. Luard for the Rolls Series Vol. III (HMSO, 1890). William Rishanger's *Chronicle* is edited by H. T. Riley for the Rolls Series (HMSO, 1865). *The Year Book of Edward I* cited in the text is that for 21–2 Edward I (1292–3) ed. H. J. Horwood (HMSO, 1873). Another informative source is *The Chronicle of Walter of Guisborough*, ed. H. Rothwell (Camden Society, XXXIV, 1957).

The London sources are varied. *The Annales Londonienses* can be found in the *Chronicles of Edward I and Edward II* ed. W. Stubbs (Vol. I HMSO, 1882). Regulation of City Life is described in the *Munimenta Gildhallae Londonienses: The 'Liber Albus'*, ed. H. T. Riley, (Vol. III. 1862). This can be supplemented by *Memorials of London and London Life 1276–1417*, ed. H. T. Riley (London, 1868). A valuable source is the *Liber de Antiquis legibus sue chronica Maiorum et Vicecomitum Londoniarum*, ed. T. Stapleton (Camden Society, 1846). Other valuable sources are *The Calendar of Coroners Rolls preserved amongst the archives of the Corporation of the City of London 1300–1378*, ed. R. R. Sharpe (London, 1913), *Calendar of Early Mayors' court rolls preserved among the archives of the Corporation of the City of London 1298–1307*, ed. A. H. Thomas (London, 1924), *Calendar of Letter Books preserved among the archives of the Corporation of London: 1275–1498*, ed. R. R. Sharpe, 'Books A–L' 2 volumes (London, 1899–1912). The relevant volumes are Letter Books A. B. and C. Finally the *Calendar of Wills proved and enrolled in the Court of Hustings London 1258–1358*, ed. R. R. Sharpe, 2 vols. (London, 1889) is also useful. An excellent cartographic survey is *The City of London from prehistoric times to c. 1420*, ed. Mary Lobel (Oxford, 1989). *The London Assize of Nuisance 1301–1431*, eds H. M. Chew and W. Kelloway (London Record Society, 1973) and *The London Eyre of 1276*, ed. M. Licinbaum (London Record Society, 1976), both provide a powerful insight into living conditions in thirteenth century London. Fitzstephen's description of London is published in John Stow's *Survey of London,* ed. C. L. Kingsford (Oxford, 1908] volumes I and II. The description is printed in Latin as an appendix of Volume II, which I have translated and is given in full in an Appendix in this book.

The judicial aspects of Edward I's reign are also valuable. Many of these records are printed. *The Lincolnshire Assize Roll for 1298* is edited by W. S. Thomson for the Lincoln Record Society: Volume 36 (1939). Other important sources are *Select cases in the Court of King's Bench under Edward I,* ed. G. O. Sayles (Selden Society, 1936], vols. I–III, and *State Trials of the Reign of Edward the First,* ed. By T. F. Tout and H. Johnstone (Royal Historical Society, 1906). References to the surname Puddlicott may be found in *The White Books of Peterborough,* ed. Sandra Rabans (Northamptonshire Record Society, 2001) pp. 305, 310.

The lives of Drokensford, Bakewell and the rest can be traced in the *Dictionary of National Biography.* However, for Drokensford we have his register when he was later appointed Bishop of Bath and Wells: *Calendar of the Register of John de Drokensford: Bishop of Bath and Wells,* ed. Bishop Hobhouse (Somerset Records Society, 1887) vol. 70. Another relevant source is *The Knights of Edward I,* ed. C. Moor (Harleian Society, 1926–53) vols. I–V.

Puddlicott's robbery is mentioned by Antiquarians whilst T. F. Tout wrote a short paper on it which was published in his *Collected Papers,* vol. III (Manchester, 1934) pp. 93–115. However, what is crucial in understanding the different feast days of that period is that invaluable compendium, *A Handbook of Dates for Students of British History,* ed. C. R. Cheney and rev. Michael Jones (Cambridge, 2000). For the rest I have quoted relevant books and articles but, to keep footnotes to a minimum, only quoted to confirm an important point.

References

Prologue

1. For the Crypt of Westminster Abbey. H. Harrod, 'On the Crypt of the Chapter House at Westminster', *Archaeologia*, Vol. XLIV. J. Burtt, *On some discoveries in connection with the Ancient Treasury at Westminster – Gleanings from Westminster Abbey*, ed. G. G. Scott (London), pp. 282–90, and *An Inventory of the Historical Monuments in London*. Vol. I, 'Westminster Abbey' (Royal Commission on Historical Muniments, HMSO, 1924) p. 81.
2. Dean Stanley, *Westminster Abbey* (John Murray, 1924), p. 368. Rishanger, *Chronicle*, pp. 69–70.

1 The King's Tale

1. *Calendar of Patent Rolls (CPR, 1301–7)*, p. 192.

2. The struggle is described in F. M. Powicke, *Henry III and the Lord Edward* (Oxford, 1947), vols. I–II.

3. F. M. Powicke, *The Thirteenth Century* (Oxford, 1962), pp. 322–76.

4. *Ibid.*, pp. 560–71.

5. *Ibid.*, pp. 581ff.

6. *Ibid.*, pp. 571–613 and pp. 683–706.

7. *Ibid.*, pp. 445–96.

8. J. Bellamy, *Crime & Public Order in England during the Middle Ages* (Routledge, 1973), p. 45.

9. *The Chronicle of Walter of Guisborough*, ed. H. Rothwell (Camden Society, LXXXIX, 1957), p. 198.

10. P. Binski, *The Painted Chamber at Westminster* (1956).

11. Nicolas Trivet, *Annales* ed. T. Hog (1846), p. 282.

12. H. M. Colvin, *The King's Works* (London, 1963), I. pp. 559–61. A. J. Taylor, 'Edward I and the Shrine of St Thomas of Canterbury', *British Archaeological Association Journal*, vol. LXXXII (1979), p. 26.

13. For Minstrels and Music at Edward I's Court, C. Bullock Davies, *Menestrallorum, Multitudo* (Cardiff, 1978).

14. *Guisborough's Chronicle*, pp. 298–303.

15. *Ibid.*, pp. 325-8.

16. H. G. Richardson "The Coronation of Edward I", *Bulletin of the Institute of Historical Research*, vol. XV 1937–1938.

17. Colvin, vol. II pp. 416–17. *Flores*, III, p. 114.

18. *Cal. Pat. Rolls*; 1292–1301, p. 218.

19. Palgrave, *Kalendars*. This is the most quoted source and will be referred to as this. pp. 288–9, nos. 73 and 74.

20. Matthew Paris, *Chronica Majora* ed. H. R. Luard (Rolls series 1873–83), vol. V, p. 598.

21. Nicholas Trivet, *Annales*, pp. 281–3 and the National Archives Mss. C.47/4/5 Fl. 47^v – and British Library Additional Mss. 7965 f15^v and 18. Payments made including the repair of the coronet. The reason of Edward

I's temper against his daughter Joanna was that she had fallen in love with a relative commoner Ralph de Monthermer – however, the story ended happily enough.

22. Pierre Chaplais, 'Some Private Letters of Edward I', *English Historical Review* [*EHR*], LXXVII, 1962, pp. 82–5.

23. He was hired by Edward III to hunt down his father's killers. Paul Doherty, *Isabella and the Strange Death of Edward II* (Constable, 2003). pp. 166–7.

24. Sophie Page, *Magic in Mediaeval Manuscripts* (British Library) pp. 59–60.

25. Desmond Seward, *The Monks of War* (Penguin, 1995) pp. 215–16.

26. *Flores*, III. p. 320.

27. Guisborough, p. 369: *Flores*, III p. 135.

28. *Cal. Close Rolls* (1288–96), p. 55.

29. Palgrave, *Kalendars*, pp. 251–3.

2 The Monk's Tale

1. *Flores*, III, pp. 115–17. E. H. Pearce, *The Monks of Westminster*, p. 70.

2. Pearce, *The Monks of Westminster*, p. 60.

3. B. Harvey, *The Obedientiaries of Westminster Abbey*. A survey of the biographies in Pearce's *Monks of Westminster* show different individuals on their travels, for example, Robert de Bures p. 58.

4. Westminster: Domesday Cartulary f. 417^v.

5. Westminster: Domesday Cartulary f. 150.

6. Harvey, *The Obedientaries*, p. XXII.

7. Harvey, *Documents Illustrating the accounts of Walter de Wenlok*, p. 34 *el seq.* 'Wenlok's Intinerary'.

8. Pearce, *Monks of Westminster*, p. 60: Pearce's index lists four other Wenloks around this period, *ibid.*, pp. 223–4

9. Harvey, *Walter de Wenlok* has the Norman French original. p. 241 *et seq.*
10. *The Customary of St. Peters Westminster*, vol. II.
11. William of Huntingdon was an old man: he died aged sixty-five in 1305. *Pearce, Monks of Westminster*, p. 55.
12. *Ibid.*, p. 62.
13. *CPR* [1292–1301], p. 228. Nat. Archives C 47/3/31.
14. Cal. Close Rolls 1251–3, p. 259. 'Liber de Antiquis Legibus, Chronicles of the Mayor and Sheriffs of London', pp. 15 and 110.
15. National archives Curia Regis Roll No. 115. (18–19 Henry III. M. 33^d); Matt. Paris, *Chronica Majora*, vols III, p. 327: IV 193–6.
16. A colourful but fairly accurate description of the right of sanctuary at Westminster is given by Walter Besant *Westminster* (Chatto, 1897), p. 136 *et seq.* For a more scholarly analysis, see M. B. Honeybourne, 'The Sanctuary boundaries and environs of Westminster', *British Archaeological Association Journal*, no. 38 (1932) p. 316 *et seq.*
17. All the matters mentioned here are dealt with in detail later on.

3 The Clerk's Tale

1. Westminster Abbey Muniments 31388 and 24502.
2. For Drokensford's biography in total, see *Dictionary of National Biography* (Oxford, 1993), vol. 6, pp. 19–20 and Bishop Hobhouse's edition of his register in the Somerset Record Series [see above] (1887), vol. I. pp XVII–XLI. As Bishop of Bath and Wells, Drokensford later patronized his nephews, Michael and Andrew, but they laboured for God and his Church, whilst his brother Richard became the Diocese's industrious Chancellor.

3. T. F. Tout, *The Administrative History of Mediaeval England*, (Manchester, 1920), vol. II, pp. 16–17.

4. *The Chronicle of Pierre de Langtoft*, ed. T. Wright (Rolls series, 1868), vol. II, pp. 344–6.

5. T. F. Tout, *Administrative History*, vol. II, p. 141.

6. M. Prestwich, 'Exchequer and wardrobe in the later years of Edward I', *Bulletin of the Institute of Historical Research*, 1973, XIVI.

7. T. F Tout, *Administrative History*, vol. II, p. 52 *et seq.*

8. T. F. Tout: *Ibid.*, pp. 53 *et seq.*

9. Palgrave, *Kalendars*, pp. 273–4.

10. *Annales Londonienses*, p. 92.

11. A. J. Taylor 'Royal Alms and Oblations' in *Essays presented to Marc Fitch*, ed. F. G. Emmison and R. Stephens (1976), pp. 119–20.

12. *Liber Quotidianus Contrulatoris Garderobae [1299–1300]*, ed. The Society of Antiquaries (1787), pp. XLVII–XLIX 'Jocalia', pp. 332–53. A fascinating analysis of the royal regalia and jewellery can be found here such as, 'Five Serpent tongues in a standard of silver, supposed to have been St Richard's, in a painted wooden case'. [*Liber*: pp. 349–50).

13. The information contained in these indictments and allegations will be discussed later. However the inability of law officers, sheriffs or otherwise to interfere with Westminster was fully checked by Henry III who thundered in his edict: 'It is our will, however, that the said Sheriff [of London] shall, with the liberties of Westminster, in no way interfere.' [Liber de Antiquis Legibus, p. 90].

14. *Liber de Antiquis*, p. 226.

15. Palgrave, *Kalendars*, p. 267, no. 50.

16. Pearce, *Monks of Westminster*, pp. 67–8.

17. Palgrave, *Kalendars*, p. 277, no. 18.

18. *Ibid.*, p. 291, no. 80.

19. *Ibid.*, p. 283, no. 50.

20. Westminster Abbey Muniments: 9496 Membrane 3.

21. *Flores*, III, p. 115.
22. Palgrave, *Kalendars*. p. 284, no. 52. The actual declaration of the Westminster jury is *E dient ausige Adam de Warfeld sacrestyn savoit de la burger n enchseon qil concela ptie du tresor ge estoit trovelee countre les ministris nost Seigneur Le Roy.*
23. This is the famous indenture, see H. Cole, *Records*, pp. 277–84: Adam of Warfeld's 'finds' are on p. 283.
24. Palgrave, *Kalendars*, p. 269, no. 52.
25. Pearce, *Monks of Westminster*, pp. 64–5.
26. H. Cole, *Records*, p. 277 *et seq.* describe in Latin the sequence of events explained here.
27. *State Trials*, pp. XXX–XXXI.

4 The Sheriff's Tale

1. Fitstephen's description of London is printed in Latin in the Appendix of Volume II of the Elizabethan John Stow, *Survey of London*, ed. C. L. Kingsford, p. 219 *et seq.*
2. *The Chronicle of Richard of Devizes*, ed. J. A Giles (London, 1841), p. 60.
3. One of the best and most recent studies of Medieval London is Caroline M. Barron's *London in the Middles Ages* (Oxford University Press, 2004). For Thomas Mocking's House. *Calendar of Pleas and Memoranda Rolls of the City of London 1364–81*, pp. 154–6. His Will is contained in Sharpe's, *London Court of Hustings: Calendar of Wills*, vol. II p. 153. For Le Botonner's Shop, *The London Assize of Nuisance*, p. 43.
4. *Rotuli Hundredorum* (Records Commission, 1812–1818], vol. 1, p. 148.
5. *Letter Book A of the City of London*, pp. 216, 217, 220. *The London Assize of Nuisance*, p. 13. The different Letter Books and *The Assize of Nuisance* are crammed with this sort of incident.
6. *Liber Albus*, pp. 36–9, 257–60.

7. *Calendar of Early Mayor Court Rolls*, p. 255.
8. *Letter Book C*, pp. 15–17.
9. *Calendar of Coroners Rolls of the City of London*, pp. 14–15.
10. *The London Eyre of 1276*, no. 20 and *Annales Londonienses*, pp. 92–3.
11. *Annales Londonienses*, pp. 94–5. Andrew Horn succinctly describes events inLondon with a list of 'happenings'.

5 The Justice's Tale

1. *CPR, 1272–1281*, p. 381. *Calendar of Letter Books*, A, p. 227, *Annales Londonienses*, p. 89. These sources together with the 'potted' biography of Bakewell in *Knights of Edward I*, ed. C. Moor (Harleian Society, 1929), vol. I, pp. 59–60 provide an overview of this royal favourite. The spelling of his name varies from Bakewell to Bauquell.
2. *Lincolnshire Assize Roll*, p. 15.
3. Please note specific dates are not given in these indictments that have to be worked out with the help of Cheyney's *Handbook of Dates*. According to the original document from the National Archives (Kings Remembrancer 332/8) which Palgrave transcribes, the aldermen gave their evidence on the Saturday after the Feast of St Peter and Paul in the 31st regnal year of Edward I. The 31st regnal year was 20 November 1302 to 19 November 1303. The Feast of St Peter and Paul is 29 June so it must be 29 June 1303. Easter in 1303 was 7 April (Cheyney, p. 188), the 29 June was a Saturday, so the Saturday after this was 6 July – this is the method by which correct dating is established.
4. Palgrave *Kalendars*, p. 253, no. 5.
5. *Ibid.*, pp. 253–4.
6. *Ibid.*, pp. 254–5. no. 9.

7. *Ibid.*, pp. 255, nos 10 and 11.
8. *Ibid.*, pp. 255–6, nos 12–14.
9. *Ibid.* pp. 256–8, nos 13–15.
10. *Ibid.*, p. 257, no. 19.
11. *Ibid.*, pp. 258–60 nos 24–5.
12. Guisborough's, *Chronicle*, pp. 249–50.
13. Palgrave, *Kalendars*, p. 270, no. 60.
14. *Ibid.*, pp. 261–5, nos 27–46.
15. *Ibid.*, pp. 260–1, no. 26.
16. *Ibid.*, p. 268, no. 51.
17. *Ibid.*, p. 269, no. 54.
18. *Ibid.*, p. 270, no. 60 and p. 271 no. 61.
19. *CPR, 1303–7*, p. 289.
20. Palgrave, *Kalendars*, pp. 270–1, nos 60–2.
21. Palgrave, *Kalendars*, pp. 266–7, no. 47.
22. Westminster Abbey Muniments 580 and J. F. Tout, *The Place of Edward II in English History* (Manchester), p. 342. Foxley held a post which, according to Wenlok's ordinances, put him in rank after the Abbot in the latter's household. Richard de Burgh disappears from Wenlok's accounts.
23. Palgrave, *Kalendars*, pp. 266–7.
24. *Ibid.*, p. 24.
25. *CPR, 1303–1307*, pp. 194–5.

6 The Constable's Tale

1. Palgrave, *Kalendars*, pp. 271–2, no. 64.
2. *Ibid.*, p. 269, no. 52.
3. *Ibid.*, p. 269, no. 53.
4. *Ibid.*, p. 270, no. 55.
5. *Ibid.*, p. 270, no. 56.
   '*Nomina earum sunt indicate et adhuc non sunt inventi* – Names of

those indicted and still not found'. For Kynebaston, see Cal. of Close Rolls, 1302-1307, p. 112.

6. Palgrave, *Kalendars*, p. 270, nos. 57–60 and p. 271–2, no 64. '*Postea ad Mandatum Dominae Reginae predict Castanea et Alicia, soror ejus dismissive sunt per Mancaptores* – Afterwards, at the command of the Queen, the said Castenea and Alice her sister were released on sureties.'

7. *Select cases in the Court of King's Bench of Edward I*, vol. I, pp. LXV–LXVII.

8. *Ibid.*, 101–2.

9. *CPR*, 1301–7 p 194–5. The full list is given here to demonstrate the commonalty of names, to show how individuals such as Gerin the Linen draper were included to underline the solidarity of the Westminster community, to exemplify the Crown's exasperation as well as its covert plan to make a thorough sweep and search of the entire Abbey buildings.

10. Harvey, *Walter de Wenlok*, pages 30–2.

11. Westminster Abbey Muniment 23631 (expenses going to Scotland).

12. Palgrave, *Kalendars*, p. 273, part II, no. 1.

13. For Ralph de Sandwich, see *Dictionary of National Biography*, vol. XVII, pp 769–70; C. Moor, *Knights of Edward I*, vol. IV, pp. 210–11.

14. *Calendar of Early Mayors and Coroner Rolls of the City of London*, pp. 146–7.

15. Rishanger, *Chronicle*, p. 225.

16. *Select cases in the Court of King's Bench*, vol. 1, p. IXIV.

17. *Statutes of the Realm* (1810), vol. I, pp. 89–90. (Statute of Westminster II capitulum 38).

18. Palgrave, *Kalendars*, p. 258, no. 23: p. 264, no. 39 and p. 265 no. 45.

19. Palgrave, *Kalendars*, part II, pp. 273–93.

20. *Ibid.*, p. 293, no. 93.

21. *Ibid.*, p. 281, no. 38, and p. 292, no 85. '*Dicunt eciam quod quidam Johes le Macoun fregit Murum dicte thesauri cum instrumentis*

suis et quod idem Johannes hoc fecit per abettum dictorum monachorum
– They [the jurors] also say that John the Mason broke the
wall of the said treasury with his instruments and the same
John did this abetted by the said monks'.

7 The Thieves' Tale

1. Palgrave, *Kalendars*, II, p. 292, no. 86 '*Dicunt eciam quod Wills de Palaco fuit consensus ipso facto in toto* – They also say William of the Palace was consenting to the deed [the robbery] in its entirety'.
2. Palgrave, *Kalendars*, II, p. 292, no. 89; p. 291, no. 82; p. 283, no. 50; p. 280, no. 3.
3. National Archives [Kew]: King's Remembrancer E/101/332/8.
4. *The Rolls and Register of Bishop Oliver Sutton 1280–1299*, ed. Rosalind Hill (Lincolnshire Record Society, 1965), vol. v, p. 154.
5. Frederick C. Hamill, 'The King's Approvers: A Chapter in the History of English Criminal Law', *Speculum*, vol. II, 1936, p. 238 *et seq.*
6. Palgrave, *Kalendars*, II, p. 288, no. 72. '*Et il [the jurors] dient ausi qu si nul de estrange pais Chivaler. Esquire ou autre que a la diste brusure eust este* – and they also say that no stranger, be he Knight, Squire or other, were present at the said robbery'.
7. National Archives [Kew]: King's Remembrancer E/101/332/8.
8. Palgrave, *Kalendars*, II, p. 284, no. 51 '*John de Lynton fust a la burgerie et fust compaignon Ric. de Puddlicote . . . E ge une clef fust trovee en Le cofre mesme celi Johan accordant a mesme le clef du avandit freytour* – John le Lenton was involved in the robbery, he was a companion of Richard de Puddlicott – and that a key was

found in the Coffer of the same John which matched the key to the refectory.'

9. *Two Cartularies of Abingdon Abbey*, ed. C. F. Slade et al., Oxford Historical Series [n.5] XXXIII, Vol. II 1992, pp. 107, 125, 186, 238, 240–1, 256.

10. Palgrave, *Kalendars*, p. 269, no. 54.
    '*In domo sua luxta Douneg* – in his house near Dowgate'.

11. Palgrave, *Kalendars*, II, p. 284, no. 51.
    '*Ge hanaps de mazer et XXXII quilers d'argent furent emblez en abbaye de Westminster hors du freytour e furent trovee od mesme celi Rici* – basket of mazers and 32 silver spoons emblazoned with the Abbey arms which came from the Abbey's refectory were found in the possession of the said Richard'.

12. Calendar of Close Rolls 1302–7, p. 486.

8 The Tangled Web

1. Sophie Page *'Astrology in Mediaeval Manuscripts'* (The British Library, 2004), p. 29.

2. Thomas Wright, *The Political Songs of England* (Camden Society, 1839), pp. 194–7.

3. *Ibid.*, p. 141.

4. Westminster Abbey Muniments: 24490.

5. *Flores*, III, p. 140.

6. 14 July 1308. *CPR 1307-1313*, p. 124, and 23 May 1310: Westminster Abbey Muniments: 12786.

7. Westminster Abbey Muniments: 9496–9499C.

8. Palgrave, *Kalendars*, II, p. 288, nos 72–4; *Ibid.* I, p. 254, no. 9.

9. Westminster Abbey Muniments: 9499C.
    '*De infamis Vero ordinetur quod omnes et singuli cuicimque accusacione et denunciacioni infamie incontinencie contra Fratrem A. De Perchore de Beatrice de Baldok et Mathilde de Dunelmia falso et maliciose preposite*

a eciam contra fratrem Wde Chalk de Roisia de Gysore pure et absolute reminicient de aliis infamis fiat renunciacio generalis – As to reports about scandals, a decree should be issued that all and each, sincerely and absolutely renounce any action, allegation and denunciation of infamy and incontinence against Brother Alexander de Pershore as regards to Beatrice de Baldock and Mathilda of Durham and also against William de Chalk concerning Roesia de Gisors, there must be a general renunciation of such charges.'

10. Pearce, *Monks of Westminster*, p. 62. Harvey, *Walter de Wenlok*, p. 17 *et seq*.

11. *The Customary of St Peter's Westminster*, the section on the refectory is p. 90 *et seq*.

12. Harvey, *Walter de Wenlok*, pp. 210, 211, 213, 214.

13. Domesday Cartulary [Westminster] fo. 147 'The Year Book of 21 to 22 Edward I', pp. 254–6.

14. Westminster Abbey Muniments. 31494.

15. Westminster Abbey Muniments. 28852.

16. *CPR*, 1292–1301, p. 218, John Le Keu [the Cook]: A John Cook witnessed a Westminster Charter [Domesday Cartulary of Westminster fo. 3456] and held land at Knowle. A Nicholas Cook of this period is mentioned in the Domesday Cartulary fos. 459, 515, 536[b]. For Edelina's guilt, see Palgrave, *Kalendars*, II, p. 283, no. 48.

17. National Archives E/101/375/3. 'Inventory made by Ralph de Manton at Westminster during the month of November at the beginning of the 28th year of King Edward concerning all the jewels of the said King . . . Found in the treasury of the Wardrobe of the said King under the Chapel of the Monks.'

18. 'Grant to William de Huntingdon from the Abbot of Westminster of a plot of land in Eye on the way towards Eybury, once the property of Alan de Eye'. (Domesday Cartulary of Westminster 1298 f. 333[b]). One wonders whether this grant was a bribe or diversion, for William

becomes more absorbed with that piece of land than anything else (Domesday Cartulary), fos. 332, 328ʰ, 328 etc.

19. *CPR*, 1292–1301, p. 24.

20. H. T. Riley, *Memorials of London and London Life* (London, 1868), pp. 57–8.

21. Guisborough, *Chronicle*, p. 248.

22. '*Et quod quidam Monachus Westm fuit special amicus ejusdem Ricardi [Puddlicott] set nomen ignorant* – that a certain monk of Westminster was the special friend of that same Richard but they [the jury] do not know his name.'

23. Westminster Domesday Cartulary, fo. 403.

24. John received the land in 1295. Domesday Cartulary, fo. 515.

25. Palgrave, *Kalendars*, p. 265, no. 46.

26. *The Customary*, p. 52 *et seq.*

27. The information given in earlier footnotes will not be repeated here.

28. On Convers' work. The Pipe Roll of 32 Edward II '*Il dient qe il unt grant suspicion vers un qe est vallet John le Convers* – they say they entertain great suspicion about the valet of John le Convers', Palgrave, *Kalendars*, II, p. 291, no 81.

29. '*Leur rigolage*', Palgrave, *Kalendars*, II, p. 284, no. 54.

30. *Ibid.*, pp. 285–6, no. 60.

31. '*Parmi sa bouche* – through his own mouth,' *Ibid.*, p. 286, no. 63.

32. G. A. Williams, *Mediaeval London* (London, 1963), pp. 99, 126 and 228.

33. T. H. Lloyd, *The English wool trade in the Middle Ages* (Cambridge, 1977), p. 75.

34. Palgrave, *Kalendars*, II, p. 287, nos. 66–7.

35. *Ibid.*, p. 257, no. 19, '*imprisonatur per quinque dies* – and he [Puddlicott] was imprisoned there [Pourte's house] for five days.'

36. *Ibid.*, p. 285, no. 56. G. A. Williams, *Mediaeval London*, p. 328.

37. *Annales* in *Chronicles of the Reign of Edward I and Edward II*, p. 130.

38. Palgrave, *Kalendars*, p. 25, no. 19.

39. *Chronicles of Edward I*, vol. I, Introduction, p. XLI.

40. On conditions in Newgate, see M. Bassett, 'Newgate Prison in the Middle Ages' [*Speculum* 18, 1943], p. 233 *et seq*. On the Sheriff's rights, see *Liber Albus*, pp. 215–17.On Sandwich being responsible for gaol delivery, see *Liber Albus*, p. 406.

41. *Letter Book B of the City of London*, p. 215.

42. *Ibid.*

43. *The Register of John Peckham, Archbishop of Canterbury*, ed. C. T. Martin (Rolls Series ,1884), vol. II, p. 968.

44. *Letter Book C of the City of London*, p. 83.

45. *Chronicles of Edward I*, vol. I, p. 130.

46. *Letter Book B of the City of London*, pp. 151, 165, 178.

47. On Southcote: Hundred Rolls, I, pp. 148–9. On the attack in Middlesex, *CPR, 1301–7*, p. 349.

48. Palgrave, *Kalendars*, p. 269, no. 52. On Richard de Caumpes, see *Letter Book C of the City of London*, p. 79.

49. *Ibid.*, p. 114.

50. *Ibid.*, p. 227.

51. 'Statutum de Nova Costuma' in the *Munimenta Gildhallae Londonienses*, ed. H. T. Riley (Rolls Series, 1859–62], vol. II, 'Liber Custumarum', pp. 205–11.

52. *Letter Book C of the City of London*, p. 122.

53. *Ibid.*, p. 132.

54. *Ibid.*, p. 135.

9 Retribution

1. *Calendar of Early Mayors' Coroners Rolls for the City of London*, pp. 11, 31, 61-62, 126 and 143–5. All these references illustrate and develop how very dangerous it was to be a royal tax-collector in London at the beginning of the fourteenth century.

References

2. *Parliamentary Writs and Writs of Military Summons*, ed. F. Palgrave (Records Commission, 1827–34), vol. I, p. 406.
3. *Letter Book C of the City of London*, pp. 117–18.
4. *Annales Londonienses*, p. 132.
5. Rishanger, p. 420.
6. *Annales Londonienses*, p. 143.
7. Rishanger, p. 420.
8. *Annales Londonienses*, p. 143.
9. *Register of Drokensford*, p. 95.
10. L. Gabel, *Benefit of Clergy in Late Mediaeval England* (1929), p. 64.
11. *Select Cases in the Court of King's Bench*, vol. III, pp. 4–5.
12. *London Eyre of 1276*, pp. 32–3.
13. *Select Cases in the Court of King's Bench*, vol. III, p. 171.
14. Westminster Abbey Muniments no. 16932.
15. Harvey, *Walter de Wenlok*, pp. 30–3.
16. *Ibid.*
17. *Flores*, III, p. 321; Rishanger, p. 225.
18. *Annales Londonienses*, pp. 139–42.
19. *Ibid.*, p. 143.
20. Cal. Of Close Rolls 1302–1307, p. 486.
21. *Flores*, III, pp. 116–17

The Aftermath

1. Paul Doherty, *Isabella and the Strange Death of Edward II*, p. 23 *et seq.*
2. G. W. S. Barrow, *Robert de Bruce and the Community of the Realm of Scotland* (1965), pp. 212–29 is one of the most lucid accounts of this fresh crisis in Scotland.
3. Doherty, *Isabella*, p. 33.
4. J. Moorman, 'Edward I and Lanercost Priory 1306–1307', English Historical Review, LXVII (1952), pp. 161–74, and Guisborough, *Chronicle*, p. 379.

5. *Chronicles of England, France and Spain of Sir John Froissart*, trans. and ed. T. Johnes, 1839, p. 38.

6. J. Ayloffe, 'An Account of the Body of Kind Edward I – as it appeared on the opening of his tomb in the year 1774,' *Archaeologia*, vol. III, 1786, pp. 398–412.

7. Doherty, *Isabella* provides an account of the friction between Edward and his French wife Isabella.

8. Drokensford's *Register* and the *Dictionary of National Biography*, vol. 6, pp. 19–20.

9. Most of the references to Pourte have been cited before. However, for his Will (1307), see *London Court of Hustings: Calendar Wills*, ed. R. Sharpe (1889), vol. I '1258–1358', pp. 192 and 196.

10. For these four servants of Edward I, see *Knights of Edward I*, vol. I, pp. 59–60, 81, 131 and vol. IV, pp. 210–11.

11. The most dramatic account of proceedings is given by the 'Annales Paulini' [Chronicle of St. Paul's] in the *Chronicles of the Reigns of Edward I and Edward II*, vol. I, p. 315 *et seq.*

12. Pearce, *Monks of Westminster*, pp. 60–76 provides details about each of the monks.

13. Harvey, *Walter de Wenlok*, provides a pithy summary of the dispute, p. 17 *et seq.*

14. Calendar of Close Rolls 1302–1307, p. 244; T. Madox, *History and Antiquities of the Exchequer* (1769), vol. II, p. 278 and note.

Appendix

Fitzstephen's Description of London

Amongst the noble and famous cities of the world, London, the capital of England, is one of the most outstanding. It possesses above all others, abundant wealth, wide commerce, great grandeur and magnificence. It enjoys a healthy climate, professes the Christian religion and possesses strength in its fortresses, its location, the honour of its citizens and the chastity of its matrons. In sports, too, it is most pleasant and, in the rise of illustrious and famous men, most fortunate. Its citizens are not addicted to licentiousness or lewdry nor are they savage or brutal but kind and generous . . .

As regards to Divine Worship they have St Paul's Church, an episcopal see. There are also in London and its suburbs, thirteen larger conventual churches besides one hundred and thirty-six parish churches. On the east rises the great Tower, a fortress of huge size and strength. Its courtyard and walls were established upon very deep foundations, the mortar used on the buildings was tempered with the blood of beasts. On the west are two Castles strongly fortified [Montefichet and Castle Baynard]. The city walls are high and thick with seven double gates having, on the north side, towers placed at proper intervals. London used to have such walls and towers along its south side but, because of the excellent river Thames (rich in fish, whose waters ebb and flow with the tide), the southern walls have long disappeared. Further west high up on the bank of the river Thames, stands the royal palace of Westminster. An incredible structure furnished with bastions, the palace is situated in a popular suburb about two miles distant from the city. Adjoining the houses of the citizens are spacious and beautiful gardens, well endowed with fruitful trees. On the north side lies fresh pasture, delightful meadow land, cut by flowing streams on which stand mills whose clatter is most pleasing to the ear. Near the city lies a stretch of immense forest, with densely wooded thickets where game of every kind, stag, deer, boars and wild bulls are to be found.

The arable land beyond the city is very fertile and produces abundant crops and fills the barns of their owners. All around London, on every side, are excellent springs; their water is clear, sweet and very healthy. Amongst these are Holywell, Clerkenwell and St Clement's well, often visited by scholars from the schools of the city when they go out to take the air during the summer evenings. The city is ennobled by her men and peopled by such a multitude of inhabitants that, in the recent wars, King Stephen [1135–54] was able to field armed horsemen mounting to twenty thousand and sixty thousand infantry. The citizens of London are respected and noted above all other cities for the elegance of their manners in dress, table and conversation, whilst the matrons of the city are like the Sabine women of Ancient Rome. The three principal churches in the city possess celebrated schools. On festival days the masters send all their pupils to these churches where the Feast of the Patron Saint is honoured and the scholars dispute, some in an open way and others more logically . . .

The workers of the different crafts, the sellers of various commodities, and the labourers of every kind, each have their separate station which they take up every morning. There are also in London, on the north bank of the river, wine-shops and public eating houses. Every day, according to the season there can be found there meats of all kinds: roast, fried and boiled, fish large and small, coarser meat for the poor and more delicate for the rich, such as venison, fowl and other small birds . . .

If friends, tired after their journey, should unexpectedly come to a citizen's house, and, being hungry, do not want to wait till fresh meat be bought and cooked, bread is immediately served. Whatever the number of soldiers or strangers who enter or leave the city at any hour of the day or night, they may go to these eating-houses if they please, and refresh themselves on the delicacies set before them. Such public cuisine is very convenient to the city, and a distinguishing mark of its civilized character. Outside one of the gates lies a certain smooth field in name and in reality [Smithfield]. There, every Friday, unless it be one of the Holy days, well-bred horses are shown for sale. The earls, barons, and knights resident in the city at the time, as well as most of the citizens, flock there either to stare or buy. It is pleasant to see the horse with their sleek and shining coats, smoothly ambling along . . .

According to the evidence of the chroniclers, London is more ancient than Rome: indeed, both derive their origin from the same Trojan ancestors. So it is, that even to this day, both cities use the same ancient law and ordinances. London, like Rome, is divided into wards; it has annual sheriffs instead of consuls; it has an order of senators and inferior magistrates . . . Every type of business, be it administrative, executive or judicial, has its own appropriate place and proper court. On stated days it has its own assemblies. There is no city in which more approved customs are observed; attending churches, honouring God's ordinances, keeping festivals, giving alms, receiving strangers, confirming betrothals, contracting marriages, celebrating weddings, preparing entertainments, welcoming guests, as well as the ordered arrangement of its funeral ceremonies and the burial of the dead. The only inconveniences of London are the immod-erate drinking of foolish persons and its frequent fires. Moreover, almost all the bishops, abbots, and great men of England are, in a manner, citizens and freemen of London. They own magnificent houses in the city to which they resort, spending large sums of money whenever they are summoned to London for councils and assemblies by the King, or their archbishop, or are compelled to go there for their own business.

Let us now proceed to the sports of the city; London, instead of theatrical shows and scenic entertainments, stages dramatic performances of a more sacred kind, either representations of the miracles which Holy Confessors have wrought or the passions and sufferings in which the constancy of martyrs was especially displayed.

To begin with, the sports of the boys (for we have all been boys). Annually, on Shrove Tuesday, the boys of the different schools each bring a fighting cock to their master and the whole of that forenoon is spent by the boys in seeing their cocks fight in the school-room. After dinner, all the young men of the city go out into the fields to play at the well-known game of football. The scholars belonging to the several schools, each have their ball and the city tradesmen, according to their respective crafts, have theirs. The more aged men, the fathers of the players and the wealthy citizens, come on horseback to see the contests of the young men, with whom, after their manner, they participate, their natural heat apparently aroused by the sight of so much agility, as well as their involvement in the amusement of unrestrained youth.

Every Sunday in Lent, after dinner, a company of young men enter the fields, mounted on warlike horses. The sons of the citizens hasten out of the gates in crowds equipped with lances and shields, the younger sort with pikes from which the iron head has been taken off. They all indulge in sham fights and exercise themselves in military combat. When the king happens to be near the city, most of the courtiers attend, and the young men from the households of the earls and barons, who have not yet attained the honour of knighthood, also participate in order to test their skill.

The hope of victory animates every one. The spirited horses neigh, their limbs tremble, they champ their bits, and, impatient of delay, cannot endure standing still. When at length, the young riders having been divided into companies, some pursue those that go before without being able to overtake them whilst others throw their companions off their mounts and gallop past them.

During the Easter holidays they play at a game resembling a naval engagement. A target is firmly fastened to the trunk of a tree which is fixed in the middle of the river. In the prow of a boat, driven along by oars and poles, stands the contestant, if he hits the target, breaking the lance, yet keep his position unmoved, he gains his points and achieves victory. However, if his lance be not shivered by the blow or he is tumbled into the river and his boat passes by, he loses. Two boats are always placed, one on either side of the target, in them are a number of young men ready to take up the fallen striker, when he first emerges from the stream . . . On the bridge and in balconies along the banks of the river, stand the spectators . . .

During the holidays in summer the young men exercise themselves in the sports of leaping, archery, wrestling, stone-throwing, slinging javelins beyond a mark, and also fighting with shields. The maidens dance merrily, tripping along the ground beneath the rising moon. Almost on every holiday in winter, before dinner, foaming boars and huge-tusked hogs, intended for bacon, fight for their lives. When the marshy pools which wash the walls of the city on the north side are frozen over, the young men go out in crowds to divert themselves upon the ice. Some, having increased their speed by a run, place their feet apart and, turning sideways, slide a great way: others make a seat of large pieces of ice like mill-stones, with a great number of them pulling before or, holding each other by the hand, draw one of their companions seated on the ice: if, at any time, they slip in moving so swiftly, all fall down together. Others are more expert in their sports upon the ice; they lash under their feet the shinbones of some animal and, holding poles shod with iron, they strike these against the ice and are carried along as swiftly as a flying bird or a bolt loosed from a cross-bow. Sometimes two of the skaters, having placed themselves a great distance apart by mutual agreement, come together from opposite sides: they meet, raise their poles and strike each other; either one, or both of them fall, not without some bodily hurt, even after their fall they are carried along to a great distance from each other by their impetus so, whatever part of their heads comes in contact with the ice, is laid bare to the very skull. Very frequently legs or arms, if the skater falls on them, are broken. However, youth is always eager for glory and ardent for victory, so these young men engage in these mock battles, where they conduct themselves more courageously than in real ones. Most of the citizens amuse themselves by sporting with Merlins, hawks, and other types of hunting birds as well as with dogs when they go hunting in the woods. Londoners have the right of hunting in Middlesex, Hertfordshire, all the Chilterns and Kent, as far as the river Cray . . .

Index

NB: page numbers in italic indicate illustrations

233

DATE DUE